Egypt
and the United States

The Formative Years

Egypt
and the United States
The Formative Years

Gail E. Meyer

Rutherford • Madison • Teaneck
Fairleigh Dickinson University Press
London: Associated University Presses

Associated University Presses, Inc.
Cranbury, New Jersey 08512

Associated University Presses
Magdalen House
136-148 Tooley Street
London SE1 2TT, England

Library of Congress Cataloging in Publication Data

Meyer, Gail E   1942-
    Egypt and the United States.

    Bibliograhy: p.
    Includes index.
    1.   United States--Foreign relations--Egypt.   2.   Egypt--Foreign relations--
United States.   3.   United States--Foreign relations--1953-1961.   I.   Title.
E183.8.E35M49   327.73'062   77-78012   ISBN 0-8386-2018-3

PRINTED IN THE UNITED STATES OF AMERICA

In memory of J. S. and M. I.

Contents

Preface

As the events triggered by the October War of 1973 build to a dramatic if uncertain climax, the Middle East is once again at the center of the world's political attention. What distinguishes the aftermath of the October War, however, from the periods following the crises of 1956 and 1967 is the radical change in the political approach of the United States toward the Arab world in general and toward Egypt in particular. This change, which is characterized by greater sensitivity to the Arab view of the region's traditional problems and by American efforts to conceive and implement a policy having truly regional dimensions, was brought about by the realities of oil politics.

The historical significance of this development cannot fully be grasped without an understanding of America's policy toward Egypt and the Arab world prior to the October War. Central to such understanding is an analysis of the relations between Egypt and the United States in the formative years 1952-1958, when all the problems that were to keep America from attaining its goals emerged to light.

The period selected for study is unified by a number of factors. It opens with major political changes in both Egypt and the United States. In July 1952 the Free Officers seized power in Egypt and overthrew the old regime. In January 1953 the Eisenhower Administration took office, the Dulles era in American foreign policy got underway, and the American leadership began to take a "new look" at the Middle East. Equally important for all the nations caught up in the cold war struggle of the time was the end of Stalin's rule in March 1953.

The period ends in 1958 with the union between Egypt and Syria. Cairo began to re-evaluate its relations with the Soviet Union, whose regional maneuvers, especially in Iraq, alarmed the Egyptian leadership. In Washington, not long after the death of Secretary of State John Foster Dulles, another reassessment of American Middle East policy was about to be undertaken.

The period as a whole has, in some studies, been divided into two phases: a cordial phase extending from mid-1952 to early 1955 and a phase in which relations deteriorated dating from February 1955 to 1958. However, this division is artificially symmetrical since American-Egyptian relations were in fact intermittently good and bad during both phases.

It seems more accurate to say that during the "first phase" interactions between the two countries occurred more or less on the level of direct exchanges. Egypt was chiefly concerned with the domestic problems of consolidating its

9

Revolution, of ending British occupation, and of promoting economic development. Hence Egypt's leaders devoted marginal attention to the Arab world and
entered a self-imposed period of relative aloofness in which they looked to the
United States for aid in achieving their objectives.

By the second half of 1954, domestic order was achieved and an agreement
providing for the withdrawal of British troops was concluded. Soon Egypt
launched itself into Arab politics, and from this point on American-Egyptian
relations must be considered within the broader context of the respective policies
of the two countries toward the Arab Middle East.

Even this rough chronological division of the period selected, however, gives a
false impression of logic and order that does not correspond to the perceived
realities of the day. To correct this impression, the present study proceeds
chapter by chapter to disentangle the many strands that are interwoven in the
complex history of this region during this period. The strands thus singled out
for separate analysis include America's role in the Anglo-Egyptian dispute; the
Arab-Israeli conflict; America's defense objectives in the Middle East;
neutralism as an Egyptian weapon against the West; the Suez Canal Crisis of
1956; and the Eisenhower Doctrine that followed this crisis. Inevitably, this approach carries the reader backward and forward in time as each separate strand
is examined. Yet, because the end result is to reproduce a pattern that could only be Middle Eastern in design, the extra burden this method imposes on the
reader seems more than justified. Indeed, failure to discern the intricate con-
tours of this pattern as a reflection of the outlook and aspirations of the Arab
peoples was one of the root causes of American reverses in the formative years
under review.

Both American and Egyptian sources have been used to document this study.
Official publications as well as the memoirs of key decision-makers, such as
British Prime Minister Anthony Eden and United States President Dwight D.
Eisenhower, were extensively consulted. A careful sifting of *The John Foster
Dulles Oral History Collection* and *The Papers of John Foster Dulles, 1888-1959*
at Princeton University's Seeley G. Mudd Manuscript Library revealed in-
valuable and little known information, including the comments and thoughts of
Secretary Dulles's closest associates and the reasoning behind many decisions.
Books by Gamal Abdel Nasser, Mohammed Naguib, and Anwar El Sadat, the
leading figures of the Free Officers' Revolution, shed light on the Egyptian point
of view, with the insights gained from Anwar El Sadat's contribution of particular interest in view of his pre-eminent role in current events.

Another rich store of data was found in both American and Egyptian
newspapers and journals of the day. Monitoring the Egyptian press in particular
proved an effective means of verifying the Egyptian leadership's attitude toward
American policy owing to the censorship it practiced and to the official direc-
tives given to the press during the period in question.

Finally, a great deal of information, some of it never before published, was
gathered by the author through interviews with prominent personalities who

participated either directly or indirectly in the events described. Foremost among the Americans consulted were John Badeau, former Ambassador to Cairo; Raymond Hare, former Ambassador to Cairo; Dr. Harry N. Howard, former State Department official; Donald Burgess, former Chief of the American Interests Section of the Spanish Embassy in Cairo; and Loy Henderson, former Under-Secretary of State. Among the Egyptians interviewed were Mohammed Riad, former Secretary to Foreign Minister Mahmoud Fawzi; Ahmed Anis, spokesman for the Ministry of Information; Dr. Boutras Boutras-Ghali, recently Acting Minister of Foreign Affairs; plus a number of distinguished Egyptian journalists active during the selected period, such as Mohammed Hakki, former foreign editor of *Al Ahram* and currently Press Counsel of the Egyptian Embassy, Washington, D. C.; Klouvis Maksoud, former political editor of *Al Ahram*; Ahmed Baha Al Din, former editor-in-chief of *Al Ahram*; and Amin Abul Einein, editor of the *Egyptian Gazette*.

Although it must be borne in mind that personal roles are sometimes exaggerated and events reconstructed in the light of subsequent developments, these interviews at the very least gave new insights into the factors that influenced decisions at the time they were made. Such insights proved all the more useful in view of the large number of documents still subject to government classification, a handicap that made it especially necessary to test official and unofficial statements against the actual course of events in order to draw independent if tentative conclusions.

Acknowledgments

This study is based on a dissertation entitled "American-Egyptian Relations, 1952-1958" prepared by the author for the Graduate Institute of International Studies, University of Geneva. The present volume, a revised and developed version of the original thesis, was undertaken in collaboration with Jerome H. Reichman.

The Graduate Institute of International Studies provided guidance and financial assistance for which the author is deeply grateful. Professors Jacques Freymond, Boutras Boutras-Ghali, Harish Kapur, and George Abi Saab merit special thanks for their help and suggestions.

Mariangela Zerioli deserves special mention for the invaluable editorial advice and assistance she provided throughout the preparation of the book in its present form. The help of Judith Noebels and Mathilde Finch in finalizing the text for publication is also gratefully acknowledged. Many others, too numerous to mention, contributed to the long and difficult process of documentation that forms the basis of this work.

Finally, without the moral support and encouragement of Mr. and Mrs. William P. Meyer, this book could never have been written.

Introduction

The Middle East in Perspective

The Middle East is not a precise geographical entity but rather a political and diplomatic term used to encompass an area with constantly changing limits that reflect the interests of the great powers in Africa, Asia, and Europe. For the purpose of this study the Middle East has been defined as the area whose northern limits run from Turkey to Pakistan, extending southward to the Saudi Arabian Peninsula, Ethiopia, and the Sudan, and westward to Libya.[1] Situated at the junction of three continents, this vast region, which holds over 60 percent of the world's estimated oil reserves, is one of the most strategically important in the world.

Within this region, it is the Arab world with which Egypt has, in recent times, closely identified itself. Divided into four principal subareas—the Nile Valley, the Arabian Peninsula, Mesopotamia, and the North African Maghreb—the Arab world is in turn comprised of eighteen states in varying stages of political, economic, and social development. Their affinity derives from their common language and religious traditions, and from their shared experience of colonial domination.

The Middle East has been a coveted prize throughout history. Many of the factors that have traditionally affected the struggle to dominate this area were at work in the early nineteenth century when the Ottoman Empire, which for nearly 500 years had controlled the Mediterranean Basin, began to disintegrate. The intense rivalry between two of the great powers of Europe—Britain and Russia—to determine which country was to gain control of both this region and the Balkan Peninsula became known as the "Eastern Question".

Britain, a great power situated far from the Middle East, was initially concerned with this region because of its imperial interests in India. These interests could have been threatened if another great power gained control of the route to India that traversed the Middle East. Napoleon's occupation of Egypt in 1798 and the French attempt to enlist Persia in a joint invasion of India stirred British anxieties in this regard.[2] However, as the decline of the Ottoman Empire progressed, Britain's rulers realized that the chief threat came from Russia.

To circumscribe Russian penetration of the region Britain enlisted the aid of Ottoman Turkey, whose own conflict with Russia had extended over four centuries and had involved numerous wars.[3] Any Russian pressure on Constantinople was met by equal, if not stronger, British backing for the Ottoman Sultan.

Later, expanding British interests in the Mediterranean led Britain to reinforce its support of Turkey, since Turkey controlled the Bosphorus Straits and
could therefore prevent naval access to the Mediterranean. Turkey thus became
a bulwark against Russia and a guardian of the British imperial lifeline at
minimal cost to Britain. This tactic of enlisting regional states to protect the interests of the Western great powers continued to be used throughout the cold
war period with which the present study is concerned.

Britain's Middle East policy was greatly influenced by the opening of the Suez
Canal in 1869 and the resulting diversion of British trade to this shorter, more
economical route to India and the Orient. By 1882, when more than 80 percent
of the total traffic through the Canal was of British registry,[4] British interests in
Egypt were considered so vital that local developments there could no longer be
ignored. After crushing a nationalist revolt viewed as a threat to the canal, Britain began a "temporary" occupation of Egypt that was to last for 72 years. The
Suez Canal, and with it, Egypt, thus became of crucial importance to the whole
British imperial system. Even after the wane of British power, the
canal—through which much of the Western world's oil was transported—remained a factor of paramount importance to Western economic and strategic
interests.

After the First World War and the dismemberment of the Ottoman Empire,
Britain profited from Russia's need to consolidate the Soviet Revolution at home
by securing dominance over former Ottoman Middle East territories through the
League of Nations Mandate System. The administration of the Palestinian,
Transjordanian, and Iraqi mandates was allotted to Britain; France received the
mandates for Syria and Lebanon. In Egypt and Iraq, as well as in other countries, Britain chose to rule from behind the facade of constitutional or treaty
provisions or by manipulating a pro-British Arab government. Its hegemony, extending from Egypt and the Sudan to India, was supreme during the interwar
period, and no power was strong enough to challenge it.

During the Second World War the strategic and energy requirements of the
Allied forces accentuated the importance of the region. The nearly successful attempt of the Axis enemy to take control of the area's resources was not to be
forgotten by the Western powers in the bipolar struggle with Soviet Russia in the
postwar period.

When the Middle East is viewed from the Russian perspective, it is evident
that any event occurring in the region that borders its own southern flank would
keenly interest that power. The northward expansion of the Ottoman Empire
was finally halted by a strong Russian response. Later, trade in the Ottoman territories led Russia to conquests of its own as it began to drive southward in search
of warm-water ports in the Black Sea and the Persian Gulf. Once Russia reached
the Black Sea, its desire for free access to the Mediterranean heightened Russian
interest in the Turkish Straits and led to conflict with Britain. However, Russian
fears that the British fleet would gain access to the Black Sea if, for example, the

Straits were internationalized helped to induce Russia to alleviate its pressure on Turkey.

After the 1917 Revolution, the new Soviet leadership began to inveigh against the "evils of British imperial colonialism" in the Middle East and ideology became the chief Soviet arm for the moment. England thus came to replace Czarist Russia as the "symbol of oppression" in the eyes of many Moslems. In practice, however, the Anglo-Russian agreement of 1907 continued to restrain Soviet Russia's southern ambitions.[5]

With the outbreak of the Second World War, the Soviet Union's conditions for agreeing to enlarge the 1939 Germano-Soviet Non-Aggression Pact into a four-power pact with the Axis nations smacked of Russia's traditional imperial ambitions — control of the Straits and of an undefined territorial sphere "south of Batum and Baku in the general direction of the Persian Gulf" — were reportedly demanded.[6] After Hitler broke this pact and the German army penetrated deep into Soviet territory, Iran became the principal Allied supply route to the Soviet Union whose vital strategic interest in the Middle East was thus dramatically confirmed.

In the postwar period, the Soviets soon found themselves in a position to re-enter the Middle East as a major force. Nevertheless, a prudent policy was once again adopted when their southward probing brought an anxious America to the scene. Fearing that communist-linked subversive activity would drive local governments toward the West, the Soviet Union often gave only token support to communist exponents in the region.

Besides Britain and Russia, it should be remembered that Ottoman Turkey was the third party involved in the historic "Eastern Question". In the Middle East, the historical and cultural consciousness of the Arabs as such had all but died out with the fall of the once mighty Arab Empire.[7] Non-Arab Turkey could thus strengthen its role as a regional power by its ability to identify itself with the Arab peoples through the call of pan-Islam. However, when inefficiency and corruption weakened Ottoman rule, centrifugal forces began to organize.[8] The formation of the Young Turk movement, with its policy of Turkification and centralization of the Ottoman territories, further alienated the Arab world. Turkey then had to maintain its dominance by force alone, and its gradual estrangement from the peoples under its sway contributed to its defeat in the First World War.

To conclude this sketch of the Middle East's geopolitical setting, certain parallels between the situation at the time of the "Eastern Question" and that existing after the Second World War may be drawn. The pressure exerted by Russia, in its concern to protect its southern flank, remained a constant in both periods. Another constant was the presence of a Western power seeking to enlarge its sphere of influence in the area and to contain Russian or Soviet pressure — Great Britain at the time of the Eastern Question, the United States after the decline of the British Empire. A third constant appears to be the role played by a local power seeking to maintain its hegemony by exploiting the rivalry of the great powers—Ottoman Turkey in the period of Russian-British conflict, Egypt in the cold war between the Soviet Union and the United States. Whether or not these parallels reflect a more general hypothesis about the geopolitical principles operating in the Middle East is an intriguing question, but one that reaches beyond the scope of the present study.

The Rise of Egyptian Nationalism

Egypt may fairly be considered one of the oldest "nations" in history. Even when the political attributes of what is conventionally termed nationhood were lacking, the Egyptians were ever aware of their separateness and uniqueness. This self-awareness was formed in the Valley of the Nile.[9]

Situated in the northeastern part of the African continent, bordering the Mediterranean and Red Seas, and linked to Asia by the Sinai Peninsula, Egypt was separated from its neighbors by vast stretches of desert. In their fertile, ribbon-like valley, the people of the Nile—surrounded by natural bar-riers—were protected from the hordes of foreign invaders long enough for an Egyptian identity to emerge. Once established, this identity survived the many cultural waves that finally swept over Egypt. Although the Arab occupation left the greatest mark, the Egyptian ability to absorb rather than be absorbed was the means by which much that is distinctive in the character of the people (originally of Hamitic origin) was preserved against the Persian, Greek, Roman, Byzantine, Arab, and Turkish assaults.

Historically, the region to the east, which included the Valley of the Tigris and Euphrates, the Negev, and the Sinai Peninsula, served as the principal cor-ridor for foreign invasions as well as for the expansion of Egypt's own influence. When Egypt flourished, one of its constant objectives was to exercise some form of control over the cities, plains, harbors, and caravan routes of this prosperous region.[10]

The region to the south was also a traditional Egyptian concern. As far back as the Pharaonic period, Nubia and the Sudan were the objects of frequent cam-paigns in quest of gold and to secure trade routes to Africa for ivory, ebony, and, later, slaves. In the modern period, Mohammed Ali's victory in 1820 unified the Sudan with Egypt until 1882. In 1898, when the possibility that an enemy might divert the flow of the Nile River had been recognized by Egypt's British occupier, a joint British-Egyptian force restored nominal Egyptian rule over the Sudan.[11] More recently, control of the Sudan was a major issue in the dispute between Egypt and Britain after the Free Officers' Revolution.

In the contemporary period Egypt's role in the region that surrounds it greatly exercised the imagination of its leaders, including Gamal Abdel Nasser:

> We are in a group of circles which should be the theatre of our activity. . . .
> We cannot look stupidly at a map. . .not realizing our place therein, and the

role assigned to us by that position. Neither can we ignore [the] Arab Circle surrounding us and that this Circle is as much a part of us as we are a part of it; that our history has been merged with it and that its interests are linked with ours. . . .

Can we ignore. . .Africa in which fate has placed us and which is destined today to witness a terrible struggle for its future? This struggle affects us whether we want it or not.

Can we ignore. . .[the] the Moslem World to which we are tied by bonds forged not only by religious faith but also by the fact of history?[12]

In retrospect, the logical nexus between Egypt's ability to identify with Arab nationalist goals and sentiments and the extent to which it could influence events in the postwar Arab world seems clear. However, this task of relating to and identifying with the peoples to the east was more difficult than is commonly supposed. Even though the Egyptians speak Arabic and belong, for the most part, to the Moslem faith, their distinctive identity prevented them from readily and wholeheartedly embracing the tenets of Arab nationalism. The states of the Arab world were equally skeptical about accepting Egypt into their fold, partly on the grounds that power politics, rather than pan-Arabism, was that country's real motivation.[13]

In tracing the path by which these obstacles were overcome it must be borne in mind that, among the states of the Arab world, Egypt was the first in the modern era to revive its own particular brand of nationalism and to develop its own autonomous political personality.[14] This was largely due to Mohammed Ali whose visions of empire and greatness captivated the Egyptian imagination. National consciousness continued to evolve; an organized movement sprang up during the 1870s; and the nationalists experienced their first taste of power in the early 1880s. But this ended abruptly when Britain crushed the nationalist forces and occupied the country in order to protect what it considered its own vital interests.[15]

The British occupation, which was to last 72 years, was the primary factor in determining the growth of modern Egyptian nationalism as a separate and distinct concept from Arab nationalism. Cut off from the mainstream of Arab resistance to Ottoman rule, Egypt was even driven into an alliance with the Ottoman Sultan in order to stave off formal British annexation. Paradoxically, Egypt had given refuge to many exponents of the Arab nationalist revival during the last quarter of the nineteenth century; yet its principal concern was that of ridding itself of the British occupier. Egypt thus remained "immune to the impact of emerging Arab nationalism and the idea of a larger Arab fatherland,"[16] and pan-Islam rather than pan-Arabism remained the link between Egypt and the rest of the Middle East during this period.

Egypt's own brand of nationalism was further fanned during the First World War when Britain declared Egypt a protectorate following Turkey's commitment to the Central Powers. The development of a constitutional system was brusquely arrested. British occupation became the overriding concern of Egyptian politics; and Egypt drifted further from the currents of opinion stirring the Arab world.[17]

The Egyptian nationalists emerged from the First World War as an organized front for independence under the leadership of Saad Zaghloul and his Wafd (Delegation) group. Zaghloul led an Egyptian delegation to the Paris Peace Conference in 1919 where his demands for independence went unheeded; nevertheless the Wafd grew to become the chief political party of the nationalists.[18]

A series of riots and strikes finally persuaded Britain to terminate its protectorate in 1922. Under the "conditional" form of independence now granted Egypt, Britain still retained the right to safeguard Egyptian communications and defense, to protect foreign national interests, and to control the Sudan. British troops continued to occupy Egyptian soil, and the "regime of capitulations," which served as the instrument for foreign control of Egyptian commercial life, remained in force.[19]

In the ensuing period of frustrated nationalist aspirations, attitudes were formed that strongly affected Egyptian political behavior in the years to come. Among these was the Egyptian reluctance to take sides in struggles between great powers, an attitude that emerged during the Second World War when many nationalists even hoped that Axis pressure would force Britain out.[20] After the war the failure of early efforts to settle the dispute with Britain[21] hardened Egypt's determination to refuse to collaborate with the West until its demands for complete independence were met.

Even after the Anglo-Egyptian settlement of 1954, Egypt's long experience with Britain — a tale of frustrated national ambitions, capitulations, colonial occupation, unequal treaties, and unfulfilled promises — continued to color its future relations with the great powers in general. Ever skeptical and hesitant in their regard, Egypt feared that close collaboration with any great power would develop into the old "master-servant" relationship it knew and detested.

The Merger of Egyptian and Arab Nationalism

Several factors combined to change Egypt's attitude toward Arab nationalism. After the Second World War, Egypt found that Arab support was useful in its struggle against Britain. Another factor was the creation of the state of Israel and Egypt's involvement in the Palestine War of 1948. Still another was the desire to influence major regional developments, such as the formation of the Arab League, and Egypt's growing realization that it had a major role to play among the emerging Arab states.

The circumstances surrounding the creation of the Arab League are particularly relevant. Both Iraq and Egypt, which were traditional rivals, had been encouraged by the wartime British government to take the lead in projects for future Arab unity. While its promises of Arab independence were intended to counter Axis propaganda, Britain seems to have calculated that its position in the Arab world would be easier to maintain through an instrumentalized or at least easily influenced Arab League. Faced with this challenge, Egypt made its own bid for leadership in order to prevent Iraq from unifying a "Greater Syria" under Iraqi hegemony.[22]

In the 1944 Alexandria Protocol, which called for a loose association of Arab states, Egypt succeeded in imposing its will on Iraq. The formative meeting was held in Egypt; it was decided to locate the secretariat of the new League in Cairo; and it was also agreed that the Secretary-General would always be an Egyptian national. Furthermore, 60 percent of the members of the secretariat were to be Egyptian, and Egypt agreed to contribute about 42 percent of the League's budget.[23]

The League of Arab States, as thus obviously dominated by Egypt, came into being in March 1945. It was heralded as a "League. . .of the independent Arab States" that sought "to coordinate their political programs. . .to effect real collaboration. . .to preserve their independence and sovereignty."[24] In this way Egypt's leaders began to lay the foundation for a united front against colonial domination, and a long aloof center of pan-Islam at last drew a little closer to the Arab world.

Opposition to Zionism was another link between Egypt and the cause of Arab nationalism that was destined to grow stronger over time.[25] After joining the Arab states that entered into war against the new Jewish state in May 1948, Egypt shared the bitterness and resentment engendered by the humiliating defeat of the combined Arab forces. This resentment extended to the great powers that had contributed to Israel's creation. In the end, it was the Arab-Israeli problem, more than any other factor, that became the vehicle for focusing Egypt's attention eastward.

Egypt on the Path to Revolution

The precarious internal balance between the king, the Wafd Party, and those who represented British interests was shattered by the Second World War. The king was humiliated by harsh British tactics—including a military demonstration that had compelled him to accept Nahaas Pasha's pro-British government. Since Nahaas Pasha headed the Wafdists at the time, this party emerged from the war tainted by the charge of having collaborated with Britain. The Wafdists thus forfeited much of their initial power and following, and in the early postwar period internal dissent split their ranks into two main factions neither of which was able to regain the party's previous strength. Control of the government subsequently oscillated between these two factions until the final collapse in 1952.

The king despised both the British and the Wafdists. Profiting from the division within the traditional ruling party, he systematically obstructed all reformist efforts. The growing political vacuum, unheeded demands for reform, and

public disillusionment with the Wafd Party all favored the rise of ex-
traparliamentary militant groups. The most powerful was the Moslem
Brotherhood, which boasted a membership ranging between 300,000 and 1.5
million in the early 1950s. The communists, who also benefited, were influential
in Egyptian trade unions and among the intellectual community; but they were
never strong in terms of numbers, and the party had been officially outlawed.[26]

The group ultimately destined to play the decisive role was that of the
clandestine Free Officers within the Egyptian army. The origins of this group
may be traced back to 1939 when, at Mankabad in Upper Egypt, Gamal Abdel
Nasser and a number of fellow officers formed a secret society for the avowed
purpose of liberating Egypt.[27] The rise of these young officers had been favored
by a reform law of 1937 that opened the Military Academy to all classes. The
"new" Egyptian army that resulted began to reflect the interests of the middle
class and to share its frustrations over slow-to-come social and economic reforms.
While the doctrinal inspiration of the original conspirators varied from Moslem
Brotherhood leanings to communism, their common denominators were Egyptian nationalism and dissatisfaction with economic mismanagement, with corruption, and with the inequitable distribution of land that characterized the existing order.

Anwar El Sadat, one of the original members, described the goals of the
clandestine cells that were organized during the war under the control of a central committee of twelve persons:

> The aim of the Committee was to establish by force a democratic and
> republican government, which implied the expulsion of the British from
> Egyptian soil and the destruction of the feudal oligarchy which ruled our
> country. . . .It was a long-term plan, and Gamal Abdel Nasser was to be the
> architect and strategist.[28]

Israel's victory in 1948 and the blame placed by corrupt political leaders on
the Egyptian army and its officers reinforced the Free Officers' movement and
increased its animosity toward the existing order. The mood of these officers was
described by Abdel Nasser in *The Philosophy of the Revolution*: "We have been
duped — pushed into a battle for which we were unprepared. Vile ambitions, in-
sidious intrigues, and inordinate lust are toying with our destinies, and we are
left here under fire, unarmed." He went on to quote the words of a dying com-
rade: "Listen. . .the supreme struggle is in Egypt."[29]

Anwar El Sadat echoed his sentiments:

> After the Palestine campaign, Egypt moved rapidly toward revolution. The
> humiliation, frustration, and anger aroused by the incompetence of the men
> who had led Egypt to defeat instead of victory provoked a passionate desire
> to overthrow a regime which had once again demonstrated its complete
> incompetence.[30]

The Free Officers concluded that only radical action would suffice. "The war revealed the extent of evils which pervaded the court and government, and stirred the nation to protest."[31] The army, as the only organized "force equipped and capable of swift and decisive action,"[32] was called to play the major role. The executive committee of the Society of Free Officers was duly formed, and in January 1950 Abdel Nasser became its first chairman, to be re-elected in January 1951 and 1952.[33]

As the internal economic and political situation continued to deteriorate, the Wafd Party tried to regain its popularity by exploiting anti-British sentiments. However, extremists took matters into their own hands, a campaign of violence and sabotage against the British canal base ensued, and a clash between British forces and the Ismailia auxiliary police resulted in the death of over forty Egyptians on 25 January 1952. Next day, known as "Black Saturday," Egyptian mobs burned and ransacked everything in Cairo that symbolized foreign control.

King Farouk took advantage of the chaos to dismiss Wafdist Prime Minister Nahaas Pasha, who was a symbol of the king's own wartime humiliation. With the fall of the Wafdists, a succession of weak caretaker governments held out until the eve of the Revolution:

> Egypt consisted of a hated King, hated Government and a sullen, docile people permeated by groups plotting in secret. The end was near. It only required the folly of the King and a new period of Wafd misrule to bring it about.[34]

Thus the stage was set for the first Egyptians to rule Egypt since the last Saite Pharaoh submitted to the Persians nearly 2,500 years earlier.

The United States Enters the Middle East

The Middle East swiftly became one of the theaters of the global cold war confrontation between the United States and the Soviet Union after the Second World War. By 1946 the French had lost their hold on Syria and Lebanon, and Britain was fast assuming the role of "sick man" formerly attributed to Ottoman Turkey. Britain's ability to resist nationalist demands for independence was weakened by growing criticism of nineteenth century colonialist methods both at home and abroad. As Britain became more and more dependent on the economic and moral support of its American ally and progressively less capable of exercising a stabilizing influence in its colonies, political upheavals in the poverty-ridden Middle East became more frequent.

Seeking to expand its sphere of influence southward, Soviet Russia began to test the weakened British position in the Middle East. In Iran it sought to set up a communist government in the north, using its wartime occupation of that area as a springboard. In Greece it assisted the revolutionary forces that tried to bring a communist government into power. In Turkey it combined diplomatic pressure with encouragement of non-Turkish minorities to exact important concessions.

These moves elicited a strong reaction from the United States. On 12 March 1947 the Truman Doctrine was announced to prevent "a revival of American isolationism" and what it "would mean for the world". President Truman later spelled out his intentions in blunt terms:

> Inaction, withdrawal, "Fortress America" notions could only result in handing to the Russians vast areas of the globe now denied to them.[35]

The Truman Doctrine, termed a "Marshall Plan for the Near East," was an extension of America's global containment policy. After an appropriation of $400 million in May 1947, Congress enacted the Point Four Program and later the Mutual Security Act of 1951 to implement the Doctrine.[36] Soon the United States pressured the Soviet Union to withdraw its troops from Iran, dispatched American naval units to the Eastern Mediterranean to back Turkey, and bolstered anti-communist forces in Greece.

Despite this successful display of strength, subsequent events—such as the communist coup in Czechoslovakia, the Berlin blockade, the collapse of the Chiang Kai-shek regime on Mainland China, and especially the Korean War—reinforced and magnified American fears of world communist expansion. The cold war soon dominated America's perception of events in the Middle East as well, and this area's defense capabilities became an overriding concern.

The British defense system was based on bilateral agreements, the renewal of which depended upon the whims of increasingly nationalistic local governments. Hence the feasibility of extending a NATO type of defense scheme to this area was considered as early as May 1949 at a conference of American envoys to the Arab world.[37] By 1950 the concept of an Allied Middle East Command had evolved. It envisaged a line-up of British and Commonwealth country forces that would be reinforced by NATO air and sea power as well as by local forces.[38] Although this plan was finally jettisoned, NATO's impact on the Middle East was greatly strengthened when Turkey became a member in February 1952. The paramount strategic importance of the Suez Canal was nonetheless recognized and, during the first half of the 1950s, the Allies continued to regard Egypt as the key to Western defense of the region.

This purely strategic viewpoint, however, clashed with the "special" relationship between America and Israel that had become a constant feature of American foreign policy after the creation of the Jewish state in 1948.[39] On 31 August 1945, after public sympathy for the survivors of Nazi persecution and growing Zionist pressure had rallied the political spokesmen for 41 states to support the creation of a Jewish national homeland,[40] President Harry Truman called on Britain to allow the immediate admission of 100,000 Jewish refugees into Palestine. When, however, Britain insisted that the United States share responsibility for this decision in view of mounting hostility between the Arab and Jewish communities in Palestine, the United States declined to risk political or military engagements and agreed only to participate in a Joint Anglo-American Commission of Inquiry.[41]

Truman's notion of the complicated issues at stake is evident in a statement to the press upon his return from Potsdam:

> The American view on Palestine is that we want to let as many of the Jews into Palestine as it is possible to let into that country. Then the matter will have to be worked out diplomatically with the British and the Arabs, so that if a state can be set up they may be able to set it up on a peaceful basis. I have no desire to send 500,000 American soldiers there to make peace in Palestine.[42]

He later added: "My basic approach was that the long-range fate of Palestine was the kind of problem we had the U.N. for."[43]

Truman acknowledged that officials in the Pentagon and the State Department feared his position "would prejudice British and U.S. interests in much of the Middle East" and that these agencies were primarily concerned about oil and potential Soviet influence.[44] But he upbraided "the striped-pants boys in the State Department [who] didn't care enough about what happened to the thousands of displaced persons who were involved."

The sincerity of Truman's humanitarian impulse, as thus formulated long after the events, is beyond question. Still, the fact that his political instincts were equally involved is shown by many other statements, some of them singularly lacking in restraint. For example, William Eddy, then American Ambassador to Saudi Arabia, recounts that he and three other ambassadors to the Middle East were recalled in October 1946 to hear Truman brush aside their fears in these terms: "I'm sorry, gentlemen, but I have to answer to hundreds of thousands who are anxious for the success of Zionism; I do not have hundreds of thousands of Arabs among my constituents."[45]

The same view was expressed in more subdued tones in a conversation between Secretary of the Navy Forrestal and American Senator and Democratic National Chairman J. Howard McGrath:

> In the first place, Jewish sources were responsible for a substantial part of the contributions to the Democratic National Committee, and many of these contributions were made with the distinct idea on the part of the givers that they would have an opportunity to express their views and have them seriously considered on such questions as the present Palestine question.[46]

Others professed concern about the so-called "Jewish vote," although the Jewish community represented only 3.5 percent of the American population and the political weight of this component may have been overestimated even on matters directly affecting Israel.[47]

One immediate consequence was that the United States took the lead in pushing the Palestine Partition Plan through the United Nations General Assembly:

> The United States not only stood on the side of partition but in the crucial moments before the decision threw her full weight into the effort to mobilize the votes that were still needed. Without this effort, it is very doubtful whether the partition resolution would have obtained the statutory two-thirds majority of the General Assembly.[48]

That the Soviet Union cast a decisive vote in favor of the Plan and that Eastern Bloc military aid helped the nascent Jewish state to resist Arab armies are less widely known facts.

By March 1948, when an American proposal to the Security Council called for a United Nations Trusteeship for Palestine,[49] Truman appeared to be more receptive to warnings from various agencies that the Palestine crisis could damage American interests in the Middle East. Two months later, however, the British Mandate for Palestine was terminated, and Israel's proclamation of independence on 14 May elicited immediate *de facto* recognition by the United States. A few days later *de jure* recognition was granted by the Soviet Union.

The Arab-Israeli war of 1948 left Israel in possession of a vastly greater territory than it had been allotted under the Partition Plan that was rejected by the Arabs. This conflict also touched off an exodus of Arab refugees from Palestine and, later on, a wave of Jewish immigration from Arab countries whose Jewish communities had previously lived without fear of the persecutions inflicted upon the Jews in Europe.

After it became evident that the Armistice Agreements of 1949 would not assuage the bitter enmities this tragedy left in its wake, the United States, together with Britain and France, issued the Tripartite Declaration of May 1950. The Declaration represented a major American commitment to stabilizing the situation. It recognized the need of both the Arab states and Israel "to maintain a certain level of armed forces for internal security and. . .legitimate self-defense. . . ." However, the three powers expressed their "opposition to the development of an arms race" and laid down that any country purchasing arms had to warrant "that the purchasing state does not intend to undertake any act of aggression against any other state." Should the three signatory governments "find that any of these states was preparing to violate frontiers or armistice lines, [they] would. . .immediately take action, both within and outside the United Nations, to prevent such violation."[50]

Despite President Truman's bland assurances that this measure was intended to heighten the confidence of both the Arab states and Israel,[51] inherent weaknesses caused the Tripartite Declaration to fall short of the principles it embodied. For example, the Soviet Union had not been included and was not therefore even formally subject to its limitations when Moscow's Middle East line veered sharply in favor of the Arabs. Again, since no means of enforcement had been agreed upon, France was able to violate the Declaration with impunity when it entered into its own conflict with the Arab world.

Above all, the Tripartite Declaration did not lessen the anti-American sentiments that had begun to take root in large segments of the Arab world. America's material, diplomatic and moral support for Israel, which was of crucial importance in ensuring the continued existence of the latter country, tarnished the American image in the eyes of the Arabs and shattered the goodwill that had been won through cultural, educational, and philanthropic work in the Arab world. The resentment generated by the alleged American "sin against the Arab nation" was destined to haunt American-Arab relations for more than two decades.

The Evolution of American-Egyptian Relations

It seems useful to conclude these introductory remarks by noting a few general principles that ought to be borne in mind as American-Egyptian relations in the period 1952-1958 are examined in the rest of this book. To begin with, it may be inferred that the erratic nature of these relations in the formative years was largely due to the inability of either side to elaborate a clearly defined policy toward the other. After the Revolution, when the two countries' reciprocal expectations were high, the establishment of a solid relationship was deferred pending settlement of the Anglo-Egyptian dispute. However, settlement of this dispute led to disappointed expectations, and other issues soon emerged to sour their relations. As each side sought to make the other accept its own view of the region's political situation, their attitudes toward each other reflected their different regional commitments, and their policies tended to become ad hoc reactions or adjustments to events rather than steps toward predetermined objectives. The interim character of the post-Revolutionary period was thus indefinitely retained, and America's traditional allies were often no less confused by the resulting contradictions than the countries of the region.

> What we have failed to see in the Middle East. . .is the need to set our own priorities, our own policies. . .through our own initiative — instead of merely reacting to the actions of somebody else, whether a Khrushchev or a Nasser.[52]

After the Second World War, the political and strategic interests of the United States in the area were mainly an outgrowth of the cold war, and America's chief objective was to prevent the Soviet Union from taking advantage of diminishing British influence. Egypt's primary objective, instead, was to rid itself and the Arab world of the vestigial manifestations of colonialism, a desire that sprang from considerations unrelated to the cold war struggle. Conflict arose when the measures adopted by the United States to accomplish its objectives appeared inimical to Egypt's own goals and Egypt reacted by trying to frustrate implementation of America's decisions.

The tendency of the United States, often under extreme internal pressure, to regard ad hoc positions as ends in themselves rather than as means to an end added to the friction. Similarly, once Nasser had assumed the role of charismatic and heroic leader of the Arab world, he was increasingly driven by the need to sustain his own image. The growing inflexibility that characterized these interactions was at the root of American-Egyptian disaccord.

The situation in the Middle East was further complicated by a number of local issues. Besides the rise of Arab nationalism and the persistence of the Arab-Israeli dispute, the following complex interrelations at both the global and regional levels had, to varying degrees, an impact on American-Egyptian relations during the period in question: those between the United States and the other Arab nations; between the United States and its NATO allies; between Egypt and the Soviet Union; between Egypt and Israel; between Egypt and the other Arab states; between Egypt and the nonaligned world; and finally, between the Soviet Union and the other Arab states.

American-Egyptian relations must also be understood as the interaction of a superpower, which viewed the Middle East as but one region among many, with a leading regional power, for which any event that occured within the Arab Middle East was of vital importance. In this perspective, the difference in sheer power between the two countries was largely offset by Egypt's ability to exploit such countervailing factors as America's rivalry with the Soviet Union, Egypt's own support for the Arab nationalist cause, and Egypt's courtship of the nonaligned nations in order to increase its prestige and overall capacity to resist. Thus, when Egypt found itself in opposition to American policy in the Arab Middle East, it was often in a position effectively to hinder the implementation of that policy.

Another problem for American-Egyptian relations was America's great power complex and Egypt's inferior power complex. Although the United States made no secret of its distaste for nineteenth century colonial tactics, it nonetheless fell into the habit of approaching countries that emerged from colonial rule with a patronizing air, and it proved capable of establishing only a mentor-pupil type of relationship rather than a relationship between equals. With specific regard to the Middle East in the 1950s, Secretary of State Dulles appeared to push for an American solution to Arab problems, whereas Egypt's President Nasser naturally wanted an Arab solution; the more determined Dulles was to make Nasser yield, the more inflexible Nasser became.

Another major cause of frustration was the different priorities the two countries attached to the problem of communist expansion. Just as the United States was obsessed with communism, so Nassar was obsessed with any potential threat to Egypt's nascent sovereignty; and just as America's obsession often seemed irrelevant to the Egyptian leadership, so Egypt's obsession seemed equally irrelevant to Dulles. A comment by Dulles at an important Background Press Conference on 24 March 1957 suffices to show this annoyance and the attitude from which it sprang:

> Now the thing we are up against is a rather extreme view which the Arab countries in general, and Egypt in particular take on this thing which they call nationalization and "sovereignty." Nasser can hardly speak more than a couple of sentences but what he has to bring in "sovereignty"— "sovereignty"— they apparently conceive it as being the right to prove that you can step on other people's toes with impunity. But we all know, who have some maturity in these matters, that sovereignty—its best expression involves the harmonization of policies, coordinating them and working for the common good. But countries that have newly won their wings of independence incline toward taking initially an extreme view. They are hypersensitive about this thing. But it is so demonstrable that in the long run it is going to hurt Egypt and the other Arab countries.[53]

One far-reaching consequence of this attitude was that the American leadership usually failed to make any practical distinction between communists and Arab nationalists. American support for unpopular regimes that tried to repress the second group drove the wedge between the United States and these same nationalists ever deeper and actually forced the nationalists to turn to the Soviet Union for help.

For obvious reasons, America's aversion to Arab nationalism was bound to damage its relations with Egypt, whose own prestige and influence grew the more it became the acknowledged champion of that very cause. Apparently convinced that, left to his own devices, Nasser could not help but favor the spread of Soviet influence,[54] America's leaders attached little importance to the fact that Nasser was not a communist, a fact they themselves clearly recognized. On this assumption the United States proceeded to bolster more conservative regimes to the point where they became potential challengers of Egypt's regional hegemony. Nothing could have been more odious to Egypt nor more counterproductive for America's avowed Middle East goals.

Fortunately for the United States, many of these goals were attained despite the failure of its own initiatives. The story of how this came about, from the Egyptian Revolution in 1952 to the death of John Foster Dulles in 1958, is told in the chapters that follow, often through the voices of both the apparent protagonists and those operating behind the scenes. Yet, as the curtain rises and the players take their places, it is worth pausing to mark the historical irony in the fact that America's primary goal—that of containing Soviet expansion in the Middle East—was largely the achievement of those very nationalist forces that were so feared, and often so contemptuously treated, by what was then a very distant Washington indeed.

Notes

1. J. F. Dulles in U.S. Congress, Senate, *The President's Proposal on the Middle East: Hearings before the Committee on Foreign Relations and the Committee on Armed Services*, 85th Cong., 1st sess., S. J. Res. 19 and H. J. Res. 117, Pt. 1, 14 January-4 February 1957. Washington D.C.: Government Printing Office, 1957, p. 11. Hereafter referred to as *Hearings, 1957*.

2. H. L. Hoskins, *The Middle East, Problem Area in World Politics* (New York: The Macmillan Co., 1957), p. 6.

3. See Ivar Spector, *The Soviet Union and the Muslim World: 1917-1958* (Seattle: University of Washington Press, 1959), p. 3.

4. W. L. Langer, *European Alliances and Alignments* (New York: Knopf, 1962), p. 252. Britain also held a 44 percent interest in the Maritime Suez Canal Company, having profited from Egyptian financial difficulties to purchase the Khedive's shares. France held the majority interest.

5. See *Great Britain: Parliamentary Papers*, vol. 125, Cd. 3750 (1908).

6. U.S. Department of State, *Nazi-Soviet Relations: 1939-1941*, Publication 3023, pp. 258-59.

7. See generally George Antonius, *The Arab Awakening* (London: Hamish Hamilton, 1945).

8. Ibid., pp. 80, 93.

9. Tom Little, *Modern Egypt* (London: Ernest Benn, 1968), p. 28. From the earliest period this feeling was expressed in a vigorous self-awareness and complacent pride as "men" in contrast with Egypt's Nubian, Libyan, and Asiatic neighbors. G. Steindorff and K. G. Seele, *When Egypt Ruled the East* (Chicago: University of Chicago Press, 1963), p. 10.

10. For the Pharaonic period, see Steindorff and Seele, *When Egypt Ruled*. Egyptian frontiers extended to the Euphrates at various points during this period, i.e., Egypt under Tuthmosis I, Tuthmosis III and Ramses III. For the Islamic period, see Philip Hitti, *The History of the Arabs* (New York: Macmillan, 1956). For examples under the Fatamid Caliphs and Salah El Din, see Little, *Modern Egypt*, pp. 21-29. For Egypt under Mohammed Ali, see ibid., pp. 30-36.

11. W. L. Langer, *The Diplomacy of Imperialism* (New York: Alfred A. Knopf, 1965), pp. 103-10.

12. Gamal Abdel Nasser, *The Philosophy of the Revolution* (Cairo: The National Publication House, n.d.), pp. 51-53.

13. See, for example, Pierre Beyssade, *La Ligue Arabe* (Paris: Editions Planète, 1968), p. 110.

14. Tom Little sets the date for the beginning of modern Egyptian nationalism as 1805, when the Egyptians reasserted themselves against Turkish domination to select Mohammed Ali as their leader. Egypt at this point began to reestablish itself as a self-contained political unit. (*Modern Egypt*, pp. 20-39). See also Peter Mansfield, *Nasser's Egypt* (Baltimore, Md.: Penguin African Library, 1965), pp. 17-18.

15. Langer, *European Alliances*, p. 272.

16. Hisham B. Sharabi, *Nationalism and Revolution in the Arab World* (New York: D. Van Nostrand, 1966), pp. 8-9.

17. Patrick Seale, *Struggle for Syria* (London: Oxford University Press, 1965), p. 16.

18. Little, *Modern Egypt*, p. 74.

19. Mansfield, *Nasser's Egypt*, p. 27. For text of the 1922 Agreement, see Royal Institute of International Affairs, *Great Britain and Egypt, 1914-1936*, Information Department Papers, No. 19 (London: Chatham House, 1937), p. 11.

20. Anwar El Sadat, *Revolt on the Nile* (New York: J. Day, 1967), pp. 81-98 and 107.

21. See Bevin-Sidqi Negotiations, 1946-47 and the resulting draft agreement, Great Britain, Foreign Office, *Papers Regarding the Negotiations for a Revision of the Anglo-Egyptian Treaty of 1936, Cd. 7179, London H.M.S.O., 1947.* British withdrawal from Alexandria and Cairo to the Suez Canal Zone in March 1947 did little to quell Egyptian hostility. See George Kirk, *The Middle East, 1945-1950, Survey of International Affairs* (London: Oxford University Press, 1954), pp. 116-36.

22. Beyssade, *La Ligue Arabe*, p. 45.

23. B. Boutras-Ghali, *Egyptian Foreign Policy and the Arab League* (Cairo: University Press, 1956), cited in Beyssade, *La Ligue Arabe*, p. 111.

24. Sharabi, *Nationalism and Revolution*, pp. 153-54.

25. See Round Table Conference (February 1939) and Arab Conference in Bludan (1937); J. C. Hurewitz, *The Struggle for Palestine* (New York: W. W. Norton and Co., 1950), pp. 98-102.

26. Manfred Halpern, *The Politics of Social Change in the Middle East and North Africa* (Princeton, N.J.: Princeton University Press, 1965), p. 150; J. C. Groves, "The Arab Attitude to Communism with Special Reference to Nasser's Egypt." Unpublished Memoire de Diplôme, no. 88, Geneva, IUHEI, 1962.

27. William Spencer, *Political Evolution in the Middle East* (New York: J. B. Lippincott, 1962), p. 380; El Sadat, *Revolt on the Nile*, pp. 11-17.

28. El Sadat, *Revolt on the Nile*, pp. 13-14.

29. Abdel Nasser, *Philosophy of the Revolution*, pp. 13-14.

30. El Sadat, *Revolt on the Nile*, p. 109.

31. Abdel Nasser, "The Egyptian Revolution," *Foreign Affairs* 33 (January 1955): 203.

32. Abdel Nasser, *Philosophy of the Revolution*, p. 28.

33. The ten original members of the executive committee were Gamal Abdel Nasser, Abdel Hakim Amer, Anwar El Sadat, Salah Salem, Kamal El Din Hussein, Gamal Salem, Abdul Moneim Abdel Raouf, Hassan Ibrahim, Khaled Mohieddin, and Abdel Latif El Boghdadi. Later they were joined by Hussain Shafi and Zakariyya Mohieddin. El Sadat, *Revolt on the Nile*, p. 112.

34. P. I. Vatikiotis, *The Modern History of Egypt* (London: Weidenfeld and Nicolson, 1969), pp. 265-66.

35. H. S. Truman, *Memoirs: Years of Trial and Hope, 1946-1955* (Garden City, N.Y.: Doubleday, 1955), 2:102. See also President Truman's official statement at the time in U.S. Department of State, *Bulletin*, 23 March 1947, pp. 534-37.

36. *Public Law 75*, 85th Cong., 1st sess., *Documents on American Foreign Relations*, ed., R. Dennett and R. K. Turner, vol. 11: January 1 - December 31, 1949 (Princeton, N.J.: Princeton University Press, 1950), p. 10; ibid., 13: 128-39.

37. J. C. Hurewitz, *Middle East Dilemmas, the Background of United States Policy* (New York: Harper and Brothers, 1953), p. 92.

38. R. P. Stebbins, *The United States in World Affairs, 1951* (New York: Harper, 1952), p. 284.

39. Although no official obligations or engagements were made, verbal support was given for the establishment of a Jewish national home in Palestine even before the war. See Lodge-Fish Joint Congressional Resolution (1922) quoted in Hurewitz, *Middle East Dilemmas*, p. 118. American support for the Balfour Declaration was declared in a letter from President Wilson to Rabbi Wise (29 October 1918) quoted in George Lenczowski, *The Middle East in World Affairs* (Ithaca, N.Y.: Cornell University Press, 1958), p. 81.

40. Samuel Halperin, *The Political World of American Zionism* (Detroit, Mich.: Wayne State University Press, 1961), p. 186.

41. Hurewitz, *Middle East Dilemmas*, p. 132.

42. Truman, *Memoirs*, 2: 162.

43. Ibid., p. 140.

44. Ibid., p. 149.

45. William Eddy, *F.D.R. Meets Ibn Saud* (New York: American Friends of the Middle East, Inc., 1954), pp. 36-37.

46. *The Forrestal Diaries*, ed., Walter Millis (New York: Viking Press, 1951), p. 345.

47. A case in point was the re-election of President Eisenhower by a wide margin despite America's position in the Suez Crisis of 1956; see chapter 7 *passim*.

48. Nadav Safran, *The United States and Israel* (Cambridge, Mass.: Harvard Univesity Press, 1963), pp. 3-4. See also U.S. Department of State, *Bulletin*, 21 September 1947, pp. 546-61.

49. *U.N. Security Council Official Records*, 3d year, 271st meeting, 19 March 1948, p..167.

50. U.S. Department of State, *Bulletin*, 5 June 1950, p. 886.

51. Ibid.

52. Eric Johnston, "Formula for a Mideast Settlement," *New York Times Magazine*, 10 August 1958, p. 46.

53. Unpublished Background Press Conference, 24 March 1957, John Foster Dulles, *The Papers of John Foster Dulles, 1888-1959*, Seeley G. Mudd Manuscript Library, Princeton University, Princeton, N.J. (hereafter referred to as *Dulles Private Papers*).
54. Loy Henderson to the author.

Egypt
and the United States

The Formative Years

1

American-Egyptian Relations before and after the Revolution

The United States long avoided political involvement in Egypt as in other colonialized countries that had not yet become independent of European control.[1] Faithful to the traditional tenets of American hemispheric isolationism, it looked upon Egypt as a British preserve.

In the nineteenth century, when Egypt had little control over its foreign policy, American activity in Egypt was chiefly confined to private initiatives in the commercial, educational, religious, and philanthropic spheres. The function of the State Department's representative was mainly to protect these private interests. Indeed, American involvement in Egypt at this stage was so limited that its first representative there was of British nationality, and it was not until 1848 that an American took charge as Consul General.[2]

At the inaugural celebration of the Suez Canal in 1869, the United States was the only sizable power without official representation. America's use of the canal subsequently accounted for a small share of the total traffic that flowed through this artery.[3] The fact that the United States was not even a signatory to the 1888 Constantinople Convention, which established the international status of the canal, shows the minor role it played in America's foreign policy at that period.

Until 1918 official business with Egypt was transacted through Constantinople.[4] Benefiting from a most-favored-nation clause in the 1830 Capitulation Treaty signed by the Ottoman Sultan, the United States was represented at the Egyptian Mixed Court of Appeals.[5] By 1914 America's gradually expanding interests warranted the establishment of a consulate in Alexandria in addition to the Cairo representation.

Private American undertakings grew in the commercial field. Although the total volume of trade was modest, Egyptian long-staple cotton found an early market in the United States. When the Civil War disrupted cotton supplies from the Southern States, the British textile industry as well as that of the Northern States turned to Egypt, which became a major source of high-quality cotton.[6] Later on, and especially in the period between the two world wars, American businesses such as Socony Vacuum, Singer Sewing Machines, General Motors, and Kodak established branch offices in Egypt.

35

American Protestant missionary groups, having begun their work in Syria as early as 1820, gradually extended educational and missionary services to Egypt after 1854. Numerous schools and medical and charity centers were set up, mainly under the auspices of the United Presbyterian Church. The American University in Cairo, founded in 1919, soon became an important intellectual center.

By 1938 total American business investment in Egypt was estimated at $14 million. Missionary, philanthropic, and educational properties were valued at less than $4 million.[7]

During the First World War, Egyptian nationalists believed their aspirations for independence might be supported by the United States, which had temporarily abandoned its isolationist stance. However, America had never declared war on Turkey and could not therefore participate directly in the Allied-Turkish peace negotiations that significantly affected Egypt. The hopes raised by President Wilson's "Fourteen Points", proclaimed in January 1918, proved empty. The United States rejected its extrahemispheric commitments shortly after the war and reverted to its long-standing policy of noninvolvement under which Egypt was considered part of the British Empire.[8] Following the proclamation of conditional Egyptian independence in 1922, the new government was recognized "subject to the maintenance of the rights of the United States in Egypt as they had hitherto existed,"[9] and the United States diplomatic representation was soon raised to legation level.

The discovery of petroleum in the period between the two world wars elicited keen American interest in the Middle East. Intensive efforts were made by American oil companies to expand their share in exploitation rights. Often blocked by their European counterparts, larger companies increasingly relied on State Department support in order to assert the principles of "open door" and equality of treatment for American citizens and their interests. By 1939 American oil companies had acquired exclusive concessions in Bahrain and Saudi Arabia, and a 50 percent interest in a concession in Kuwait. Through the Iraq Petroleum Company, Americans participated in oil explorations not only in Iraq but also on the fringes of the Arab Peninsula.[10]

This development did not directly affect American-Egyptian relations until the events of the Second World War demonstrated the importance of the Suez Canal and, with it, Egypt. The advance of Rommel's desert army into Egypt threatened the Allies' energy supplies and dictated American acceptance of joint strategic responsibilities with Britain. For the first time the United States agreed to undertake defense commitments concerning the Middle East.

Egypt became of vital importance to Allied war efforts in the Middle East. Cairo was the center for the Allied Intelligence Headquarters, for lend-lease distribution and propaganda operations, and Britain built one of the world's most extensive military bases on the banks of the Suez Canal. Three miles wide and 65 miles long, this base became the cornerstone of the Allied defense system in the region.[11]

Although Egypt was still regarded as primarily Britain's responsibility, by 1942 the United States had assumed a joint obligation for its defense. The United States Armed Forces in the Middle East (USAFIME) were established in Cairo to coordinate and control military activity in the region, and an American air base was constructed in Cairo.[12]

By 1945 America's contacts with Egypt had harvested a store of good will. Its educational, missionary, and philanthropic endeavors had established an image untarnished by a history of colonial domination. Hence, on the eve of the postwar period, America stood high in the esteem of the average Egyptian citizen.

The wartime lesson concerning Egypt's strategic value in a global power struggle was not to be forgotten in the postwar period. The gigantic military base along the Suez Canal was seen as vital to the defense of the region. Ensuring Egypt's commitment to the Western camp soon became a major preoccupation of both Britain and the United States.

Egypt, instead, was chiefly interested in terminating British occupation of its territory and in achieving union with the Sudan. It viewed America's traditional opposition to European colonialism as a possible source of support for Egypt's position against Britain. But this required cultivation[13] and induced Egypt to tone down the hostility that American sympathies for Israel would otherwise have provoked.

American-Egyptian relations evolved slowly after the war through a series of bilateral agreements that covered a wide range of subjects. In 1946 an air transport agreement was signed, and the American air base in Cairo was turned over to Egypt. Both countries elevated their diplomatic representation to embassy level later that year. In July 1947 the Export-Import Bank granted a loan of $5.6 million (subsequently increased to $7.3 million) for the reconstruction and repair of Egyptian fertilizer and chemical industries.[14] Agreements concerning educational exchanges and war surplus purchases furthered the development of cordial relations.

Trade, although still modest, improved. Between 1948 and 1952 Egyptian exports to the United States showed a fourfold expansion by value, while imports from America nearly trebled.[15] In 1947 the United States became Egypt's second largest supplier after Britain.[16] Growing American interests in Middle East oil led to a substantial increase in American use of the Suez Canal, and this was reflected in the appointment of an American national to the Board of Directors of the Maritime Suez Canal Company in June 1948.[17]

On 5 May 1951, by means of the Technical Cooperation Agreement, America's "Point Four" Program was extended to Egypt.[18] Grants of large-scale American aid normally followed political or strategic commitments by the recipient country. In Egypt's case, however, truly substantial aid was postponed pending solution of the Anglo-Egyptian dispute, cessation of Egyptian-Israeli hostilities, and an Egyptian commitment to a Western defense system.

Despite Egyptian attempts to gain American sympathy, the United States preferred not to interfere in the affairs of its British ally during the postwar Anglo-Egyptian negotiations. In other words, so long as Britain appeared to be in control of the situation, the United States chose to maintain its traditional low-key policy toward Egypt.

> The American Government refused to compete with Britain in what was believed to be a British preserve. It was reluctant, moreover, to create a precedent which might affect its own position in Panama.[19]

This contrasts with what had happened in Palestine, Iran, Turkey, and Greece where Britain, unable to cope with the situations that arose, was forced to turn to America for aid.

Only a combination of unfavorable developments, including Soviet and communist successes elsewhere, finally led the American leadership to decide that its own interests in Egypt and the Middle East were such that it could no longer afford to remain aloof from the ever more bitter dispute between Britain and Egypt. As Egypt hardened its attitude and the impasse in negotiations drove Britain to maintain its occupation by force alone, acts of sabotage and guerilla warfare began to render the Suez Canal Base more of a liability than an asset to Western defense.[20] It was clear that unless Britain swiftly pacified Egypt, the latter would become a center of resistance to the very Western defense system that was in theory to be extended from Egypt throughout the Arab world.

Accordingly, the United States set out to find a workable compromise between the strategic needs of the West and the national aspirations of Egypt. It began to lend its good offices to the disputing parties and to step up its own activities with a view to finding a satisfactory solution to the defense needs of the region.

In early 1950 British Foreign Minister Bevin suggested that a settlement based on the replacement of British troops in Egypt by an integrated force of Egyptian and British troops under a supreme commander might offer a way out of the impasse.[21] The American Pentagon and a British working group duly planned a Middle East command that was in principle to satisfy all the interested parties. American Secretary of State Dean Acheson described the results:

> [It would consist of] a Supreme Allied Commander Middle East and his headquarters, which would be in Cairo and include Egyptian officers and be directed by a Middle East Chiefs-of-Staff Committee. The British base in Egypt would be given to Egypt, which would put it under the Supreme Commander with Egyptian participation in its operation. British troops not allocated to the Supreme Commander should be at once withdrawn from Egypt; the number remaining would be determined by the Commander in agreement with the Egyptian Government.[22]

Intensive diplomatic activity followed, with conferences in Ankara and London of the Chiefs-of-Staff of Britain and the Commonwealth, the United States, France, and Turkey. This gave rise to a Four-Power Proposal for a Middle East Command, which was presented to Egypt on 13 October 1951. Emphasizing that "Egypt belongs to the free world and, in consequence, her defense and that of the Middle East in general is equally vital to other democratic nations," the proposal invited Egypt "to participate [in the projected Allied Middle East Command] as a founding member" with Britain, the United States, France, and Turkey, on the "basis of equality and partnership."[23]

The Egyptian contribution was to consist of "such strategic defense and other facilities on her soil as are indispensable for the organization in peacetime of the Middle East" and "all necessary facilities in the event of war, imminent menace of war or apprehended international emergency. . . ." Inducements to win Egypt's assent included provisions for "facilities to train and equip her forces" and for "supercession of the 1936 Treaty" as well as the stipulation that the Suez Canal Base "would be formally handed over to the Egyptians on the understanding that it would simultaneously become an Allied Base within the Allied Middle East Command with full Egyptian participation in the running of this base in peace and war."[24]

However, the Commander under the plan was to be British; hence Britain, whose defense plans heavily depended on retention of the Suez Canal Base, could have maintained control albeit in coordination with the other founding members and without the sting of "occupation". Furthermore, the Western desire to link the Command to NATO as a first step in extending it throughout the region was apparent in the overlapping membership scheme as proposed.

If these papier-mâché arrangements appealed to those in Washington, they merely succeeded in angering the Egyptian government, which rejected the proposal two days after it was presented. Egypt's Ambassador to the United States explained that his country had neither been consulted when the proposals were drafted nor guaranteed its independence and sovereignty by them.[25] On the same day the Egyptian Parliament adopted decrees unilaterally abrogating the 1899 and 1936 Anglo-Egyptian Treaties, and Farouk was declared King of Egypt and the Sudan.[26]

Officially, the American leadership expressed disappointment over the hastiness with which the proposal was rejected and remained hopeful that the Egyptian government would reconsider its position.[27] At the same time efforts were made to devise a more flexible approach that toned down and interpreted away some of the more objectionable aspects of the original project.[28] The minimum requirements, however, added up to an arrangement similar to that of the preceding plan: a safe, secure, and functional base should be maintained on the canal as part of the Allied defense structure; its control should be placed in what the promoters considered reliable hands.[29]

American optimism about this modified plan appeared to be based on the belief that a "package deal" could be arranged. Egyptian sovereignty over the

Sudan would be recognized and British occupation terminated in exchange for an Egyptian agreement to join a Western defense system. Responsibility for the Suez Canal Base would have been internationalized.[30]

In reality both the British and the Egyptian governments were now dissatisfied for different reasons. The former viewed the Americans' willingness to cede British interests, especially in the Sudan, with dismay.[31] The latter derided the scheme as yet another "device to prolong British occupation of Egyptian territory with the added backing of the United States."[32] Moreover, the successes of nationalist movements elsewhere in the world had hardened the Egyptian will to resist any solution that would mean less than total independence, while the precarious internal situation obliged the government to avoid appearing in any posture that might be interpreted as yielding to colonialist pressure.

The uprising against Britain at the end of January 1952 and the ensuing deterioration in Egypt's domestic political situation appear to have heightened America's concern about the impact of the Anglo-Egyptian dispute on Western relations with Egypt. Fears mounted that only local extremist elements, including the communists, might benefit from continued British occupation of the canal base by force. Now the United States began to press Britain to adopt a more compromising attitude,[33] and the American leadership energetically sought to foster a solution that would satisfy both Egyptian nationalist aspirations and Western defense needs. Besides lending his good offices, American Ambassador to Cairo Jefferson Caffery at times virtually assumed the role of mediator. As will be seen, long, hard negotiations lay ahead before the basis for a settlement was finally to be found.

On the eve of the Revolution this strategically vital part of the region had begun to seethe with instability. Egyptian demands remained unsatisfied, the Anglo-Egyptian dispute still festered, and the vaunted Middle East Command was no more than a fading illusion. The Suez Canal Base was held by British force alone, and American reluctance either to back its ally fully or to discourage Egyptian nationalist demands had earned it the title of "meddler" in British eyes.[34]

The Free Officers took action on the evening of 22 July 1952. Within four hours (23 July), and with a minimum of bloodshed and resistance, Cairo had been occupied and the reins of power were firmly in the hands of the army. Three days later King Farouk left the country.

The fall of Egypt's corrupt and feudal regime presented the American leadership with an opportunity to undertake the major policy reassessment that had by then become imperative.

It was not doctrine that subsequently guided the Free Officers so much as the need to react to the chain of events their initial moves had touched off.[35] Nasser later referred to the Egyptian Revolution as a "Revolution without a plan".[36] What began as a coup d'état appears to have resulted in the overthrow of the old order mainly because the political survival of the Officers' group rendered this mandatory.

Although it took several months before the implications of these events became clear, the United States government had every reason to view them with optimism. Intelligence reports prior to the coup had stressed the moderation that was likely to characterize a Junta formed by the young army officers.[37] Besides, the old regime was discredited in American eyes by its unwillingness to compromise with Britain; by its refusal to participate in a Western defense system or even to preserve the effectiveness of the Suez Canal Base; and by the debauchery and corruption that rendered it easier for extremist elements to extend their influence or perhaps to seize power. In a word, the Americans hoped the new leaders would be moderate enough to cooperate with them and yet powerful enough to take certain unpopular decisions that would remove the obstacles to Western defense plans for the region.

Egypt's new leaders in turn had their own grounds for being optimistic about relations with the United States. American sympathy for the Egyptian goal of complete independence seemed consistent with the revolt that the United States had itself staged against Britain.[38] Americans traditionally viewed European colonialism with distaste and their activities in the Middle East were still free of a colonialist taint. The American leadership's preoccupation with building up a defense system for the Middle East had already led the United States to support Egyptian aspirations for the Sudan and to urge Britain to compromise on other key issues as well. On the reasonable assumption that fewer concessions would have to be made if Egypt could induce America to adopt a benevolent attitude, the Egyptian leadership chose not to stress American support for Israel and aimed instead to persuade the United States that satisfaction of Western strategic needs would be forthcoming once legitimate Egyptian nationalist interests had been secured.[39]

To bolster its internal position, the Egyptian Junta also needed the kind of technical, financial, and military aid the United States had been granting to other countries in order to reinforce the world's "soft spots".[40] Egypt hoped that the basic agreement for the allocation of such aid, which the old regime had already concluded with the United States, would be expanded in the future.

At what point contacts between the Free Officers and the United States were established and to what ends they were pursued remain controversial issues that only information still classified can settle. The fact that the two sides believed they shared certain common interests has led to speculation that a relationship existed between them prior to the Revolution. Many specialists in Egyptian affairs contend that American diplomats had been in contact with the Free Officers months before the coup d'état;[41] some even claim that the United States was directly involved.[42]

Miles Copeland, a former American diplomat and CIA agent, asserts that it was the mission of Kermit Roosevelt, also a diplomat and CIA agent, to help pave the way for a strong leader to come to power. Copeland holds that meetings between Roosevelt and select members of the Free Officers' group began as early as March 1952. By May 1952 the American Ambassador, Jefferson Caffery, was reportedly convinced "that only the army could cope with the deteriorating situation and establish a government with which the Western powers could talk sense."[43]

None of these claims has been completely substantiated. Nevertheless, the important role the Junta assigned America's diplomatic representatives in Cairo from the earliest hours of the coup is indirect evidence that the American position was already known to the Free Officers prior to the events of 23 July. This is the opinion of Jean and Simone Lacouture, who wrote that American intelligence agents had been taken into the confidence of the Free Officers at least two or three days before the coup.[44]

Mohammed Hassanein Heikal, Nasser's friend and confidant, stated that the American Deputy Naval Attaché, David Evans, had been contacted on the night of the coup and asked to convey a message to Ambassador Caffery, who was absent.[45] But Mohammed Naguib, the nominal leader of the Junta, asserts that the primary concern was to allay fears that the Free Officers were acting on behalf of the communists or Moslem Brotherhood and to assure the interested powers, especially Great Britain, that the rights and property of foreigners in Egypt would be protected.[46] This message was in fact delivered and, according to Naguib, American diplomatic representatives in Cairo were active in forestalling possible British intervention.[47] The same source holds that the Egyptian leadership was also informed that so long as the situation remained under control and no harm came to King Farouk or his family, who were to be allowed to leave Egypt "with honor", the United States would consider the coup a purely internal matter.

Once contact between the two sides had been officially established, the American Ambassador became the intermediary between the Junta and Britain's own representatives. Signs of the new Egyptian leaders' confidence in Ambassador Caffery and of their initial willingness to cultivate warm relations with the United States were abundant in this period. Caffery conveyed messages from the Junta to the British Embassy and assured Britain that its interests would be respected. He arranged for the safe departure of the royal family, after having previously received calls from King Farouk begging him to ask the British to intervene.

Naguib described Caffery as "one of the few foreign diplomats in whom we believed that we could trust."[48] Whereas the Soviet press grumbled about the links between the coup d'état in Egypt and "Anglo-American imperialists",[49] Mohammed Heikal later extolled the role of the United States at the time of the coup. This role, in Heikal's eyes, attained symbolic importance: "her representative was the last man to see off the remains of the old regime and the first in contact with the new."[50]

In Washington, meanwhile, a benevolent but prudent "wait and see" attitude was officially adopted toward the Junta in line with the State Department's desire to know more about how the situation would develop.[51] Important organs of the American press were less reserved. The *New York Times* saw the Egyptian development as the

> consequence both of the King's laxness in observing the proprieties and responsibilities of his office and of a drive for power that overshot its objectives. . . .He supported the "old guard" of the Egyptian Army, many members of which had been discredited by charges of graft and corruption, rather than the younger officers in the ascendancy who were seriously concerned with the state of the Egyptian Armed Forces.

The same paper further depicted the coup d'état as "an expression of the upheaval that is going on all over the Middle East. The peoples of this area are becoming aware of the evils that have been apparent to visiting Westerners — corruption, backwardness, disease."[52]

The *Washington Post* predicted that the future role of General Naguib would be that of "a benevolent despot on the Ataturk model." *US News and World Report* censured Farouk's Egypt as a "welter of corruption and graft" and predicted that the new Egypt would enjoy greater stability and show more moderation toward Britain in the future.[53]

What Americans found appealing in the Free Officers' cause is suggested by George Kirk:

> Many of the cherished stereotypes of American tradition were reproduced in the person of General Naguib — the serious soldier assuming the highest responsibilities in the state in times of crisis, the supplanter of the tyrannical King. . .the abolisher of medieval titles. . .the buster of trusts and privilege. . .and Egyptian publicity for its part did not fail to involve, in favor of its national aspirations, the Declaration of Independence and the Atlantic Charter, precedents dear to American minds. An American correspondent reduced the British case for being [in the Canal Zone]. . . to a mere survival of "old-style" colonialism.[54]

An acceptable international image of this kind was actively sought by the Junta, which emphasized the bloodless character of the revolt. Appointing the older, well-liked General Mohammed Naguib to be the nominal head of the new regime favored the image of moderation that was desired and inclined the Free Officers to overlook the fact that he had only joined the group after the coup.[55] In describing his role, Naguib candidly indicated who their leader really was:

> Abdel Nasser. . .realized that a successful revolution could not be carried out

by a group of junior officers unless they were led by a senior officer with special qualifications. I was that senior officer.[56]

Similarly, Ali Maher, a political leader in the old regime known to be ardently nationalistic, was designated Prime Minister,[57] and the system of monarchy was provisionally retained.

By maintaining links with the old order, the young officers helped to allay Western fears that the new regime would be extremist.[58] At the same time, the Free Officers quickly rejected the terms set by the Moslem Brotherhood for their collaboration and the Communist Party remained outlawed. Workers' riots in August led to strong government action and Naguib announced in September that the army would "crush" anyone spreading lies that the army was influenced by communism. However, there was no interest in a Western-style parliamentary system either. The political parties were deemed incapable of ridding themselves of corruption, and they were disbanded in early 1953.

A series of measures during the first weeks of its rule sought to strengthen the impression that the Junta was a dynamic group with a reformist and progressivist outlook. The cumbersome system of shifting government offices to summer and winter quarters was abolished, as were all civil titles. The foreign hold on Egyptian industry was limited by a governmental decree that at least 49 percent of the shares of limited liability companies had to be in Egyptian hands.[59] The most radical action of all was the proclamation of the Agrarian Reform Law on 7 September 1952, which the government claimed would end the feudal heritage in Egypt.[60]

At length, on 3 September 1952, Secretary of State Dean Acheson clarified the Truman government's more considered estimate of the Egyptian Revolution:

> There have been some encouraging developments in Egypt. . .including the reform program announced by the Egyptian Government. . . .Relations between the United States and Egypt remain most friendly and cooperative. I am hopeful that in the interest of our Countries these relations. . .will be increased and strengthened. We look forward to an era in which new areas of cooperation and mutual benefit can be brought into being.[61]

A wide range of official and unofficial exchanges followed in an atmosphere of good will and cordiality that was to last for the next two and a half years.[62] In retrospect the reason is plain: each of the two countries believed the other would serve as an instrument for the accomplishment of its immediate goals.

One area in which American-Egyptian relations advanced during this early period was that of economic cooperation. Soon after the new regime took power, the American government signaled its willingness to expand the scale of its economic and technical assistance to Egypt.[63] The nature of this assistance was defined in a series of agreements based on the May 1951 Point Four Technical

Cooperation Agreement, and in 1952 the United States Operations Mission became the implementing agency.[64] After an October announcement that Egypt's share of Point Four aid would be increased, projects covering a broad spectrum of economic activity were initiated.[65] However, the thorny question of military aid was bequeathed to the next administration.

When the Eisenhower government took office, State Department officials urged that Egypt, "the leader among the countries of the Arab world," should be given far more substantial assistance than before. The Director of the Mutual Security Administration, Harold Stassen, argued before the Senate Foreign Relations Committee that "special" attention should be given to Egypt where "there has emerged a new government which has already made significant strides toward better understanding with the West and has shown a determination to improve the lot of its people."[66]

But this recommendation went unheeded and the financing of large-scale aid schemes was deferred until the dispute between Britain and Egypt was settled. Instead, numerous undertakings of a demonstrative and exploratory nature were carried out. For example, in November 1952 the State Department announced that a group of American experts would assist an Egyptian group in a joint survey to assess the potential for rapid development of Egypt's resources, chiefly industrial.[67] By 1953 a major project — the construction of the Aswan High Dam — had become the subject of various surveys and feasibility studies. In March 1953 a new Point Four agreement, described as "the most important of its kind so far entered in the Middle East," led to the creation of the Egyptian-American Rural Improvement Service (EARIS). An initial American grant of $10 million matched an Egyptian appropriation of $15 million for the reclamation of marsh land in the Delta and the Fayyum Province. Various other technical assistance projects were subsequently sponsored by EARIS,[68] a number of training and educational programs were carried out under other auspices, and an American-Egyptian Society for Trade Promotion sought — without much success — to stimulate American private investment in Egypt.

How, from these promising beginnings, American-Egyptian relations went downhill on a zigzag course that often played havoc with America's global cold war strategy is the disconcerting tale to be related in the following chapters. Three basic, unresolved problems were to destroy the optimism that had seemed a natural outcome of the Revolution. The first was the Anglo-Egyptian dispute, which rendered the United States reluctant to satisfy Egypt's plea for large-scale economic aid lest such aid strengthen Egyptian resistance to British demands. The second was Egypt's concomitant refusal to make a commitment to the Western defense system without receiving the aid it wanted and without achieving true independence. The third was the protracted state of war between Egypt and Israel, which made it politically dangerous for the American leadership to provide Egypt with the unrestricted military hardware Egypt insisted it needed to defend itself and to ensure the credibility of its bid for regional leadership.

Pending the solution of these problems, an interim policy consisting of ad hoc reactions to situations as they arose remained *the* United States policy toward Egypt for nearly two decades. There was always some other obstacle just around the corner—like Gatsby's green light "that year by year recedes before us"[69]— that had to be removed before the true policy could be elaborated. As a result, events moved forward with a logic of their own, improvisation became the hallmark of the world's greatest power in its dealings with one of the world's most strategically vital areas, and a fledgling Egyptian army officer, still in his thirties, ran rings around the American political leadership.

Notes

1. J. A. DeNovo, *American Interests and Policies in the Middle East: 1900-1939* (Minneapolis: University of Minnesota Press, 1963), p. 19.

2. Hurewitz, *Middle East Dilemmas*, pp. 58-59. The formal designation of a United States representative to Egypt received Congressional approval only in 1864.

3. A. T. Wright, *The Suez Canal, Its Past, Present, and Future* (London: Oxford University Press, 1939), pp. 135-36.

4. Georgiana G. Stevens, "Middle East Perspectives," *The United States and the Middle East*, ed. G. G. Stevens (Englewood Cliffs, N. J.: Prentice-Hall, 1964), p. 1.

5. DeNovo, *American Interests*, p. 321.

6. "The Americans in the U.A.R.," *Egyptian Economic and Political Review* (Cairo), January 1961, p. 3.

7. DeNovo, *American Interests*, p. 379.

8. Ibid., p. 368. The United States neither became a member of the League of Nations nor signed the Versailles Treaty of Peace.

9. *Papers Relating to the Foreign Relations of the United States, 1922* (Washington, D.C.: G.P.O., 1938), 2: 105.

10. DeNovo, *American Interests*, p. 202.

11. Brian Horrocks, "Middle East Defense—A British View," *Middle Eastern Affairs*, February 1955, p. 33.

12. Hurewitz, *Middle East Dilemmas*, p. 80.

13. Egyptian Prime Minister Noqrashi's personal trip to the United States in 1948.

14. U.S. Department of State, *Bulletin*, 23 June 1946, p. 18.

15. Egyptian exports to the United States (Egyptian £ 1000): 1938—708; 1945—2,914; 1947—5,570; 1948—4,456; 1949—19,507; 1950—15,377; 1951—19,507; 1952—16,784.

16. Hurewitz, *Middle East Dilemmas*, p. 86.

17. D. A. Farnie, *East and West of Suez* (Oxford: Clarendon Press, 1969), pp. 646-59.

18. See Truman's Inaugural Address, *Documents on American Foreign Relations, 1949*, p. 7. See also "Point Four: An Experiment in International Collaboration," *Revue Egyptienne de Droit International* (1951), pp. 89, 339, for American-Egyptian Agreement.

19. H. L. Hoskins, "The Guardianship of the Suez Canal," *Middle East Journal*, April 1950, p. 143.

20. An Egyptian blockade deprived the base of 18,000 of its Egyptian workers and interrupted its fresh water supply. Farnie, *East and West of Suez*, pp. 698-700. Other hostile acts resulted in an almost daily loss of British lives.

21. *Anglo-Egyptian Conversations on the Defense of the Suez Canal and on the Sudan*, December 1950-November 1951; Egypt, no. 2, 1951, Cmd. 8419 (London: Oxford University Press, 1952), p. 148.

22. Dean G. Acheson, *Present at the Creation* (New York: New American Library, 1970), p. 563.

23. U.S. Department of State, *Bulletin*, 22 October 1951, p. 647.

24. Ibid., pp. 647-48. At the same time, Britain offered a new proposal for the establishment of an international commission, to include Egypt, that would investigate and advise on constitutional developments in the Sudan. *Anglo-Egyptian Conversations*, pp. 43-46.

25. *Crisis in the Middle East*, ed., Edward Latham (New York: H. W. Wilson, 1952), p. 95; *The Times*, 26 October 1951.

26. Egypt, Ministry of Foreign Affairs, *Records of Conversations, Notes and Papers Exchanged Between the Royal Egyptian Government and the United Kingdom Government*, March 1950-November 1951, Cairo, 1951, pp. 167-79. The timing of the proposal was especially bad since it was presented shortly after the Egyptian government, perhaps in a bid to regain popular support, had publicly declared its intention to abrogate the Treaties. See *Egyptian Gazette*, 9 October 1951.

27. Statement by Acheson, 21 October 1951; see U.S. Department of State, *Bulletin*, 29 October 1951, p. 686.

28. Ibid., 19 November 1951, pp. 817-18.

29. *New York Times*, 15 January 1952.

30. Sir Anthony Eden, *Full Circle* (London: Cassel, 1960), 3: 230; See also Acheson, *Present at the Creation*, pp. 726-27.

31. *New York Times*, 1 and 2 January 1952; Acheson, *Present at the Creation*, p. 727.

32. J. C. Campbell, *Defense of the Middle East* (New York: Frederick A. Praeger, 1960), p. 44.

33. Eden, *Full Circle*, 3: 233-34; Acheson, *Present at the Creation*, p. 727. Reportedly, the United States advocated "an immediate start on the withdrawal of [British]. . .forces from Egypt" and British acceptance of a United Kingdom of Sudan and Egypt under King Farouk.

34. Eden, *Full Circle*, 3:238.

35. Abdel Nasser, *Philosophy of the Revolution*, pp. 10, 22, 26, and 28; Keith Wheelock, *Nasser's New Egypt* (New York: Frederick A. Praeger, 1960), pp. 10-13.

36. *The Times*, 12 October 1970.

37. Miles Copeland, *The Game of Nations* (London: Weidenfeld and Nicolson, 1969), p. 59.

38. The Egyptian press did not hesitate to draw similarities between the American and Egyptian Revolutions: "America, which fought so long for independence and freedom, realizes today the meaning of our struggle." (*Al Ahram*, 5 September 1952).

39. *Al Akhbar Al Gadida*, 5 November 1952. "All Islamic and Arab states have to confess that the American foreign policy toward the Middle East, if compared with that of other big powers, has been nearer to justice and more in favor of small countries."

40. At this time the United States was the chief source for Egypt's development aid. Only after 1955 did the Soviet Union begin to extend substantial aid to developing countries.

41. For example, H. B. Ellis, *Challenge in the Middle East* (New York: Ronald Press Co., 1960) and Miles Copeland, *The Game of Nations*.

42. This opinion, which is shared by many high-level Egyptians interviewed by the author, could not be substantiated. Jean and Simone Lacouture believed these rumors were well-founded. *Egypt in Transition* (London: Methuen and Co., 1962), p. 212.

43. Copeland, *The Game of Nations*, pp. 51-53.

44. Lacouture, *Egypt in Transition*, p. 212.

45. Mohammed Hassanein Heikal, *The Cairo Documents* (Garden City, N.Y.: Doubleday and Co., 1973), p. 34.

46. Mohammed Naguib, *Egypt's Destiny* (Garden City, N.Y.: Doubleday and Co., 1955), p. 110.

47. Ibid., pp. 119 and 135; see also *Al Ahram*, 25 July 1952.

48. Naguib, *Egypt's Destiny*, pp. 118-19; *New York Times*, 27 July 1952; Clarence Sulzberger, in *A Long Row of Candles* (New York: Harper and Row), p. 805, quoting interview with Caffery. *Al Ahram* commented further: "We find it our duty to pay tribute to the noble efforts of the American Ambassador to Egypt. Mr. Jefferson Caffery understood the spirit of the struggle and the meaning of the new era." *Al Ahram*, 5 September 1952.

49. *Tass*, quoting Middle East leftist journals. It was felt that the advent of the new military dictatorship would open the way to Egyptian entry into the Middle East Defense Organization. *The*

Current Digest of the Soviet Press, vol. IV, no. 30, p. 13, 6 September 1952, and vol. IV, no. 31, 13 September 1952, p. 24.

50. Heikal, *The Cairo Documents*, p. 36.

51. *New York Times*, 27 July 1952.

52. Ibid., 27 July and 3 August 1952.

53. *Washington Post and Times Herald*, 25 July 1952; *US News and World Report*, 8 August 1952. See also *Time*, 4 August 1952 and 8 September 1952.

54. George Kirk, "The Egyptian Revolution and National Aspirations," *Survey of International Affairs, 1951*, ed., Peter Calvocoressi (London: Oxford University Press, 1955), p. 220.

55. El Sadat, *Revolt on the Nile*, p. 31.

56. Naguib, *Egypt's Destiny*, p. 29.

57. Ali Maher had served as Prime Minister several times in the past. The fact that he had no links with any political party made him an acceptable candidate. He continued as Prime Minister until September 1952 when, after allegedly refusing to approve a sweeping land reform act, he was replaced by Naguib himself. *Egyptian Gazette*, 9 September 1952.

58. Wheelock, *Nasser's New Egypt*, pp. 14-16; *New York Times*, 23 August and 28 September 1952.

59. *Egyptian Gazette*, 25 and 31 July 1952; Decree Amending Article 6 of Law 138, 1947.

60. Decree Law No. 178, 1952 Land Reform; *Al Ahram*, 9 September 1952: "No person may possess more than 200 feddans of agricultural land." The Act also called for the extension of cooperative services in rural areas to improve the standards of the fellahin, whose political support was canvassed.

61. U.S. Department of State, *Bulletin*, 15 September 1952, p. 406.

62. For examples, see Prime Minister Ali Maher, *Egyptian Gazette*, 5 September 1952; Deputy Secretary of Defense William Foster, *New York Times*, 11 November 1952; Under-Secretary of State Henry Byroade, U. S. Department of State, *Bulletin*, 15 December 1952, p. 933; Prime Minister Naguib, *Egyptian Gazette*, 21 September 1952; President Eisenhower, *New York Times*, 27 July 1953; Secretary of State Dulles, U.S. Department of State, *Bulletin*, 15 June 1953, p. 851.

63. *Egyptian Gazette*, 9 October 1952; see statement by Henry Byroade, *New York Times*, 5 December 1952.

64. It continued operations until the Suez Crisis in 1956.

65. Acheson, *Present at the Creation*, p. 727.

66. U.S. Department of State, *Bulletin*, 25 May 1953, pp. 740-42. See also comment by Henry Byroade, *New York Times*, 5 December 1952.

67. *New York Times*, 12 November 1952. Agreement was reached with Egypt on 23 February 1953 for Arthur D. Little, Inc. to carry out a joint survey for which the United States allocated $240,000. U.S. Department of State, *Bulletin*, 9 February 1953, pp. 223-24. This study resulted in 33 special reports plus the book *Opportunities for Industrial Development in Egypt*. "Point Four and the UAR," *Egyptian Economic and Political Review* 7 (January 1961): 15.

68. U.S. Department of State, *Bulletin*, 6 April 1953, p. 498 and *New York Times*, 23 March 1953. EARIS projects included the construction and development of housing and community facilities, health improvements, development of small industries and management training programs, vocational training, aid to agricultural cooperatives and extension services, the resettlement of landless farmers, improvement of the water supply and the rural road system. "Point Four and the UAR," p. 8; Wheelock, *Nasser's New Egypt*, pp. 99-102.

69. F. Scott Fitzgerald, *The Great Gatsby* (Harmondsworth: Penguin Books, 1950), p. 188.

2

America between Britain and Egypt

The Suez Canal Base exemplified the British practice of constructing a permanent defense installation within the framework of bilateral treaties that were limited in time. By 1953 this sprawling base was worth over $1.5 billion and housed an estimated 75,000 British troops.[1] As the largest Western military base outside Britain and the United States, it seemed a strong link in both the regional and global defense structures established by the West.[2]

After Egypt unilaterally abrogated the 1936 Anglo-Egyptian Treaty of Alliance in October 1951, Britain's position in Egypt was maintained by force alone. Pressures against continued occupation mounted both locally, where paramilitary harassment was now frequent, and at home, where public opinion was critical of such a massive peacetime commitment. The value of the canal base as an asset to British defense needs and to those of the West in general became increasingly dubious. The fact that the abrogated treaty had in any case been due for revision only made it more imperative that Britain should come to terms with Egypt.

The American leadership viewed the lingering dispute over the base as a primary source of regional instability. Unsatisfied Egyptian demands for British withdrawal had been a major factor in the overthrow of the old regime and now seemed to menace the future existence of the new regime. As then Assistant Secretary of State Henry Byroade clearly recognized, the long-run prospects were even more alarming:

> If there is actual guerilla fighting I think the tenseness in the Arab world and the entire Near East is such as to have a great effect upon the maintenance of any Western interests in that part of the world.[3]

These fears were later made still more explicit by Secretary Dulles himself: "We did not believe that the base would be a usable and effective base unless it could be maintained with the goodwill of the Egyptian people."[4]

American concern was heightened by the knowledge that the Arab peoples were eager to break their ties with Britain and France at a time when the cold war with the Soviet Union began to have regional implications that could not be ignored.[5] The United States therefore determined that settlement of the Anglo-Egyptian dispute was an urgent matter, and it resolved to secure the reconciliation of legitimate national Egyptian interests with Western strategic requirements for the region.[6]

In this context America welcomed the advent of the Free Officers' Junta as an opportunity to break out of the impasse that had troubled Britain's relations with the old regime. The Junta needed to consolidate its power as rapidly as possible in the face of strong domestic opposition, most notably from Wafdist sympathizers, the Moslem Brotherhood, and the communists. Hence the Free Officers feared that a delay or renewed deadlock in the withdrawal negotiations might expose them to the same discontent that had contributed to the fall of the old regime. Conversely, an early and favorable settlement would have enhanced their position and prestige and might also have led to the release of frozen Egyptian sterling reserves that were needed to meet economic difficulties.[7]

The new leadership soon signaled its willingness to separate the Sudan question from that of British withdrawal from the canal zone. At the same time, this inclination to facilitate a renewal of the negotiations was tempered by the Junta's awareness that it could not allow the negotiations to take any direction that could be interpreted by local opposition forces as one that compromised important national interests. This made it unreceptive to the British "package deal" under which Britain had offered to withdraw its troops in return for an Egyptian engagement to join the Western defense system. The British proposal would also have entailed internationalizing the defense of the Suez Canal Base.

The Junta objected that the British proposal implied *de facto* perpetuation of foreign control over Egyptian territory. Moreover, the Junta insisted that, without a solution to the Arab-Israeli problem and the withdrawal of British troops, an alliance with the West directed solely against the Soviet Union could only benefit the Western powers and extremist elements in Egypt. An Egyptian saying that "the pointed pistol at short range appears more threatening than the cannon in the distance" was interpreted to mean that Egypt had more to fear from its British occupier and its Israeli neighbor than from the Soviet Union.

Still, the Junta recognized that it stood to gain from the key position assigned to Egypt in Western defense planning and from the fact that the West, especially the United States, was anxious to see Egypt join its "camp". Egypt's leadership accordingly adapted the British package deal to suit its own ends, counterproposing that if, but only if, British troops left Egyptian soil would it consider joining the Western defense system.

In its quest for complete independence, the Junta leaders used still other tactics to weaken Britain's bargaining position while conceding as little as possible in return. One of these was to exploit differences between the United States and Britain that came to light on a number of occasions. These differences reflected growing American concern with its ally's ingrained colonialist attitude and with the fact that Britain seemed unable to disassociate its goal of maintaining a dominant position in the region from the overriding Western objective of Soviet containment.

Another Egyptian ploy was to fan American anxieties that the new regime might easily succumb to an extremist coup. The Junta also threatened to renew guerrilla activities against the British occupier.[8] Combining flattery, warnings[9] and the lure of future cooperation in Western defense schemes with its own form of "divide and rule" tactics, the Egyptian leadership made a concerted effort to encourage the United States to push its British ally toward compromise.

These efforts struck a responsive chord in the United States where the American leadership began to frame a defense plan of its own that was thought to be more palatable to Egypt than the British proposal. Major obstacles were, of course, foreseen, including Arab suspicion of Western motives and the Arab-Israeli dispute. Nevertheless, when General Naguib requested American arms aid in early August 1952, the time seemed ripe for the United States to put forward its new scheme.

This plan envisaged a cooperative approach to defense that was to be assured "by the greatest possible number of nations in the region."[10] If the participatory role of the Arab countries was augmented within the framework of an organization that provided for mutual consultation and planning, the end result could be less offensive to local nationalist forces than previous plans, including the British package deal. A corollary of the plan was that new incentives would be offered to Egypt for its collaboration with the West, among them American military aid. The possibility that Egypt could be helped to play a leading role in the region was also intended to arouse Egyptian interest in the plan.

The Junta leaders reportedly received an encouraging answer to Naguib's request,[11] and in October they were asked to submit a list of the military equipment they wanted to the American Military Attaché in Cairo. In the course of a November visit to Cairo by American Under-Secretary of Defense William Foster, Egypt was invited to send a military mission to the United States to follow up its request. Dean Acheson writes that, at about the same time, the new regime secretly contacted the American Embassy in Cairo "with a proposal to cooperate with the United States and to undertake certain commitments," including membership in the Western defense system, "in return for military and economic aid."[12]

The authenticity of these exchanges could not be verified at the time of writing, when the relevant material was still classified. Heikal claims that a secret agreement between Egypt and the United States had existed since February 1952 and that America had agreed to supply $5 million in arms.[13] Whatever the truth may be, any show of interest in these American defense proposals should be read in conjunction with other steps taken by the Junta to resolve its dispute with Britain. Generating American support was the goal, and the indications are that Egypt's apparent willingness to cooperate did succeed in creating an atmosphere of good will.

In late Autumn 1952 an Egyptian military mission under the leadership of Ali Sabri visited the United States and reportedly discussed its requirements with General Omar Bradley. A subcommittee was formed to work out the details. In the meantime, feelers were put out by General Olmstead, Director of the

Foreign Military Aid Program, concerning the feasibility of an Islamic military pact. According to Heikal, Olmstead shocked his listeners by discussing the possibility of creating an Islamic "fifth column" to influence Moslems in the Soviet Union and China.[14]

Once the link between military aid and the kind of pact reportedly described by Olmstead in extremely blunt terms came out into the open, the Egyptian delegation evidently shrank from making the commitments that the Americans expected. Consequently, the American negotiators remained noncommittal on the question of supplying arms to Egypt, and Ali Sabri went home empty-handed.

Acheson commented afterward that "the Department of Defense told us it could not prepare a specific program of assistance to Egypt in the absence of an approved strategic plan and force requirements for the area."[15] He indicated that the granting of military aid without an Egyptian commitment to a defense system was such a complex matter that the incoming Republican administration was left to deal with it.

Egypt's reaction to the latest Western defense proposals was confirmed by a statement issued in Khartoum by Junta spokesman Salah Salem: it would reject all military pacts until its national aspirations were fulfilled.[16]

General Naguib, however, subsequently tried to appear more malleable. In a December press interview he described Egypt's stance in relation to the cold war as follows:

> We realize that nowadays no country can stand alone in the world. There are only three possible courses for a free Egypt: to remain neutral — and this is at the very least extremely difficult if not impossible; to join the Eastern Bloc, which is out of the question as we are not Communists; or to join the West. It is our natural inclination to work with the West whose people we know.[17]

He nevertheless left no ambiguity as to his position on the defense of the Suez Canal: "If the idea of a joint defense of the Suez Canal is left to Egypt, we will defend it heartily and efficiently as part of our own national soil which it is."[18]

Later, in his memoirs, Naguib explained his reasoning:

> It is only as a free people capable of defending our freedom that we shall be able and willing to ally ourselves with the West, if the occasion should arise. A regional defense pact on any other terms would merely perpetuate the explosive conditions that now exist. The Americans, instead of gaining allies, would merely inherit the enmity left behind by the British and the French.[19]

The link between British withdrawal and Egyptian cooperation with the West's own defense needs was thus given an Egyptian twist designed to further its nationalist aspirations.

At this juncture, the priority that the Free Officers attached to settling the dispute with Britain led Egypt to drop its demand for unification with the Sudan in favor of Sudanese self-determination. This moderation was encouraged by the good will policy that Britain had adopted toward the new regime. By the end of January 1953, blocked Egyptian reserves worth £E 15 million had been released, and British troops had withdrawn from the El Firdan Bridge that spanned the canal near Ismailia.[20] In this more cordial atmosphere, negotiations soon recommenced and in a short time agreement on the Sudan issue was reached.[21] One of the two biggest problems troubling Anglo-Egyptian relations was thus ostensibly removed after nearly a quarter century of heated debate.

American Secretary of State John Foster Dulles welcomed the new settlement as "the first step toward the establishment of more fruitful associations in an area of critical importance to the security of the free world."[22] His satisfaction was all the greater in that the United States had played an important role in the negotiations. This was recognized by General Naguib, who praised Ambassador Caffery for "bringing closer the two viewpoints. . . ." Naguib declared that "it was through. . .[Caffery's] good offices that many difficult points were ironed out. . . .These had a direct effect on the successful conclusion of this agreement."[23] The Egyptian press echoed the official attitude and expressed gratitude to the United States for its moral support.[24]

Once the principle of Sudanese self-determination was accepted, however, the parties soon disagreed on the type of provisional government to be established there. The problem was that Britain and Egypt vied with each other for influence in the Sudan, and this rivalry continued to be a source of friction until 1956. Extremist groups, especially the Moslem Brotherhood, expressed displeasure with the agreement concerning the Sudan.[25]

The residual friction between Egypt and Britain did not diminish the warmth of American-Egyptian relations at this time. One reason was that the Eisenhower administration began to take a "new look" at the Middle East and certain other areas shortly after the inauguration in 1953. The new American leadership was particularly concerned by the marked decline in Western and, with it, American prestige in the Middle East. The region as a whole also appeared to constitute a major gap in the Western defense system,[26] and the possibility that the Soviet Union might make inroads upon this region greatly troubled Secretary Dulles. In his words, "if all of that [the Middle East] passed into the hands of our potential enemies, that would make a tremendous shift in the balance of economic power."[27]

The Dulles-Stassen mission to the Middle East and South Asia was launched only four months after the Eisenhower administration took office. Dulles explained his objectives when he announced the coming trip in March:

President Eisenhower is keenly aware of the importance of the Near East and

South Asia. . . .[He] has therefore asked me to go personally. . .to show our friendship for the governments and peoples of these areas. . . .

I am going to get first hand information. I shall listen carefully to what I am told and consider the problems presented to me with utmost sympathy. I shall not bring with me any specific plan or program, nor do I expect to ask the governments I visit for any decisions. I am going to renew old friendships and, I hope, make new ones. . . .

I look upon this trip as an opportunity to dispel misunderstandings and to develop close relations between the United States and these friendly nations.[28]

Among the "misunderstandings" Dulles probably had in mind was an ill-fated Western attempt, initiated only two months before, to organize the Middle East countries into a regional defense system. Turkey had been the principal organizer, apparently in the belief that, as the regional representative of NATO, it would have more success than its Western partners in persuading Arab neighbors of the advantages to be gained from a regional defense system.[29] However, Turkey's efforts had been opposed by Egypt. While a special Turkish envoy shuttled between Beirut, Cairo, and Baghdad from March until May 1953,[30] Egypt convoked a meeting of the League of Arab States in March, ostensibly for the purpose of determining a common attitude toward both the Turkish initiative and the Dulles visit.

The participating Arab delegations arrived without either the prime ministers or the foreign ministers of the states they represented. Egypt remonstrated in strong terms. In his opening speech before the League Council, Egyptian Foreign Minister Mahmoud Fawzi called for "a renaissance of the Arab nations through strength and unity" and "the end of the days of Arab puppets of the imperialist powers." He also urged that a strong Arab bloc was the only means of survival.[31]

This vehement Egyptian reaction reportedly elicited apologies from the states concerned as well as pledges of solidarity and allegiance to the ideal of Arab unity. At the next meeting of the Arab League, four days before the Dulles mission arrived in Cairo, all participating states were represented by their foreign ministers. Unanimity was then reached on five points, namely: that Britain should withdraw without prior conditions; that Arab countries had the right to defend themselves through the Arab League's Collective Defense Pact; that United Nations resolutions on Palestine should be enforced; that West German reparations to Israel should be opposed; and that Arabs who still lived under colonial domination possessed the right of self-determination.[32]

From 11 to 28 May 1953 Dulles, accompanied by Harold Stassen, then Director of the Mutual Security Administration, visited twelve Middle East[33] and South Asian countries. Before this fact-finding tour, no American official of comparable rank had ever spent so lengthy a period in the Middle East gathering on-the-spot information.

It may be inferred from comments made during the course of his trip that Western defense needs were foremost in Dulles's mind. A typical statement was that given during a New Delhi press conference:

> I believe it is important that there should be established a regional defense organization in the Middle East. It is too costly for these countries individually to have adequate defense establishments of their own. I have no firm views as to the precise type of organization that should be sought, but I hope there can be some sort of regional development towards collective security.[34]

While in Egypt, Dulles had one meeting with Nasser. According to Mohammed Heikal, Nassar's friend and confidant, three principal topics were covered: British occupation of Egypt; Egypt's need for arms; and Western proposals for a Middle East defense organization. The interrelated nature of these issues is illustrated by something Dulles said to Nasser: "The question of selling arms to Egypt would be easier if Egypt could come to an agreement with Britain, especially if this agreement was within a system of collective defense of the Middle East."[35]

In explaining the Egyptian attitude to Dulles, Nasser reportedly declared that so long as 80,000 British troops were in his country, Egypt would not accept the British package deal. This was because any deal that involved the withdrawal of British troops in exchange for Egyptian membership in a defense system plus the internationalization of responsibility for the canal base would appear to have been forced on the Egyptian leadership by the presence of these same troops. The package deal as proposed implied not only that the occupation of Egyptian soil by British troops wearing different uniforms would continue, but also that they would be joined by troops from still other countries.

Nasser went on to observe that communism was an internal rather than external threat to Egypt. He stressed that acceptance of the British solution would give rise to public dissatisfaction from which only extremist groups, especially the communists, stood to gain. However, Nasser allowed for the possibility of future cooperation between Egypt and the West with the proviso that "we are not ready to discuss pacts or any security measures unless we do it of our own free will."[36]

Six years later Nasser commented on this historic meeting in the following terms:

> I told him (Dulles) my opinion frankly. . . .There would be no aggression from outside for the simple reason that methods of modern warfare with its nuclear weapons have changed the whole art of war, and rendered any foreign aggression a remote possibility. I then added that internal fronts were of highest priority as regards defense and security. I also told him that he could by his own ways and means exert pressure on any Arab government to join the Western camp and give them military bases on its own territory, but this would be of no avail when the decisive experience came. I also added that he would find that the government which submitted to their pressure would be divorced from its popular support, and would be unable to lead the people.[37]

He added that military bases would prove useless when needed because hostile local elements would be working against them.

Since this later statement was made at a time when the Iraqi Revolution was a logical point of reference, it is instructive to note the themes that Nasser then stressed. He took credit for having suggested that the usefulness of foreign bases needed to be reassessed in light of conditions in the nuclear age. Emphasizing that any real threat would be an internal one, he claimed to have warned Dulles that Arab leaders who submitted to Western pressures to obtain bases would lose popular support.

The extent to which Secretary Dulles's conversations with Nasser and the leaders of other states visited during the mission affected Dulles's thinking about the Middle East is seen in both his "Report to the Nation on the Middle East," delivered on 1 June 1953, and a private memorandum concerning his trip.[38] In the Report, Dulles's discussion of American interests in the Middle East revealed a marked change in the American approach to regional defense. Holding that the Arab peoples ". . .are more fearful of Zionism than Communism," he found that

> a Middle East Defense Organization is a future rather than an immediate possibility. Many of the Arab League countries are so engrossed with their quarrels with Israel or with Great Britain or France that they pay little heed to the menace of Soviet Communism.

He noted that proximity to the Soviet Union made the Northern Tier of nations more aware of the danger. Hence in these countries

> there is a vague desire to have a collective security system. But no such system can be imposed from without. It should be designed and grow from within out of a sense of common destiny and common danger.

As an interim measure, he suggested that "the United States can usefully help to strengthen the interrelated defense of those countries which want strength, not as against each other or the West, but to resist the common threat to all free peoples."[39]

Dulles recognized, however, that the countries of this region were suspicious of the United States because of its association with the colonial powers. He added that "United States policy has become unnecessarily ambiguous in this matter," and that "the Western powers can gain, rather than lose, from an orderly development of self-government."[40]

In his private memorandum, Dulles was even less guarded:

> We must also accept the fact that the political situation is such that the Arab states will not, at this time, openly join defensive arrangements with a combination of Western powers. . . .We must therefore avoid becoming fascinated with concepts that have no reality.[41]

Discussing Egypt's dispute with Britain, he expressed concern that open hostilities might recommence between the two countries if Egyptian nationalist aspirations remained unsatisfied. At the same time he queried Egypt's ability to maintain operational efficiency of the canal base without outside help. He was also keenly aware of the importance of popular opinion to the Egyptian leadership both in defining an acceptable solution and in making further commitments to great powers:

Naguib and group almost pathological on British question. Would rather go down as martyr, plunging Egypt into chaos, than agree to anything which public could call infringement [of] Egypt's sovereignty.[42]

Hence, for Dulles, the crucial point in reaching a settlement was whether Egypt would agree to allow the West, including Britain, to occupy and use the base in the event of an emergency.

The American Secretary also recorded the fact that President Naguib had encouraged him to believe that "moving forward on arrangements with Israel" would not be too difficult once Naguib had solved his problems with the British. But Dulles was not convinced: "How much of this is window dressing for our present support?"

In his concluding remarks on Egypt in the private memorandum, Dulles asserted that the United States must strive to convince the British that they should ease their stance while America exerted a strong influence to "hold Naguib in line. [It is] *necessary to act soon after* [*my*] *arrival in Washington as both sides* [*are*] *awaiting U.S. position."* [43]

After his return to the United States, Dulles set out to resolve the problems that hindered the realization of a Middle East defense system. His approach was two-pronged: to facilitate an agreement that would end the Anglo-Egyptian dispute and to help resolve the Arab-Israeli dispute through a comprehensive program that would combine aid for regional development with a plan for the resettlement of the Palestinian refugees (the Johnston Plan).

The idea of centering a defense system around Egypt was temporarily shelved pending a solution of these and other problems. Having found a more receptive audience in the countries of the Northern Tier, Dulles instead appeared to favor an interim defense solution that would bolster these countries militarily and economically through informal bilateral arrangements until a multilateral system could be developed.[44]

The Dulles-Stassen visit had no less of an impact on the Egyptian leadership. In particular, the American Secretary's manifest interest in the Northern Tier countries seemed to presage a diminished interest in Egypt within the context of America's cold war strategy. This worried Egypt because American interest in and aid to Egypt was thought to be a bargaining counter that could minimize the latter's concessions to Britain.

The paradoxical result was that Egypt's leaders, who had reportedly been shocked by General Olmstead's view of Egypt's role in the previous administration's regional defense plans,[45] now undertook to convince the American leadership of the importance of Egypt and the Arab world in any effective system of regional defense. After Dulles delivered his Report to the Nation, Naguib began to stress the weakness of any system of defense that did not encompass the Arab world:

> A Middle East defense organization consisting only of Turkey, Greece and Yugoslavia cannot perform (its) functions. Nor can such an organization, from the point of view of the Middle East countries, provide more than a weak front defense line.[46]

Now Egypt attempted to revive the dormant Arab League Collective Security Pact, which it began to promote as an alternative solution to the defense of the area that—in Dulles's terms—"had grown from within."

These efforts did not succeed in diverting America's attention from the more receptive region to the north. In evaluating this and related decisions, it readily appears from the official and private remarks discussed above that the American Secretary of State was not so naive in his estimate of Middle East realities as his critics usually supposed. Rather, as will be shown, the policies chosen and the problems to which they led were largely the result of constraints placed on the American leadership by domestic considerations.

When negotiations between Egypt and Britain first resumed in 1953, they focused on the single most important regional preoccupation of the West — the Suez Canal Base. Western hopes that the solution to the Sudan question would have created the good will necessary for a quick settlement of this issue proved illusory. Not only had Britain been slow in agreeing to reopen negotiations,[47] but by March Anglo-Egyptian rivalry in seeking to influence the Sudan's choice between complete independence and union with Egypt had soured relations once again.[48] The "new era in the relations between Egypt and Great Britain," proclaimed by General Naguib on the conclusion of the Sudan Agreement, had thus borne no fruit, and the negotiations quickly broke down.

Britain hoped that America could be persuaded to take part in future negotiations and that America's presence would induce Egypt to accept the package deal. President Eisenhower agreed to American participation only on condition that an invitation would be extended by both parties.[49] However, Egypt turned the proposal down, apparently fearing lest any compromise in the presence of two great powers be made to look as though it had been imposed against Egypt's will, and the United States accordingly refused to participate.[50]

After two months of delay during which Ambassador Caffery actively attempted to bring the parties back to the bargaining table, new Egyptian moderation was evidenced in a statement by Nasser:

You ask, what is our policy? It is evacuation — complete independence. But we also want the Canal Zone Base to function efficiently
and we are willing to discuss how its efficiency can be preserved as
an Egyptian base.
We are soldiers and we are realists. We know that we cannot maintain
such an immense base as we are now. We know that we will want
technicians and since it is British equipment in the base we will need
British technicians.[51]

In the rest of his statement Nasser left little doubt about Egypt's unwillingness to
be linked with NATO, even if he did not exclude the possibility of cooperating
with "our friends" once a settlement had been reached. He also indicated that
Egypt would agree to maintain the base in readiness for war; but he rejected the
idea that Egypt's ties to a Western defense organization should be a condition for
British withdrawal.

This attitude enabled negotiations to be resumed on 26 April. It took only six
meetings for them to bog down once again. According to Naguib:

Great Britain took the position that Egypt must first agree to some sort
of military alliance before it could safely evacuate the Suez Canal Zone.
The Council of the Revolution, for its part, took the position that Egypt
would have to be given its independence before it could agree to any
sort of alliance with the West. The government of an occupied country...is no more able to negotiate a treaty of alliance with the occupying
power, — or, for that matter, with an allied power like the United States
than a prisoner is able to negotiate with his jailers, or their intermediar-
ies, the terms of his parole.[52]

Egypt's leaders may also have acted in the knowledge that the Dulles-Stassen
Mission was about to visit Egypt. On this hypothesis, the Egyptians hardened
their position in order to impress upon Dulles that the situation was urgent and
to spur the United States to exert pressure on Britain to be more flexible.

Whatever the Egyptian leaders hoped to gain from America, the statement
issued by Dulles during the first day of his visit made it clear that the United
States was by no means prepared to lend its full support to Egypt. Acknowledging that a solution consistent with full Egyptian sovereignty should be found,
Dulles nonetheless emphasized that " the important base in the Canal area, with
its depots of supplies and systems of technical supervision, should remain in good
working order and be available for immediate use in the event of future
hostilities."[53] This was the point on which Nasser had earlier shown a certain
flexibility. Yet, because Dulles linked the need to maintain the base in readiness
for war with the need to maintain a limited British presence at the base, the
statement drew fire from the Egyptian press. Moreover, the problem of defining
the nature and duration of this "limited presence" subsequently became a further source of conflict between Egypt and Britain.

It has already been seen that Dulles's Report to the Nation on his mission to
the Middle East diverged from the British insistence on a package deal. This,

plus his conciliatory remarks on colonialism and the "future rather than immediate possibility" of establishing a Middle East defense organization, may un-
wittingly have encouraged Egypt to resist a British solution.[54] If so, it defeated
the main purpose of the conversations in Cairo, which both the Egyptian and
American leaderships expected would enable the disputing parties to surmount
the impasse in negotiations.[55]

In the new phase of quiet diplomacy that followed the Dulles-Stassen Mission,
Ambassador Caffery renewed his efforts to bring about a resumption of negotiations. Through the good offices of Prime Minister Nehru of India and Prime
Minister Mohammed Ali of Pakistan a continuous if indirect exchange between
the parties was maintained. Secret diplomatic maneuvering, including a July
1953 promise from President Eisenhower to President Naguib that substantial
American aid would be forthcoming upon the settlement of the dispute,[56] was
aimed at coaxing Egypt to continue the talks.

Britain showed a greater willingness to compromise after meeting American
leaders in July and also in anticipation of the treaty to be concluded with Libya
that would give Britain the right to maintain its military establishment there for
twenty years. Reportedly, Britain would no longer insist on permanently having
its technicians at the canal base.[57] By October Egypt had conceded "the right of
unconditional return to the base" in the event of a direct land attack against any
member nation of the Arab Collective Security Pact.[58]

However, two issues created a new deadlock near the end of the month. One
was Britain's requirement that its technicians should be allowed to remain in
uniform. The other, with far more serious implications, was the demand that
British control over the Suez Canal Base could be reactivated in the event of an
attack on Turkey and Iran.[59] Britain's leaders, again under fire from the Conservative Party for allegedly capitulating to American pressure and Egyptian
threats, became intransigent on these issues.[60] A statement by Prime Minister
Winston Churchill before the House of Commons in December 1953 was typical
of many heard at this period:

> Our action will be based on a careful study of the merits of the prob-
> lem and the solution will not be dictated either by the violence of our for-
> eign enemies or by the pressure of some of our best friends.[61]

The Egyptian leadership, itself under attack from domestic opposition
groups,[62] likewise hardened its position, and guerrilla warfare was resumed in
the Canal Zone early in 1954. A power struggle between Naguib and Nasser
broke into the open in February of the same year, and this further delayed the
quest for final settlement with Britain.

Dismayed by the widening rift, America combined pressure and inducements
to bring the parties back to the bargaining table. Special efforts were made to
allay Egyptian fears that the right to return to the canal base harbored neo-
colonialist designs. This is the tenor of a statement issued by Henry Byroade,
then Assistant Secretary of State:

Our fundamental problem is to lessen suspicions and encourage agreement between the Eastern and Western powers. By every word and action of our Government, we make it clear that the old colonial relationship is dead and that it will stay dead. At the same time, we should encourage a better understanding of the possibility inherent in a new relationship based on voluntary cooperation among independent nations.[63]

Finally, Egypt attempted to break the impasse at the end of February 1954. This occurred just after the resignation of Naguib as President and the proclamation of Nasser as Chairman of the Revolutionary Council and Prime Minister.[64] The new Prime Minister agreed to the "automatic availability of the canal base for re-entry of British forces in the case of an attack on Turkey as well as on any member of the Arab League." In return, he asked Britain not to insist on having its technicians wear British uniforms.[65]

The inclusion of Turkey, a NATO member, was an important concession toward guaranteeing Western strategic interests in the Eastern Mediterranean.[66] But Britain remained unmoved, and Nasser could do no more until his dominant position in the internal power struggle was secured. Then, at the end of May, he called off the guerrilla activities that had plagued British operations in the Canal Zone for the preceding five months.[67]

A breakthrough was achieved when Churchill and Eden, apparently yielding to American pressures, finally agreed to the concessions that made an accord with Egypt possible. American influence was evident in a statement by Prime Minister Churchill to the House of Commons:

I have for some time been of the opinion that the United States has a strategic interest in Egypt, as well as interests in the international waterway of the Canal, and that responsibility for both of these matters should no longer be allowed to rest exclusively with Great Britain.

Although, of course, the strategic importance of Egypt and the Canal have been enormously reduced by modern developments of war, it cannot be wholly excluded from American thought where the recent extension of NATO's southern flank to Turkey is concerned.[68]

This face-saving interpretation of Western strategic requirements in the Atomic Age and the downgrading of the canal base that went with it helped Britain to accept a compromise on the remaining points at issue.[69] Agreement was reached on 27 July and signed on 19 October 1954. This agreement embodied the following principles:

1. Withdrawal of British troops from the Canal base within 20 months.
2. Termination of the 1936 Anglo-Egyptian Treaty of Alliance.
3. British civilian technicians to maintain certain installations.
4. In the event of war involving members of the Arab League or Turkey, the right of Britain to such facilities including ports in order to secure the operations of the Canal base.
5. Immediate consultation between England and Egypt in the event of

attack by an outside power on the above-mentioned states.

6. Immediate British withdrawal at the termination of such a war.

7. Overflight, landing, and servicing rights for announced Royal Air Force flights.

8. Recognition of the international importance of the Suez Canal, "which is an integral part of Egypt," and mutual guarantees to uphold the 1888 Constantinople Convention.

9. Agreement to remain in force for seven years.[70]

This settlement was hailed by Egypt, Britain, and the United States as the beginning of a new era of closer collaboration. Moreover, with the end of more than seventy years of British occupation in sight, Egypt was now on the way to complete independence. Nasser, in a message broadcast by Radio Cairo, expressed the Egyptian mood:

> This is a turning point . . . with this agreement, a new era of friendly relations based on mutual trust . . . opens between Egypt and Britain and the Western countries . . . . Now we want to get rid of the hatred in our hearts and start building up our relations with Britain on a solid basis of mutual trust and confidence, which has been lacking for the past seventy years.[71]

Secretary Dulles welcomed the event as:

> [A] major step in the evolution of the relations between the states of the Near East and the nations of the West. This agreement eliminates a problem which has affected not only the relations between the United Kingdom and Egypt but also those of the Western nations as a whole with the Arab states.[72]

Dulles also expressed the hope that "a new and more permanent basis had been laid for the tranquility and security of the Near East."[73]

The Egyptian leadership expressed gratitude to the United States for having helped Egypt and Britain to settle the dispute.[74] On 4 November 1954, in fulfillment of its 1953 promise, the United States agreed to grant Egypt $40 million for economic development.[75]

Now both the United States and Egypt looked forward to attaining their respective goals. Reports were circulated that America's leaders expected to persuade Egypt to join a collective defense system. From Egypt, President Nasser expressed the hope that the United States would provide military assistance — enabling Egypt to strengthen its armed forces.[76] Speculation that the United States would aid Egypt in realizing major development projects, such as the construction of the Aswan Dam, appeared in the Egyptian press. According to Egyptian diplomatic sources, it was even hoped that the United States would back an Egyptian-led Arab League Collective Security Pact as the basis for regional defense.[77]

But these expectations were destined to go unfulfilled as other issues cast their shadows on the briefly sunny horizon of Egyptian-American relations. One of the most troublesome was the Arab-Israeli problem and the "special relationship" that existed between Israel and the United States.

Notes

1. *Manchester Guardian*, 19 February 1953.
2. Eden, *Full Circle*, 3: 244; Hoskins, *The Middle East*, p. 270. Hoskins held that "both politically and strategically, Egypt had been and continues to be a prime factor in Middle East defense. . . ."
3. Statement by Assistant Secretary of State Henry Byroade, *Conference on U.S. Foreign Policy*, U.S. Department of State, 4 and 5 June 1953.
4. U.S. Cong., *Hearings, 1957*, p. 196.
5. Statement by Byroade, *Conference on U.S. Foreign Policy*, 4 and 5 June 1953.
6. See Dulles's statement implying this in U.S. Cong., *Hearings, 1957*, p. 197. Also see comments on his 1953 trip to the Middle East, John Foster Dulles, "Important Points of Trip," Unpublished Memorandum, *Dulles Private Papers*.
7. Wheelock, *Nasser's New Egypt*, pp. 12-47, 212; *Survey of International Affairs, 1953*, ed. Peter Calvacoressi (London: Oxford University Press, 1956) pp. 150-56.
8. Henry Byroade's statement, U.S. Department of State, *Conference on U.S. Foreign Policy*, 4-5 June 1953; Copeland, *The Game of Nations*, p. 72. Copeland quotes Ambassador Caffery as holding that the crucial test for the Free Officers was their success in dealing with the impasse in negotiations. If they failed there, the stability of the Junta would have been placed in doubt. American Middle East expert and later Ambassador John Badeau warned the United States that "the feeling against British occupation is not merely a trick of politicians for confusing popular feeling—it is a genuine national cause. That cause must be advanced if any new regime is to prove permanent." John Badeau, *Foreign Policy Bulletin*, 15 November 1952, p. 2.
9. For typical examples, see *Egyptian Gazette*, 2 March 1953; *Al Ahram*, 30 January 1953 and 4 October 1952; *Akhbar Al Yaum*, 11 January 1953 and 6 February 1953. Non-cooperation and neutrality in the cold war were later threatened.
10. *New York Times*, 7 and 8 August 1952.
11. Ibid., 27 August 1952.
12. Heikal, *The Cairo Documents*, pp. 36-37; Acheson, *Present at the Creation*, p. 727.
13. Heikal, *The Cairo Documents*, pp. 36-37.
14. Ibid., pp. 37-39.
15. Acheson, *Present at the Creation*, p. 727.
16. *Al Akhbar Al Gadida*, 21 November 1952.
17. *New York Times*, 11 December 1952.
18. Ibid.
19. Naguib, *Egypt's Destiny*, pp. 260-61.
20. *Egyptian Gazette*, 6 January 1953. See also ibid., 10 and 11 October 1952.
21. 12 February 1953. See *Documents on International Affairs, 1953* (London: Oxford University Press, 1954), pp. 315-24 for text.
22. U.S. Department of State, *Bulletin*, 23 February 1953, pp. 303-6.
23. *New York Times*, 13 February 1953.
24. For example, see *Al Ahram*, 26 April 1956. These comments may have overstated the American role in order to encourage further American support and thus strengthen Egypt's bargaining position vis-à-vis Britain.
25. See *Documents on International Affairs, 1953*, pp. 329-37; Robert Stephens, *Nasser: A Political*

Biography (London: Allen Lane, The Penguin Press, 1971) pp. 123, 130-31.

26. See, for example, Eisenhower's expression of concern, U.S. Department of State, *Bulletin*, 23 March 1953, pp. 440-41; Dulles's statement before the Senate Foreign Relations Committee and the House Foreign Affairs Committee, Ibid., 25 May 1953, p. 723.

27. Ibid., 9 February 1953, p. 214. See also J.F. Dulles, "The First 90 Days," ibid., 27 April 1953, p. 605.

28. Ibid., 23 March 1953, p. 431.

29. *New York Times*, 11 March and 29 April 1953.

30. His purpose may be inferred from a March press interview with Turkish Foreign Minister Koprulu: "Turkish foreign policy is a practical one which aims at providing the Middle East with security. Turkey hopes that the Arab states and Egypt in particular would join her in striving toward this practical policy." *Al Ahram*, 17 March 1953.

31. Ibid., 28 and 30 March 1953; *Akhbar Al Yaum*, 28 March 1953.

32. *New York Times*, 10 May 1953; *Al Ahram*, 4 and 12 April, and 8 and 12 May 1953; *Egyptian Gazette*, 10 May 1953. See also *Le Journal d'Egypte*, 28 April 1953 and *New York Times*, 23 and 27 April 1953.

33. Iran was excluded because of internal problems at the time, which brought that country to the verge of revolution under Mossadegh.

34. *Keesings' Contemporary Archives* (London: Keesings' Publications), 6-13 June 1953, p. 12,958. Note the similarity to Dulles's statement in Pakistan. Transcript of Press Conference, Karachi, Pakistan, U.S. Department of State, 24 May 1953.

35. Mohammed Hassanein Heikal, *Nahnu Wa Amrika* (Cairo: Al Ahram Press, 1965), p. 77, translated.

36. Heikal, *The Cairo Documents*, p. 41. See also idem, *Nahnu Wa Amrika*, p. 80.

37. *New York Times*, 3 November 1959.

38. U.S. Department of State, *Bulletin*, 15 June 1953, p. 833 and Dulles, "Important Points of Trip," Unpublished Memorandum, *Dulles Private Papers*.

39. U.S. Department of State, *Bulletin*, 15 June 1953, pp. 833-35.

40. Ibid.

41. Dulles, "Important Points of Trip," Unpublished Memorandum, *Dulles Private Papers*. He added: "The Israeli factor, and the association of the United States in the minds of the people of the area with French and British colonial and imperialistic policies, are millstones around our neck."

42. Ibid.

43. Ibid.

44. U.S. Department of State, *Bulletin*, 20 July 1953, p. 90.

45. According to Heikal; see footnote 14 above.

46. *Egyptian Gazette*, 5 June 1953.

47. The Sudan Agreement was widely criticized in Britain, especially by the Conservative Party, which made the British government hesitant to resume negotiations that would envisage a commitment to evacuate the canal base. Tom Little, "Britain, Egypt, and the Canal Zone Since July, 1952," *The World Today*, May 1954, p. 190.

48. Article 12, Anglo-Egyptian Agreement concerning Self-government and Self-determination for the Sudan, *Documents on International Affairs, 1953*, p. 318; see also the heated exchange of accusations, ibid., pp. 329-37.

49. Eden, *Full Circle*, 3: 248-53. For Eden's ideas on a general settlement, ibid., p. 248.

50. Dwight D. Eisenhower, *Mandate for Change* (London: Heinemann, 1963), pp. 152-53. The Egyptian Government announced that it was not acceptable for the United States to play more than a "good offices" role. *New York Times*, 19 March 1953.

51. *The Observer*, 12 April 1953.

52. Naguib, *Egypt's Destiny*, p. 251.

53. *Egyptian Gazette*, 12 May 1953.

54. U.S. Department of State, *Bulletin*, 15 June 1953, pp. 833-35. See Eden's comments on the

American unwillingness to put pressure on the Egyptian Government. Eden, *Full Circle*, 3: 252-53, 257.

55. These expectations appear from certain statements by General Naguib and the Egyptian Ambassador to Washington. *Egyptian Gazette*, 4 July 1953 and *New York Times*, 24 May 1953, respectively. The idea of an American peace project was frequently discussed in the press at this time. Dulles, when asked, did not deny its existence, thus contributing to the circulation of rumours, perhaps to gain time. *Egyptian Gazette*, 12 June 1953.

56. *New York Times*, 14 February 1954.

57. *The Times*, 13 July 1953.

58. *New York Times*, 11 October 1953.

59. Ibid., 10 December 1953.

60. Love holds that the British leadership believed the Junta would not last and delayed negotiations for this reason. Kennett Love, *Suez: The Twice-Fought War* (New York: McGraw-Hill Book Company, 1969), p. 185. See also Farnie, *East and West of Suez*, p. 706 and *The Times*, 9 October 1953.

61. *New York Times*, 18 December 1953.

62. *Egyptian Gazette*, 26 November 1953. The Moslem Brotherhood tried to belittle the regime; the communists feared that an accord would be followed by Egypt's association with a Western defense organization.

63. U.S. Department of State, *Bulletin*, 8 February 1954, p. 214.

64. On 24 and 25 February 1954. Nasser remained unsure of his position until mid-April, when his supremacy in the government was assured. During this period, a quick settlement would have boosted his prestige. See Wheelock, *Nasser's New Egypt*, pp. 28-36.

65. *New York Times*, 26 February and 19 March 1954.

66. Eden, *Full Circle*, 3:259.

67. Farnie, *East and West of Suez*, p. 709.

68. *New York Times*, 15 July 1954. In other developments, the British Minister of Defense announced the transfer of Britain's forces to Cyprus on 23 June (*The Times*, 24 June 1954); on 9 July Britain released £E 10 million of blocked Egyptian reserves (*Egyptian Gazette*, 10 July 1954); and Egypt lifted restrictions on trade with the sterling area (ibid., 14 July 1954).

69. Eden describes the reasoning that ultimately led to the decision to relinquish the Suez Canal Base in *Full Circle*, 3:260.

70. For document, see Great Britain, Foreign Office, *Agreement Between the Government of the United Kingdom of Great Britain and Northern Ireland and the Egyptian Government Regarding the Suez Canal Base* (With Annexes, Exchange of Notes, and Agreed Minutes), Cairo, 19 October 1954, Cmd. 9298 (London: H.M.S.O., 1953).

71. E.B. Childers, *The Road to Suez: A Study of Western-Arab Relations* (London: MacGibbon and Kee, 1960), p. 111.

72. U.S. Department of State, *Bulletin*, 9 August 1954, p. 198.

73. Ibid. See also Eisenhower's comment, *New York Times*, 12 August 1954.

74. See comments by Nasser and Fawzi, U.S. Department of State, *Bulletin*, 16 August 1954, p. 234.

75. *Egyptian Gazette*, 4 and 5 November 1954.

76. *New York Times*, 28 July and 4 August 1954.

77. *New York Times*, 28 July 1954.

3

Israel and Egypt: In Search
of an Equation

King Hussein recalls that, of the 670 miles of hostile borders between Israel and its Arab neighbors, Egypt had to defend 180 miles; Syria, 45; Lebanon, just over 50; and Jordan, 400. The Israeli-Jordanian border was in fact the site of the most frequent hostilities, and Egypt was far less anxious about its proximity to Israel than Jordan until the Israeli raid on Gaza in 1955.[1]

The relative calm that prevailed along Egypt's border with Israel in the early years of the new regime allowed the Junta to concentrate on consolidating the Revolution and throwing off the British yoke. In this perspective, it paid Egypt to tone down its belligerence toward Israel in return for American support in resolving its internal problems.[2]

This show of moderation did not signify any lessening of Egypt's moral support for the Arab cause against Israel. As long as such problems as the fate of the Palestinian refugees, the defining of permanent frontiers, and the character of Jerusalem remained unsolved, Egypt refused to consider a final peace with Israel. Of particular concern to Egypt was the fact that its present boundaries cut it off from the Arab Middle East. This was conveyed to Dulles during his trip: "He [Naguib] will insist on corridor arrangement linking Egypt with other Arab states."[3]

Egypt's leaders remained very sensitive to the Western and, in particular, American attitude toward Israel. As early as December 1952, for instance, General Naguib criticized the United States for encouraging West German reparation payments to Israel before a similar agreement was reached between Israel and the Palestinian refugees. Naguib also reminded the powers of their own regional vulnerability: "In order to create a nation of 1,000,000, you [the West] have spoiled relations with 50,000,000 Arabs who own, among other things, great quantities of oil."[4]

As the Arab-Israeli feud began to affect America's relations with the new Egyptian leadership, the American government was invariably subjected to intense domestic pressures in favor of Israel. The "special" relationship between the United States and Israel thus bred antagonism, misunderstandings and animosities in the Arab world that greatly hindered the application of American policy toward Egypt and the entire region.

These difficulties were apparent even before the Eisenhower administration took office. For example, a new realism was demonstrated in a December 1952 speech by Under-Secretary of State Henry Byroade before the Chicago Council on Foreign Relations:

> The people of the Arab States have cried out against this policy of the United States. The birth of the tragic Arab refugee problem out of the Palestine conflict has added to the real and deep-seated bitterness toward Americans throughout the Arab world, a bitterness which replaced, to some extent at least, an earlier faith in the United States. The emotions which surround this problem in the Middle East are so intense that any immediate or dramatic solution of the problem is impossible. Even progress toward solution of any segment of the problem is at best exceedingly difficult.[5]

However, the politically unpopular decision to re-evaluate policy on this issue was left to the next administration.

The inauguration of President Eisenhower in January 1953 freed the new American leadership from the immediate election concerns stirred by the charged issue of support for Israel. These leaders could also benefit from the fact that their slate was relatively clean in the eyes of the Arab world despite the Republican Party's pro-Israeli platform during the election campaign. That President Eisenhower wished to take advantage of these opportunities to improve Arab-American relations was enunciated during the March 1953 visit of Foreign Minister Prince Feisal of Saudi Arabia. On this occasion Eisenhower also admitted that the Palestine issue had left a residue of bitterness that was reflected in the negative and suspicious attitude of the Arab world toward the West. Announcing that he meant to restore the spirit of confidence and trust that had once characterized these relations, he expressed his hope for a "peace with justice."[6]

Secretary of State Dulles also demonstrated that his understanding of the problems stemming from the "special relationship" had been enlarged by his trip to the Middle East in 1953:

> The United States' position...is not good, and the loss of respect for the United States varies almost directly with the nearness of the respective Arab State to Israel.[7]

This new awareness must be viewed against the cold war background that eventually tempted the Soviet Union to exploit America's pro-Israeli stance for its own ends. Global strategy considerations seemed to require the American leadership to devise a Middle East defense arrangement that could be acceptable to the Arab nationalists. The lesson to be drawn from the failures of the previous administration was that a solution to the Arab-Israeli conflict that might satisfy both sides was a prerequisite to the kind of defense arrangement that would satisfy the United States.[8]

Efforts in this direction could be observed by early May 1953. In a discussion of the Mutual Security Program for 1954, Dulles outlined a plan to reduce tensions through "maintenance of programs of relief and rehabilitation of refugees" and "assistance in promoting plans for peace between Israel and the Arab nations."[9]

Meanwhile, Eisenhower's election victory offered Egypt's leaders a welcome opportunity to cast the blame for past difficulties in Arab-American relations on the outgoing administration. This was soon accompanied by real hope that a fresh look at the problems of the region would incline the Americans to take a more favorable view of the Arab cause.

An attempt to convince the administration, during its first month in office, of the need to re-evaluate the old attitude was made when the Egyptian Ambassador to the United States joined six other Arab Ambassadors in an appeal to Under-Secretary of State General Walter B. Smith. Drawing Smith's attention to what the delegation deemed a Zionist attempt to cloud the issues by portraying Israel as the "beachhead of democracy", they warned that the Soviet Union, which had just severed relations with Israel, stood to gain from future American aid to the latter country.[10]

The Egyptian Ambassador further expressed the hope that the Eisenhower Administration was genuinely interested in finding solutions to the problems that plagued the Middle East. His statement was seconded by the Egyptian press, which urged the United States, as "the major provider of Israel, both morally and financially," to exert its influence on that country "to accept the United Nations resolutions concerning partition and the Palestine refugees."[11]

The announcement that Dulles intended to make a personal visit to the Middle East was seen by Egypt as a concrete manifestation of America's new interest in the Arab world and its problems. The hope that Truman's pro-Israeli stand would now be replaced by greater impartiality was publicly expressed by General Naguib.[12] Thus the arrival of the Secretary of State was greeted with the message that a change in America's attitude toward Israel was essential to improving relations with the Arabs.

The first-hand information that Secretary Dulles gathered in the course of his mission included an account of the border incidents between Jordan and Israel, which flared up during his visit.[13] He returned to Washington determined to alert both his colleagues in the government and the general public to the need for urgent action to settle the problems surrounding the Arab-Israeli dispute. Some examples of the frankness and insight he showed in his "Report to the Nation on the Middle East" of 1 June 1953[14] were noted in the last chapter, in connection with the Anglo-Egyptian dispute. Here instead it seems appropriate to recall Dulles's remarks on some of the most delicate — and heretofore least talked about — aspects of the whole Arab-Israeli question.

In discussing the character of Jerusalem, Dulles knew that both Jordan and Israel, who ruled the divided city since 1948, had refused to implement United

Nations resolutions calling for the internationalization of that city. Jordan held that implementation would compromise "the security, integrity, and the interests of its country." The Israelis insisted that Jerusalem was an integral part of Israel and suggested that the "holy places" might be placed under U.N. authority.[15] By 1 January 1950 Israel had moved most government activities from Tel Aviv to Jerusalem with the exception of the Foreign Office, which was subsequently moved in 1953.

Nevertheless, the American Secretary openly reaffirmed the American commitment to the United Nations resolutions:

> Jerusalem is divided into armed camps split between Israel and the Arab nation of Jordan. The atmosphere is heavy with hate...the world religious community has claims in Jerusalem which take precedence over the political claims of any particular nation.[16]

Dulles also faced up to the question of the Palestinian refugees. The Arab states and the Palestinians themselves insisted on the refugees' right to choose repatriation in their homeland or resettlement elsewhere. Israel rejected anything more than token repatriation, arguing that mass repatriation would create a centrifugal force that would destroy the very character of the state. For Israel, the refugees had to be absorbed by the Arab states; on the basis of this solution, linked with a final peace with the Arabs, Israel expressed on various occasions its willingness to pay reparations.[17] However, the will to compromise proved to be lacking on both sides.

In considering an American-sponsored solution, Dulles thus emphasized humanitarian considerations:

> Closely huddled around Israel are most of the over 800,000 Arab refugees, who fled from Palestine as the Israelis took over. They mostly exist in makeshift camps, with few facilities either for health, work, or recreation. Within these camps the inmates rot away, spiritually and physically...Some of these refugees could be settled in the area presently controlled by Israel. Most, however, could more readily be integrated into the lives of the neighboring Arab countries. This, however, waits on irrigation projects, which will permit more soil to be cultivated.[18]

Relating the development needs of the area as a whole to the plight of the refugees, Dulles added:

> Throughout the area the cry is for water for irrigation. United Nations contributions and other funds are available to help refugees, and Mr. Stassen [who accompanied Dulles on his trip] and I came back with the impression that they can well be spent in large part on a coordinated use of the rivers which run through the Arab countries and Israel.[19]

In his concluding summary of the situation Dulles recommended that "the United States should seek to allay the deep resentment against it that has

resulted from the creation of Israel." He evoked the Arabs' past goodwill and affirmed that "the Arab peoples are afraid that the United States will back the new
state of Israel in aggressive expansion. They are more fearful of Zionism than of
communism and they fear lest the United States become the backer of expansionist Zionism."[20]

Dulles also cited and reaffirmed the American 1950 commitment to the
Tripartite Declaration:

> It must be made clear that the present U.S. administration stands
> fully behind that Declaration. We cannot afford to be distrusted by
> millions who could be sturdy friends of freedom. They must not swell
> the ranks of communist dictators....United States policies should be im-
> partial so as to win not only the respect and regard of the Israelis but also of
> the Arab people....[21]

He thus publicly acknowledged the need for evenhanded treatment of both sides
as a necessary principle of the American cold war policy applicable to the Middle East. A corollary of this policy was the suggestion that Israel "...should
become part of the Near East community and cease to look upon itself, or be
looked upon by others, as alien to the community."

Finally, Dulles offered American assistance in resolving the Arab-Israeli problem: "The United States will not hesitate by every appropriate means to use its
influence to promote a step-by-step reduction of tension." What concrete
measures this implied began to emerge from the Secretary of State's speech
before the Senate Appropriations Committee soon after his return. On this occasion, Dulles proposed a new regional approach: "We have prepared a 'single
package' program designed to lay emphasis on the need for the countries of the
region to cooperate with each other and to marshal their resources, whenever
feasible."[22]

The administration's long-term plan for regional development was unveiled
gradually. On 14 October 1953 President Eisenhower announced the appointment of Eric Johnston as Special Ambassador to the Near East. Johnston was "to
explore with the governments of . . . that region certain steps which might . . .
contribute to an improvement of the general situation . . . and to undertake
discussions with certain of the Arab States and Israel, looking to the mutual
development of the water resources of the Jordan River Valley on a regional
basis."[23]

The Johnston project was the result of a Tennessee Valley Authority desk
study of previous plans for the development of the Jordan River Valley.[24] The
United States Point-Four Technical Cooperation Mission was, at the same time,
working on a competing plan, the Maqarin Project. There is some evidence that
the different American agencies were working at cross-purposes.[25]

The Johnston Mission was primarily motivated by the desire to resolve the
Palestinian refugee problem, a root cause of regional discontent. Its task, which
presupposed a certain amount of cooperation among the belligerent parties, was

to encourage a regional effort toward development that would be coordinated with UNWRA's work to resettle the refugees.[26] It was explicitly recognized by Under-Secretary W. B. Smith that it was "unreasonable to expect Arab countries to accept refugees as workers unless means are found to improve conditions of their own citizens."[27] To enhance the possibilities for the success of this project — soon known as the Johnston Plan — the United States offered to contribute two-thirds of the costs or an estimated \$200 million.[28]

The Johnston Plan encountered serious difficulties from the outset. The Jordanian-Israeli border had been troubled by numerous Palestinian incursions followed by acts of Israeli retaliation. Israeli dissatisfaction with the work of the United Nations Truce Supervision Organization, which was sometimes hampered by Israel itself, led to an increasingly uncooperative Israeli attitude. Despite the fact that the Johnston Mission and Plan represented President Eisenhower's first major peace initiative, Israel chose this period to adopt and carry out a new, hardline policy of large-scale retaliatory attacks across the Jordanian border that began with a raid against the town of Qibya. The Israeli government also declined to heed a United Nations order to desist from Israel's own project to divert the flow of the Jordan River.[29]

Arab reaction to the American initiative was mixed. The Egyptian press conceded that "the Arab states are thankful to President Eisenhower for his careful attention toward the problems of the Middle East." The stated American intention of exercising greater impartiality in matters affecting Israel was also noted with favor. But the Egyptian commentator added pessimistically: "We are of the opinion that Mr. Eric Johnston's success does not seem very probable so long as the Palestine problem remains unsettled and as long as the United Nations resolutions remain ink on paper."[30]

The Egyptian government seems to have lent its support to the mission, both morally and materially, despite various Arab objections. According to the former British Ambassador to Cairo, Egypt privately favored the scheme and even lent Johnston considerable technical assistance, including Egyptian engineers.[31] Egypt may also have persuaded Syria and Jordan to maintain contact with Johnston.[32] However, the Egyptian government could not risk public declarations of support so long as there was substantial Arab resistance.[33]

In retrospect the fact that the Arab states actually considered the Johnston scheme and that, despite existing hostilities, each state recognized the right of all riparians to share the waters of the Jordan were accomplishments in themselves. Yet, as one observer pointed out, by drawing the question of water resources deeper into the highly explosive Arab-Israeli dispute, a basic economic issue of great importance to the region became further politicized.[34] As tension rose instead of diminishing, the mission was seen as that much "more urgent and necessary" and it was continued for two years in the hope that "the project will commend itself to the states concerned."[35] When the heightened unrest of early 1956 finally brought the endeavor to an end, the parties were no closer to an agreement on its objectives than at the beginning.

The greater impartiality with which the Eisenhower administration began to approach Arab-Israeli issues together with its declared aim of bettering relations with the Arab world were viewed with alarm by Israel. The policy of "wooing the Arabs" in order to organize a regional defense system that would satisfy American cold war needs was seen by Israeli leaders as a particularly threatening prospect, since the United States might yield to Arab demands concerning the cession of territory and the integration of a vast number of Palestinian refugees in return for Arab support of the Western defense system. It raised even greater fears that the United States would have to arm the Arab world as a necessary consequence of the same defense policy. In this case an increasingly isolated Israel could be left to face a well-armed Arab camp.

Abba Eban, the Israeli Ambassador to the United States at the time when the new administration's change of attitude began to emerge, defined the reasons for his country's uneasiness. According to him, it gave Israel's citizens the impression that America's friendship had been a casual and short-lived circumstance of history, linked organically with the Truman administration. The feeling was that Israel could no longer count on the United States to protect Israel's interests because America's cold war strategy impelled it to make a strong bid for Arab support.[36]

By the same token, the settlement of the Anglo-Egyptian dispute was viewed with misgivings, since it increased the likelihood that Egypt and, with it, other Arab states would join a Western defense pact. Moreover, the departure of British troops from Egypt, foreseen in any Anglo-Egyptian settlement, was an event that Israeli leaders felt would leave their country exposed to attack from what they regarded as potentially their most dangerous enemy.[37]

Israel's anxiety, evidently conveyed to Secretary Dulles during his 1953 visit to that country, was recorded in his private memorandum:

> Israel is jittery over fact they do not know intentions of new administration and fear that we may attempt to impose a peace settlement which they would consider to be unjust. They are particularly concerned we might attempt to take away some of the territory they now control.[38]

Israel's response to the prospects it saw as a threat to its future security was a policy of stepped-up activism and self-help. Abba Eban also explained the reasoning behind this development:

> A greater policy of militancy . . .[was to] develop in Israel for two reasons: as a compensation for American friendship, and, perhaps, as a way of forcing the United States to recoil from any change adverse to Israel.[39]

The break in Israeli-Soviet relations that occurred in February 1953 also meant that Israel could no longer count on a neutral Soviet attitude.[40]

The history of the ensuing period was largely determined by a series of actions and reactions caused by the American attempt to implement its policy of greater impartiality and the tougher, more militant tactics adopted by Israel, from 1953 on, to face what it considered a precarious situation. These tactics included the hard-hitting retaliatory raids previously mentioned. On the diplomatic plane, a prime example was Israel's 10 July decision to move its Foreign Office from Tel Aviv to Jerusalem.[41] This action, which completed the transfer of all Israeli government offices to that city, was carried out in defiance not only of the Arab states, but also of established United States policy and of the extant United Nations Resolutions.[42]

The temporal relationship between this manifestation of Israel's self-help policy on 10 July and Secretary Dulles's 9 July request that funds be allocated from the Mutual Security Program of 1954 for military assistance to the Middle East hardly seems coincidental. At any rate, the American leadership reiterated its intention to maintain an impartial stance:

> The United States does not plan to transfer its Embassy from Tel-Aviv to Jerusalem. It is felt that this would be inconsistent with the international nature of Jerusalem and that it would not observe the situation regarding Jerusalem which was set forth in the Secretary of State's address of June 1, 1953.[43]

Dulles further expressed his dissatisfaction by pointing out that the Israeli government had seen fit to carry out its move despite a request by the American government that it refrain from so doing.

> We believe that it [Israel] would embarrass the United Nations. . . .Also, we feel that this particular action by the Government of Israel at this particular time is inopportune in relation to the tensions which are rather extreme, and that this will add to rather than relax any of these tensions.[44]

For more than a year, the American Ambassador avoided Jerusalem; however, in November 1954, four months after a similar Soviet move, the newly appointed American Ambassador, Edward Larson, presented his credentials there.[45]

Still another major demonstration of Israel's policy occurred in September 1953, when it attempted unilaterally to divert the waters of the Jordan River for a Negev development project. Once this project was under way, Israel chose to resist the combined pressure of Arab protests, United Nations orders to discontinue work until agreement with the interested parties had been reached, and an official American request asking Israel to accede to the United Nations demand.[46]

Although any connection between the Israeli water diversion project and the Johnston Plan later announced by the United States has been denied,[47] it seems significant that Dulles had earlier stressed the great importance of water in any regional settlement and the need to coordinate the use of water resources among the riparians.[48] Whether or not he already had the Johnston Plan in mind remains unknown; it is a fact that Dulles did emphasize this need for cooperation in June and that the Israeli leadership decided to act independently all the same.

As a result, the United States took its firmest stand ever in support of a United Nations desist order. On 20 October, less than a month after Major General Vagn Bennike, Chief of Staff of the United Nations Mixed Armistice Commission, had requested Israel to stop its work,[49] Secretary Dulles announced the suspension of economic aid to Israel ". . .because it seemed to us that the State of Israel should respect General Bennike's decision and that as long as the State of Israel was acting in defiance of the decision, it was questionable at least as to whether we should make the allocation."[50] Fifteen million dollars from the Foreign Operations Administration and a $60 million Mutual Security Fund Loan were in fact suspended.

The stern American stand must be viewed in conjunction with other manifestations of the tough Israeli attitude toward its neighbors. Reportedly Israel began to construct fortifications in a demilitarized zone near Al Auja on its border with Egypt, perhaps in relation to the October announcement of a major breakthrough in Anglo-Egyptian negotiations and Britain's agreement in principle to withdraw its troops from Egypt. Israel's heavy retaliatory raid against the Jordanian town of Qibya shortly after the American leadership announced the Johnston Mission is another, more serious example. According to the interpretation of the Egyptian press, the Qibya raid was part of Israel's plan "to force peace" on the Arabs on Israel's own terms and, at the same time, to pressure America into forcing Arab acceptance of peace on these terms. Whether true or not, Arab resistance to a plan that called for cooperation with Israel was definitely intensified by the Israeli action.[51]

The Qibya raid so nettled the new American leadership that the United States joined France and Britain in bringing the incident before the Security Council. The official American position was set forth by Deputy Representative James J. Wadsworth in support of a United States sponsored resolution censuring Israel: "The recent action at Qibya. . .is in violation of the ceasefire resolution. . . and is inconsistent with. . .the General Armistice Agreement and the obligations of the Charter." Although he conceded that both Jordan and Israel were responsible for preventing such violations, the United States nonetheless joined with the other states of the Security Council, on 24 November 1953, in condemning Israel for the Qibya raid.[52]

In the meantime, Israel had agreed to comply with the United Nations desist order concerning its Jordan River diversion project. The American leadership responded by agreeing to resume aid to Israel.[53]

Israel's concern grew even stronger in the ensuing months as the United States proceeded to develop its regional defense plans, especially in the Northern Tier, and as the pending agreement between Britain and Egypt moved toward finalization. Then, late in 1953, Egypt decided to tighten restrictions on Israel-bound cargo allowed to pass through the Suez Canal. Israel took this opportunity to reopen the highly charged issue of Egypt's prior refusal to allow Israeli vessels to use the canal at all.

Both Egypt and Israel could muster strong legal arguments. Israel contended that Egypt failed to honor its international obligations under Article 1 of the Constantinople Convention of 1888, which stipulated that the Suez Canal "shall always be free and open, in time of war as in time of peace, to every vessel of commerce or war without distinction of flag."[54] Egypt held that under Article X of that Convention and Article 51 of the United Nations Charter on self-defense it had the right to refuse passage to enemy ships, and that a state of war still existed between Israel and Egypt. The precedents cited included Britain's own wartime policy that effectively prevented first the Central and later the Axis Powers from using the canal in the First and Second World Wars. Egypt also claimed it had the right under international law to search and seize cargo of neutral ships bound for Israel.

While these issues never reached the International Court of Justice, a 1951 Security Council Resolution stated that Egypt's practice of search and seizure of neutral ships bound for Israel was inconsistent with the Israeli-Egyptian Armistice Agreement and unjustifiable on grounds of self-defense.[55] Egypt still refused to comply and on 2 December 1953 added foodstuffs to the list of articles destined for Israel that would not be allowed to pass through the Suez Canal.[56] On 16 December 1953 Egypt intercepted an Italian freighter, *Franca Maria*, bound for Israel and confiscated its cargo.[57]

In January 1954 Israel called on the Security Council to review the Egyptian blockade of neutral ships bound for Israel, contending that such action was in violation of the Armistice Agreement of 1949 and the 1951 United Nations Resolution. This move, and the international debate it stirred up, enabled Israel to demonstrate that it was not alone in resisting United Nations resolutions.

Israel also counted on the support of America, which had consistently favored Israeli passage through both the Suez Canal and the Straits of Tiran. Israel contended the Straits were also an international waterway subject to the right of "free passage."[58] In fact, the United States lodged an official protest against Egypt[59] and voted for Israel in the Security Council debate on a resolution calling for free navigation in the Suez Canal.[60]

Egypt reacted strongly. Insisting that the blockade was within its legitimate rights, it viewed the American position as an unjustified regression to the previous administration's pro-Israeli attitude. The warm and encouraging comments that had hailed the Eisenhower administration's fresh approach to the Middle East as a step that "will do much to strengthen the faith of the Arab world in the United States"[61] ceased abruptly. Instead, the Egyptian press lashed out in strongly worded articles that contrasted with the relative moderation that had been shown until then on matters concerning the United States. Threats of Arab "non-cooperation with the United States so long as the latter supports Israel against them" were uttered,[62] and attention was drawn to new demonstrations of Soviet sympathy for the Arabs:

We must bear in mind the fact that the Arab-Israeli dispute has become an international question; Israel is supported by the Anglo-American bloc, and the Arab States are supported by the Russian bloc.[63]

The strength of the Egyptian reaction may in part have reflected the stalemate that had developed in Anglo-Egyptian negotiations and the fear that Britain would now feel encouraged to condition its withdrawal on Egypt's acceptance of the United Nations resolution concerning Israel's rights to use the canal.[64] The shift in Egypt's political humor seen in its press commentary may also have reflected the internal power struggle between Naguib and Nasser that was now coming to a head. Nevertheless, the Soviet veto of the American-backed resolution and the Egyptian "hope that the Russian veto will wake up the West to the dangers of its shortsighted policy of supporting Israel in disregard of Arab nationalist opposition"[65] were clearly a warning of things to come. From this time onward the Soviet Union gave unreserved support to Arab causes, and its championship of the Arabs against Israel provided the Soviets with a particularly effective means of asserting their influence in Arab affairs.[66]

At the very time that the new administration was obliged to test its policy of impartiality in circumstances forced upon it by local maneuvering in the Middle East, it was also running into heavy fire on the domestic front from pressure groups that traditionally supported Israel in periods of stress. Besides the Zionist organizations and the much larger body of Jewish public opinion that identified with Israel without wholly embracing Zionist ideals, these groups included heterogeneous segments of the American population that were neither Zionist nor Jewish. While the true strength of this lobby may have been exaggerated, it was perceived as being of great potential influence by the American leadership:

> Any attempt to give aid to the Arabs always met with opposition behind the scenes in Washington, where the members of Congress were acutely aware of the strong popular sentiment in this country for Israel. . .Consideration for the great body of private opinion in the United States favoring Israel was a large factor in every governmental decision on the Middle East issues.[67]

Because these pressure groups were especially effective within the Congress, where sensitivity to election needs was acute, they were able to exert a restraining influence on the new American approach to Arab-Israeli problems. Action on issues that would either have given rise to congressional debate or have necessitated congressional approval was avoided in order to spare the American leadership political embarrassment should it be charged with favoring a policy deemed contrary to Israeli interests. Such issues as the arming of Israel's Arab neighbors, American membership in the Baghdad Pact, large-scale aid to Egypt, and the creation of an effective enforcement organ for the Tripartite Declaration had thus to be approached cautiously and, in some cases, avoided entirely. As will be seen in subsequent chapters, this constraint on American policymakers remained constant throughout the period under consideration.

In 1954 the pro-Israeli lobby in America concentrated much of its efforts on preventing the United States from arming the Arab world. So long as Egypt and Britain failed to reach an agreement, these groups were able to rely on America's unwillingness to give arms to Egypt that could be used against British troops. Once an agreement was in the offing, the pro-Israeli groupings stepped up their campaign to forestall an arrangement between Egypt and the United States similar to the American-Iraqi Mutual Assistance Agreement of April 1954.[68] They were bolstered by numerous official Israeli protests to the United States against the arming of Egypt.[69]

As a result, members of both the House of Representatives and the Senate, led by Senator Saltonstall of the Senate Armed Services Committee, queried the State Department about Israeli security in the event of the conclusion of military agreements between the United States and the Arab nations. They also raised the possibility of direct American military assistance to Israel, which had so far been withheld.[70] Shortly after the Anglo-Egyptian draft agreement was accepted by both sides in July, those pleading Israel's cause increased their pressure. On 25 October 1954 — six days after the final agreement between Egypt and Britain was signed — sixteen national Jewish organizations in the United States formally protested against Dulles's policy of arming the Arabs.[71]

Meanwhile, American attempts to organize Arab defenses in a regional system geared to cold war objectives were affected by the tougher Israeli attitude toward its neighbors. During the spring of 1954, for example, after the conclusion of the American-Iraqi bilateral defense agreement in April, Israel's intensified reprisal raids against Jordan — whether or not justified by the immediate circumstances — lessened Jordan's interest in Western defense schemes despite a previously favorable response to Western overtures. In general the military muscles now flexed by Israel diminished Arab receptivity to the idea of cooperating in a Western defense system oriented primarily against the Soviet Union. Both criticism and activism on the part of Israel thus reinforced the domestic pressures that aimed to keep the American administration from implementing its policies in the manner it desired.

The American leadership did not remain passive to this interference, which it considered all the more irritating in view of growing Soviet support for Arab causes. Official American sources reproached Israel in strongly worded statements for stirring up local hostilities at a most inopportune time. Under-Secretary Henry Byroade in an April discourse explained that the American desire for a more evenhanded approach to the Middle East rested on three pillars: (1) the people — "all the 65 million souls"; (2) strategy, because of the highly important geographic significance of the region; and (3) oil. Alluding to the interests of "special groups" concerned with this region, he stressed that the policy of the United States would be shaped and conducted "to represent the interests of the majority of our people where vital issues affecting our security are concerned." Using strong language, he went on to advise Israel to "drop the attitude of conqueror and. . .make your deeds correspond to your frequent utterances of the desire for peace."[72]

In a second speech, less than a month later, Byroade warned that:

> America would back no state, including Israel, in a matter of expansive aggression and. . .its opposition would be equally strong regardless of which side started such a move.[73]

Earlier, the same Under-Secretary of State had stigmatized the Israeli raid on Qibya in the following terms:

> I think that when anything like that [Israel's raid on Qibya] happens, the net loser is the United States as well as Israel. The Arabs' first hatred and renewed passions are against Israel. But, on second thought, they say, "Well, there would not be an Israel but for the United States." And they find a United States cartridge shell and they say, "Well, look, who is really our enemy? Who has done this? The United States has done it."[74]

These statements produced a shower of protests from Israel and from pro-Israeli groups in America.[75] Nevertheless, the State Department stood behind Byroade's remarks and replied "that the American people were entitled to such information." Israel was again urged to find some way to allay Arab fears, particularly with regard to its policy on immigration and the need for territorial expansion it was alleged to imply.[76]

America's strong stand only served to fan Israel's fears that it stood alone in its battle with the Arabs. This in turn helped ensure that the American policy designed to strengthen the defenses of the Arab region was bound to become bogged down in the very regional strife that, by 1955, was about to boil over.

On 28 February 1955, two days after the signing of the Baghdad Pact, the relative calm that had prevailed along the Egyptian-Israeli border was abruptly shattered. Israeli troops, responding to the latest in a long series of incidents, launched a major retaliatory raid on the Egyptian-controlled Gaza Strip. In this raid, which was the first direct clash between Egypt and Israel since 1948, both Egyptian soldiers and Palestinians were killed.[77] A chain reaction of increasingly violent confrontations between the two countries climaxed in the Suez War twenty-one months later.

Many reasons have been advanced to explain this manifestation of Israel's hardline policy toward Egypt, which was condemned by both the United Nations Armistice Commission and the Security Council.[78] Officially, Israel contended that the number of hostile incursions originating from the Gaza Strip had increased prior to the raid. General Dayan later blamed the Egyptian Fedayeen, although there is evidence that attacks by this organization may only have begun after the raid and, in part at least, as a response to it.[79]

Perhaps a more telling reason is to be found in comments by Dayan before the raid. The withdrawal of British troops was only months away and Egypt's entry into a Western defense pact seemed a possibility that was not to be discounted. Against this background Dayan's great concern about the West's "policy of one-sided reinforcement of Israel's neighbors" suggests the hypothesis that security considerations may have dictated a policy calculated to thwart this eventuality.[80]

This hypothesis is indirectly supported by the so-called "Lavon affair" that occurred in July 1954, when Pinhas Lavon was Israeli Minister of Defense and the moderate Moshe Sharett was Prime Minister. In this controversial and still mysterious operation, Israeli agents were accused by Egyptian and, later, by authoritative Israeli sources of direct responsibility for anti-American incidents in Cairo that were allegedly designed to discredit Egypt as a potential ally of the West. Specifically, those who back this charge claim that, under Lavon's orders, Israeli agents were responsible for the burning of USIS libraries in Cairo and Alexandria and the placing of bombs in six American-owned cinemas in Egypt. In the end, this charge led Ben Gurion, whom Lavon accused of authorizing the operation, to resign from the Labour Party he headed.[81]

In retrospect, the sequence of events touched off by the Gaza Raid does in fact seem to have driven a wedge between Egypt and the United States, whether or not it was Israel's real motive. From this point until the Suez War of October-November 1956 the clashes on the Israeli-Egyptian border were numerous and constantly threatened open warfare. This threat heightened the Egyptian leaders' determination to satisfy what they considered an urgent need for arms, especially when it became known that Israel had been securing arms from France since August 1954 despite the French commitment to the 1950 Tripartite Declaration.[82] The fact that the United States continued to frustrate Egypt's quest for Western arms only increased Egypt's receptivity to the alternative source of arms and support that had presented itself on the Middle East scene—the Soviet Union.

As Egyptian-Israeli relations deteriorated after the Gaza Raid, the United States strove to reduce the explosive tensions that were building up in the area.[83] On 26 August 1955 Secretary Dulles announced the most comprehensive approach yet formulated by the United States. The occasion was an address to the Council on Foreign Relations that was delivered only four days before America officially acknowledged the existence of Soviet proposals to arm Egypt.[84] The timing of this new policy announcement suggests that it was intended to forestall any such agreement.

In this address Dulles set forth wide-ranging proposals for the solution of all the major problems stemming from the Arab-Israeli feud. The plight of the refugees required a policy of "resettlement and—to such an extent as may be feasible—repatriation." This could be brought about by rendering unproductive land arable through the development of water resources. American financial assistance for this specific purpose and for the still larger goal of helping Israel to compensate the Palestinian refugees as part of a resettlement program was now explicitly offered. For Dulles, "a solution to the refugee problem would help in eliminating the problem of recurrent incidents which have plagued and embittered the settlements on both sides of the borders."[85]

Concerning the Arab-Israeli conflict itself, Dulles offered to extend and enlarge American engagements "to prevent or thwart any effort by either side to alter by force the boundaries between Israel and its Arab neighbors." To this end, he expressed the American government's willingness to enter into a formal treaty providing for the creation of an effective control agency that "other countries would be willing to join. . .and [that]. . .would be sponsored by the United Nations."

The question of boundaries was one of the most delicate aspects of the whole problem. After their defeat in 1948, the Arab states demanded that Israel return the lands assigned to Arabs by the Partition Plan of 1947. Israel refused to consider these demands on the grounds that the Arabs had initially rejected the Partition Plan, choosing instead to fight and subsequently losing. Israel thus continued to occupy 40 percent more land than had been allocated to a Jewish state in the Plan. The resulting *de facto* borders often divided Arab villages from the farmland and water that had provided their livelihood.[86]

Redefining these borders was a topic American policymakers had understandably shied away from. Dulles, instead, now risked bringing the issue into the open as part of his comprehensive solution:

> The existing lines separating Israel and the Arab States were fixed by the armistice agreement of 1949. They were not designed to be permanent frontiers in every respect; in part, at least, they reflected the status of the fighting at that moment.
> The task of drawing permanent boundaries is admittedly one of difficulty . . . .Surely, the overall advantages of the measures here outlined would outweigh vastly any net disadvantage of the adjustments needed to convert armistice lines of danger into boundary lines of safety. In spite of conflicting claims and sentiments, I believe it is possible to find a way of reconciling the vital interests of all the parties. The United States would be willing to help in the search for a solution if the parties to the dispute should so desire.[87]

The breadth of the new Dulles approach was evident, and it was quickly endorsed by Britain, which offered "to guarantee by treaty or treaties with the parties concerned any territorial settlement so agreed."[88] However, these comprehensive proposals could only succeed if the belligerents themselves reached agreement on a whole series of extremely sensitive issues. The chances for such an agreement were very poor after the Gaza Raid and the escalation of hostilities that ensued.

In view of the half-measures, the indecisiveness, and the lack of any well-defined policy that was later to characterize the American leadership's approach to Middle East problems, it is instructive briefly to review the responses of the parties concerned to Secretary Dulles's bold plan of action. The reaction of the belligerents has been summed up in a single paragraph:

> Without satisfying Arab opinion, this proposal, as might have been expected, evoked a howl of protest in Israel. So negative was the reaction that the Western powers did not follow up these speeches with further endeavors to

promote a settlement. They were not going to try to force a solution on both sides, and any hope of agreement between the two seemed quite vain.[89]

With particular regard to Egyptian opinion, Mohammed Heikal reported that Nasser found the Americans "too concerned with. . .superficial and artificial ways of settling problems" and that he "could not take these gimmicks seriously." In Nasser's view, the Israelis had no intention of accepting the borders laid down by the Partition Plan, a condition that supposedly formed the basis for Nasser's own demands in a negotiated settlement.[90]

Nasser's views, if correctly reported, seem overly simple unless they are interpreted against the background of America's domestic pressures and policies that were weakening Arab confidence in the United States and especially in America's capacity to force Israel into making compromises that would be acceptable to its antagonists. Nearly two years earlier, the Egyptian Ambassador to Washington, Ahmed Hussein, had already formulated Egypt's expectations in this regard:

> The Arabs do not expect the United States to abandon Israel, but we do not want Israel and the American Zionists to force the United States Government to alienate the Arabs.[91]

The constraints on America's policymakers were thus clearly recognized by the Egyptian leadership.[92]

Nevertheless, this recognition was hardly a substitute for the fulfillment of Egypt's own needs, nor could it erase the impression created by the disproportionate flow of American funds to Israel as compared with the sums disbursed to the entire Arab world. This imbalance appears from the tabulation below, which shows that, in the period 1945-1955, all Near East and African countries together received about half as much as Israel alone in net United States grants and credits.

Net U.S. Grants and Credits to the Near East and Africa,
1945-1955
(In millions of dollars)

Country	Population[a] (millions)	Net Grants	Net Credits	Net Total
Egypt	23.5[b]	26	4	30
Israel	1.7[c]	233	137	370
Jordan	1.3[d]	25	— —	25
Other Near East and Africa[e]	— —	189	-7	182

Source: U. S. Department of Commerce, *Foreign Grants and Credits by the U. S. Government,* September 1955.
a. According to Encyclopaedia Britannica, *World Atlas* (London: Encyclopaedia Britannica, 1960).
b. 1956. d. 1952.
c. 1954. e. Including Egypt and Jordan, but excluding Israel.

A similar picture emerges from the following tabulation of loans made to Near Eastern countries by the American Export-Import Bank during the same period:[93]

Egypt	$ 7,335,000
Israel	$ 135,000,000
Total Arab World	$ 47,335,000

Besides these funds from official sources, Israel could also count on large private contributions from the American Jewish Community. These amounted to at least $60 million a year in the form of private gifts and another $50 million a year through the purchase of Israeli bonds. The magnitude of this assistance, both public and private, was largely a product of American sympathy for the Jewish state that arose after the holocaust of the Second World War.[94]

The United States still refused to satisfy Israel's demands for direct arms purchases in this period. But its financial generosity clearly enabled Israel to allocate funds for the purchase of arms from other willing sources, especially France from 1954 on.

This background helps to explain why Egypt's sense of frustration and estrangement from the United States was magnified in the period following the Gaza Raid. The "special" relationship established between Israel and the United States contrasted sharply with America's refusal — or inability because of internal pressures — to supply Egypt with the military equipment for which it now clamored. As the two belligerents stepped up their hostilities and the prospects for a full-scale Egyptian-Israeli war grew, the failure of American attempts to condition Nasser strained American-Egyptian relations and ultimately helped set the stage for the Suez Crisis of 1956.

The weakness that characterized the Eisenhower administration's approach to the Middle East at the end of its first term in office nullified both the bold "new look" with which it began and the "comprehensive" plan announced in August 1955. By April 1956, the only affirmative action the United States was still capable of taking was an endorsement of an Anglo-Soviet proposal for a United Nations arms embargo on the Middle East.[95]

As the November election drew near, the American leadership once more relegated the Arab-Israeli dispute to the floor of the United Nations, where it was less likely to disturb the domestic political jockeying. Echoing a similar statement by President Truman only a few years earlier, Dulles dismissed the problem with the following remark: "I feel that in a sense Israel is a ward of the United Nations."[96]

Hindsight suggests that a great opportunity had been lost. The fear of adverse public opinion had kept the administration from resolutely using all the means at its disposal to extract the reciprocal concessions necessary for a settlement. These means might have ruffled Israeli feelings without in fact endangering the security of the Jewish state; in the long run they might have avoided the bloodshed, the unrelenting hatred, and the complications of Soviet involvement that were subsequently to characterize the situation. This lost opportunity seems all the greater in view of the objective weaknesses and needs of both the Arabs and the Israelis at the time. The irony is that the "strong public opinion" that was so feared and that acted as such a constraint on those who initially desired resolute action may in reality have been much weaker than the American leadership ever suspected.

Notes

1. King Hussein of Jordan, *Uneasy Lies the Head* (New York: Bernard Geis Associates, 1963), p. 86.
2. Egypt's desire to soft-pedal the Israeli question at this time is seen in a CBS interview with General Naguib. Questioned on a renewal of the Palestine War, he commented that Egypt's relations "are friendly with the whole world." *Egyptian Gazette*, 30 September 1952. Dulles, following his trip to Cairo, summarized the Egyptian attitude: "Naguib feels moving forward on arrangements with Israel is not too difficult once he solves his problems with the British." Dulles, "Important Points of Trip," Unpublished Memorandum, *Dulles Private Papers*.
3. Ibid.
4. *New York Times*, 11 December 1952. See also *Egyptian Gazette* editorials on this matter throughout May 1953.
5. H.A. Byroade, "U.S. Foreign Policy in the Middle East," U.S. Department of State, *Bulletin*, 15 December 1952, p. 932.
6. *New York Times*, 3 March 1953.
7. Dulles, "Important Points of Trip," Unpublished Memorandum, *Dulles Private Papers*.
8. See the statement by Dulles at the Foreign Service Association luncheon, U.S. Department of State, *Bulletin*, 19 February 1953; in another statement (ibid., 8 June 1953, pp. 804-05), he recognized that the communists could make inroads upon the region by exploiting the situation of the Palestinian refugees and the Arab hatred of Israel. In still another statement on 10 March 1953, Dulles regarded the need for peace as a prerequisite for the establishment of a defense system.
9. Ibid., 28 May 1953, p. 738.
10. *New York Times*, 18 February 1953. Following the announcement of the "Doctors' Plot" in the Soviet Union (ibid., 13 January 1953), the Soviet Legation in Israel was bombed. Ibid., 13 February 1953. In reaction, the Soviet diplomatic representation was withdrawn from Israel.
11. *Al Ahram*, 3 March 1953.
12. *Egyptian Gazette*, 11 May 1953. *Al Ahram* added to Naguib's comments by writing that peace would come between Israel and the Arabs only if the problem of the Palestinian refugees were solved. If this problem and that of British evacuation were eliminated, the paper indicated that the Arab states would be more receptive to the American-sponsored Middle East Defense Pact. *Al Ahram*, 11 May 1953.
13. Numerous skirmishes were reported during the period 20-23 May. M. Mansoor, ed., *The Arab World* (Washington: NCR Microcard Editions, 1973), vol. 3, 24 May 1953.
14. U.S. Department of State, *Bulletin*, 15 June 1953, pp. 832-35. Aspects of this Report are also discussed in chapter 4.
15. *Bulletin des Nations Unies*, Volume VIII, No. 9, 1 May 1950, p. 394; ibid., No. 12, 15 June 1950, p. 529.
16. U.S. Department of State, *Bulletin*, 15 June 1953, pp. 832.
17. Israel consistently refused to implement the United Nations Resolution of December 1948, which resolved that "refugees wishing to return to their homes and live at peace with their neighbors should be permitted to do so. . . ." General Assembly Resolution 194 (III), adopted by the General Assembly on 11 December 1948.

18. U.S. Department of State, *Bulletin*, 15 June 1953, pp. 832-35.

19. Ibid. Initially, the United States contributed $48 million to the U.N. agency concerned with the fate of the Palestinian refugees (U.N. Work and Relief Agency) and yearly met around 70 percent of its budget. UNWRA, *Statistical Summary*, December 1957.

20. U.S. Department of State, *Bulletin*, 15 June 1953, p. 835.

21. Ibid. For a discussion of the Tripartite Declaration, see "The United States Enters the Middle East" in the Introduction to this volume.

22. U.S. Department of State, *Bulletin*, 20 July 1953, p. 90.

23. Ibid., 26 October 1953, p. 553.

24. K. B. Doherty, "Jordan Waters Conflict," *International Conciliation*, May 1965, pp. 22-26.

25. Miles E. Bunger, Chief of the Point-Four Mission, reportedly advised Jordanian authorities against the Johnston Plan. See Dana A. Schmidt, "Prospects for a Solution of the Jordan River Valley Dispute," *Middle Eastern Affairs*, January 1955, p. 5.

26. U.S. Department of State, *Bulletin*, 26 October 1953, p. 553.

27. Ibid., 8 June 1953, p. 824.

28. *New York Times*, 6 May 1956.

29. E. H. Hutchison, *Violent Truce* (New York: Devin-Adair, 1956), pp. 90-91.

30. *Al Akhbar Al Gadida*, 28 October 1953.

31. Humphrey Trevelyan, *The Middle East in Revolution* (London: Macmillan, 1970), p. 40.

32. Love, *Suez: The Twice-Fought War*, p. 277.

33. Trevelyan, *The Middle East in Revolution*, p. 40. Apparently, at an Arab League meeting held in February 1956 to discuss the Johnston Plan, Lebanon and Jordan were prepared to agree; Iraq and Saudi Arabia were neutral; while Syria rejected the Plan.

34. Doherty, "Jordan Waters Conflict," p. 27.

35. U.S. Department of State, *Bulletin*, 30 November and 28 December 1953, pp. 749-50, 892.

36. Abba Eban, *John Foster Dulles Oral History Collection*, Seeley G. Mudd Manuscript Library, Princeton University, Princeton N.J., hereafter referred to as *Dulles Oral History Collection*.

37. Ibid.

38. Dulles, "Important Points of Trip," Private Memorandum, *Dulles Private Papers*. See also Israeli press comments on Dulles's trip, *Jerusalem Post*, 15 May 1953.

39. Eban, *Dulles Oral History Collection*. See also the statement by Prime Minister Ben Gurion, *New York Times*, 14 March 1953.

40. See *New York Times*, 13 January and 13 February 1953; see also footnote 10 above.

41. *New York Times*, 11 July 1953.

42. See Dulles, "Report to the Nation," U.S. Department of State, *Bulletin*, 15 June 1953, p. 832 and other sources cited at footnote 15.

43. U.S. Department of State, *Bulletin*, 20 July 1953, p. 82.

44. Ibid., 10 August 1953, p. 177.

45. Despite this de facto recognition, the United States continued to deny that this represented a change in policy. See the reply by Dulles to Arab complaints, *New York Times*, 3 and 4 November 1954.

46. Mansoor, ed., *The Arab World* (3), 2 September 1953.

47. Eban, *Dulles Oral History Collection*.

48. U.S. Department of State, *Bulletin*, 15 June 1953.

49. *New York Times*, 25 September 1953; ibid., 29 September 1953.

50. U.S. Department of State, *Bulletin*, 2 November 1953, p. 590.

51. *Al Ahram*, 19 October 1953. Compare this interpretation with not dissimilar comments by Abba Eban reported above.

52. U.S. Department of State, *Bulletin*, 14 December 1953, pp. 840-41. See also ibid., 26 October 1953, p. 55.

53. Ibid., 16 November 1953, p. 675.

54. *Diplomacy in the Near and Middle East* (1), ed. Hurewitz (New York: D. Van Nostrand, 1956), p. 202.

55. U.N. Security Council, *Official Records*, 558th meeting, 1 September 1951, Resolution s/2322.

56. Mansoor, ed., *The Arab World* (3), 2 December 1953.

57. Ibid., 11 December 1953.

58. Egypt held that Israel, as a "non-existent" state that had seized the Port of Elath after the Egyptian-Israeli Armistice, did not *de jure* border on the Gulf of Aqaba; therefore, it claimed that Israel, as a non-riparian state, held no right under international law. U.N. Security Council, *Official Records*, 659th Meeting, 15 February 1954, p. 2. The United States consistently supported Israel's position on this as on the Suez issue.

59. *New York Times*, 1 February 1954.

60. See the speech of the American representative to the Security Council. U.N. Security Council, *Official Records*, 663d Meeting, 25 March 1954, pp. 1-3; see also 664th Meeting, 29 March 1954, for New Zealand proposal.

61. Statement by the Egyptian Ambassador to Washington, Ahmed Hussein. *Egyptian Gazette*, 22 October 1953. This idea was further echoed in the Egyptian press at the time: "Naturally the Arabs should feel pleased about this positive action on Washington's part. It is a step in the right direction, and should be coupled by American economic and military aid to the Arabs. Our only hope is that the United States will maintain an honest and just policy toward the Palestine Issue, since this is the only way for Washington to restore Arab confidence." *Al Ahram*, 23 October 1953.

62. *Al Misri*, 31 March 1954.

63. *Al Kahira*, 13 April 1954.

64. Compare General Dayan's comments concerning the September 1954 *Bat Galim* incident. Dayan explained that this later Israeli attempt to test the Egyptian Canal blockade was a diplomatic effort to break the Egyptian "stranglehold," aimed at bringing the matter to the Security Council. By provoking this incident just prior to final signature of the Anglo-Egyptian Agreement, Israel hoped that Britain might insist, in its final version of the agreement, that Egypt end the blockade. *Haaretz*, 17 April 1964, quoted in Love, *Suez: The Twice-Fought War*, p. 74.

65. *Al Ahram*, 3 April 1954.

66. The Soviet Union also cast a veto in January on a Western proposal, unacceptable to the Arabs, concerning the Jordan River water project. Mansoor, ed., *The Arab World* (3), 22 January 1954. This constituted a marked change in Soviet policy, all the more significant in that the Soviet Union had even abstained from censuring Israel for the Qibya Raid. For the first time, a cold war line-up was apparent in the voting pattern on an issue of great importance to Egypt.

67. Presidential Adviser Sherman Adams, *Firsthand Report* (New York: Harper and Brothers, 1961), pp. 247-48.

68. Note that by August 1953, the Zionist Organization of America had urged the United States to withhold supplies from the Arab states "in accordance with traditional American policy" of refusing assistance to those nations belligerent to a friendly nation. *New York Times*, 1 September 1953. For information about the American-Iraqi Agreement, see chapter 4.

69. See *New York Times*, 26 July 1954, for Israeli Foreign Ministry warning to the U.S; ibid., 29 July 1954, for Israeli Prime Minister Sharett's statement on new balance of power; ibid., 8 August 1954, for Ambassador Abba Eban's comments to Dulles on Israeli security. Many other instances could be cited.

70. *New York Times*, 2 August 1954.

71. Mansoor, ed., *The Arab World* (3), 25 October 1954.

72. *New York Times*, 10 April 1954.

73. U.S. Department of State, *Bulletin*, 10 May 1954, p. 709. Byroade added: "We see no basis in our acts to justify her [Israel's] fear that her legitimate interests are placed in jeopardy by United States' concern over the area as a whole. . . . When we ask the Arab States to accept the existence of the State of Israel and to refrain from hostile acts toward her, it seems only fair to me that they should have the right to know, with far greater assurances than have ever been given them, the magnitude of this new State. They look upon it as a product of expansionist Zionism. I believe the Arab world today believes that the United States would not allow an attack by them upon Israel with the purpose of driving her into the sea. I also believe, however, that in general the Arab people are

not convinced that the opposite is true — and that they question our ability to fulfill our obligations in opposing aggression under the Tripartite Declaration of 1950."

74. U.S. Congress, House of Representatives, *Hearing on the Mutual Security Act of 1954*, 83d Cong., 2nd Sess. (Washington, D.C., Government Printing Office).

75. See, for example, *New York Times*, 4, 5, and 6 May 1954.

76. Ibid., 6 May 1954. Byroade's comments on this point elicited strong Israeli protests that this issue was an internal matter. Ibid, 5 May 1954.

77. Egypt had frequently complained to the United Nations that Israel was building fortifications in the demilitarized zone near Al Auja; however, this situation had never deteriorated to the shooting stage. Border infiltrations previously involved Palestinian refugees and irregulars located in Gaza. Thirty-nine Egyptian soldiers were reportedly killed in the Israeli raid.

78. *New York Times*, 30 March 1955.

79. Moshe Dayan, *Diary of the Sinai Campaign* (London: Sphere Books, 1965), p. 40. For the view that the Fedayeen were not created until April and activated in August 1955 as an Egyptian response to the intensification of Israeli aggressiveness, see Mansoor, ed., *The Arab World* (3), 31 August 1955.

80. Moshe Dayan, "Israel's Border and Security Problem," *Foreign Affairs*, January 1955, p. 259. One author offers a counter argument, suggesting that Israel hoped to drive Egypt, which was desperately in need of arms, into a Western alliance; this was to ensure that such arms would not be used against Israel. Arslan Humbaraci, *Middle East Indictment* (London: Robert Hale Ltd, 1958), pp. 196-97. Egypt officially and frequently argued that the West used Israel to pressure Egypt into entering the Western defense grouping.

81. On this subject, see among others Love, *Suez: The Twice-Fought War*, pp. 76-80; *New York Times*, 22 August 1954 and 21 December 1960; Golda Meir, *My Life* (London: Futura Publications, Ltd, 1976), pp. 238-39.

82. See French Minister of Defense General Koenig's admission to Love, *Suez: The Twice Fought War*, p. 75.

83. An earlier attempt in July 1954 to reduce border incursions by strengthening the United Nations Truce Supervision Organization had failed. Ibid., pp. 137-38.

84. *New York Times*, 1 September 1955.

85. U.S. Department of State, *Bulletin*, 5 September 1955, pp. 379-80.

86. Hutchison, *Violent Truce*, p. xxvi.

87. U.S. Department of State, *Bulletin*, 5 September 1955, p. 380.

88. British Foreign Office statement, 27 August 1955 (*New York Times*, 28 August 1955).

89. Campbell, *Defense of the Middle East*, pp. 88-89.

90. Heikal, *The Cairo Documents*, p. 56.

91. *Egyptian Gazette*, 22 November 1953.

92. Confirmed by Mohammed Riad to the author.

93. According to U.S. Department of State, *Bulletin*, 9 April 1956, p. 600.

94. These figures were to skyrocket in crisis years. Private donations to the Jewish National Fund and the United Jewish Appeal were tax exempt because these organizations enjoyed the status of charities. See Ellis, *Challenge in the Middle East*, p. 95. Given a population of 2 million in 1962, the total official and private American capital flow to Israel up until this time represented close to $1,200 for every Israeli man, woman, and child. R.H. Nolte, "United States Policy and the Middle East," *The United States and the Middle East*, ed. G. Stevens (Englewood Cliffs, New Jersey: Prentice-Hall, 1964) p. 155.

95. Mansoor, ed., *The Arab World* (3), 25-27 April 1956; *New York Times*, 7 May 1956. The United States rejected a British proposal that would have required it to commit its troops to an organization to guarantee Arab-Israeli border peace. U.S. Department of State, *Bulletin*, 12 March 1956, p. 412.

96. Ibid.

4

Pactomania: The American Approach to Middle East Defense

The successful hydrogen bomb tests by the Soviet Union in August 1953 ended the Western monopoly on thermonuclear weaponry. This changed America's cold war priorities and led to the development of a new strategy of massive retaliation that was thought to provide a "maximum deterrent" against a Soviet nuclear strike. According to Secretary Dulles, "the essential thing is that a potential aggressor should know in advance that he can and will be made to suffer for his aggression more than he can possibly gain by it."[1]

It followed that by encircling the Soviet Union with a "decentralized system of alternative bases" capable of nuclear delivery, America's capacity to retaliate acquired greater credibility and the risk of a Soviet attack was correspondingly reduced. On the assumption that any future conflagration would be a total war of nuclear annihilation, it was thought that this strategy would discourage the Soviet Union from adventuring into the world's political and military "soft spots."

Suddenly, the Middle East acquired added importance in the eyes of the Western world:

> The Middle East is an important forward zone of the free world. Possession of this zone is, resources apart, a vital element in the early warning and forward-support point tactics requisite to free-world strategy in the event of a conflict with Soviet power.[2]

After the development of the Atlas missile in 1953, the new deterrent strategy seemed to hinge on the ability of the West to secure a series of bases as close as possible to the Soviet Union.[3] The countries of the Northern Tier of the Middle East, which directly flanked that country and which seemed the most vulnerable to any Soviet threat to the region, became of primary concern to American strategists and policymakes.[4] In order to enlist allies in the crucial Northern Tier zone, the United States began to offer these countries military and economic aid in return for facilities, including bases, that would be placed at the disposal of "free world" defense.

At the same time it was projected that the Western defense system would be extended southward. This was partly because, after the formation of SEATO, the Middle East as a whole appeared to remain the biggest gap in the system as it was now conceived. Solutions to the problems of the Arab world needed to be found that would enable it to become integrated into American strategic planning in such a way as to give depth to the forward defense system in the north.

The new emphasis on the Northern Tier significantly affected American evaluation of Egypt's role in the overall design. Earlier views that the defense of the region should center on that country, with its gigantic Suez Canal Base, were revised, since the concentration of troops and equipment merely offered the potential enemy a static target in a thermonuclear war. The premise that a system of dispersed bases presented a far better solution made Egypt's formal membership in a Middle East defense structure appear correspondingly less vital. Nevertheless, because of the Suez Canal and also because Egypt was a leader in the region destined to play an ever greater political role, its ability to influence the attitudes of the Arab states toward Western defense objectives made Egyptian policy a factor that American strategists could not ignore.

It may be inferred that the Egyptian leadership was less than pleased with the priority that the United States now accorded the Northern Tier and the downgrading of its own position this seemed to imply. In this period Egypt still counted on American support to force the British out and on American aid for economic development. Moreover, Egypt intended to promote its own organization for regional defense—a strengthened and renovated version of the Arab Collective Defense Pact—in which Egyptian hegemony would be assured. Egypt felt that its plan could be forced upon the West provided that a united Arab front prevented the West from implementing any other plan.

Soon after Secretary Dulles visited the region in 1953, the Junta leaders attempted to draw American attention to their own concept of regional defense. On 4 June 1953 General Naguib stressed that a system of defense that did not encompass the Arab world would not be effective:

> It would be an error for anyone to believe that Turkey, Greece, and Yugoslavia can constitute a Middle East defense organization [following the Balkan Pact]. The Middle East organization must first of all include the area in which it is interested. Its task is to protect the overland lines of communication and to ensure mutual assistance between the right and left wings of the defense chain.[5]

Then, on 17 June, the Egyptian government issued a decree bringing the Arab League's Collective Security and Economic Pact into force.[6]

Egypt's aims seem clear. The grouping it promoted would satisfy the Dulles formula that a regional defense organization should "grow from within." It thus offered the West a solution that could more easily be reconciled with Arab nationalist sentiments than any other. It also offered Egypt the chance to extend its influence within the Arab region as a whole.

Serious American consideration of Egypt's proposed defense scheme obviously required a solution to the Arab-Israeli conflict, since American support for an Arab pact with an anti-Israeli tinge was politically unthinkable. Yet this did not deter the Egyptian leadership from insisting that its project was the sole acceptable solution. Perhaps Egypt hoped that a united Arab front against competing solutions might one day force the United States to reconsider the Egyptian scheme, with or without a settlement of the Arab-Israeli dispute. Another, more likely explanation, is that Egypt wanted the United States to pressure Israel into a settlement with its Arab neighbors precisely because the United States would otherwise lack the means of realizing its overall cold war strategy for the Middle East.

The Egyptian proposal did not stop the American leadership from organizing the defense of the northern region after mid-1953. It will be recalled that a series of bilateral agreements was conceived as a first and provisory step toward the establishment of a more solid, multilateral defense system. These agreements would provide American military and economic assistance in return for certain commitments to aid in the defense of the "free world."

One such commitment called for the "beneficiary" country to place specified defense facilities at the disposal of the West. Although information on this subject remains classified, it seems safe to assume that these "facilities" frequently included missile bases. Another commitment specified that the country concerned would participate in a regional defense organization that would subsequently be created. In this way the resistance capacity of each country willing to accept the American offer would be strengthened, while the United States satisfied its strategic needs for a string of bases that would enhance the credibility of its own "massive retaliatory power."[7]

Four countries — Turkey, Iran, Pakistan, and Iraq — warmly received the American initiative. Each of them had its special reasons, usually local in character, for desiring American aid and support.[8] All of them were close to the Soviet Union's southern border and shared a certain awareness of what could be termed the traditional Russian threat.

By the end of 1953 reports were circulated that the United States and Pakistan had already entered into discussions on the latter's role in a Middle East defense organization.[9] A visit by Vice-President Nixon to Karachi in December emphasized American interest in that country. In February 1954 an agreement in principle was reached; however, the American National Security Council appears to have conditioned military aid on Pakistan's willingness to collaborate with Turkey in the defense of the region.[10] Accordingly, American leaders were in contact with Turkey to discuss the project,[11] and a treaty of friendship and collective security was concluded between the two countries on 2 April 1954. A nucleus for the Northern Tier collective defense scheme was thus created, and the United States promptly complied with Pakistan's request for military and economic aid.[12]

This set a pattern for the future. The United States would appear to initiate the process toward defense negotiations through inducements of aid. Its NATO regional representative, Turkey, would then carry out the negotiations. In this manner the development of the region's defense capabilities appeared to arise from within, with the American role characterized as that of supplier.

By September 1954 the gap in America's global defense system had narrowed. Pakistan had joined SEATO;[13] Turkey constituted a link to the North Atlantic defense grouping; American relations with Iran[14] and Iraq were excellent; and the adherence of both these countries to the Ankara-Karachi axis appeared to be only a matter of time.

Iraq was thus the one Arab state that seemed particularly receptive to these early American overtures. This propensity, noted by Dulles in the private memorandum drafted during his 1953 trip to the area,[15] is explained in part by Iraq's proximity to the Soviet Union and by the Iraqi leadership's own drive for hegemony within the Arab world.[16] Of equal or greater importance was the fact that military aid made it easier for Iraq to keep both the Arab nationalists and the Kurdish separatist movement under control.

Iraq's receptivity was especially useful to the American leadership since Iraq—unlike Egypt, Jordan, Lebanon, and Syria—did not directly border on Israel.[17] An American agreement to aid Iraq militarily before an Arab-Israeli peace agreement was reached thus appeared less likely to elicit serious congressional opposition than the question of aid to Israel's direct neighbors.

Moreover, it was held that Iraq, in view of its potential influence upon Syria, Jordan, and Lebanon,[18] might serve as the instrument for a later southward extension of the Turco-Pakistani Pact. With this in mind, the American leadership agreed to extend substantial military assistance to the Iraqi government in April 1954. In return Iraq pledged to put materials, services, and equipment in excess of its own requirements at the disposal of the United States and eventually of other governments, in keeping with a cooperative regional defense agreement.[19]

Opposition to this accord inside the United States was partly appeased by Iraq's acceptance of a clause limiting the use of American aid "solely to maintain its [Iraq's] internal security and its legitimate self-defense" and by its promise not to "undertake any act of aggression against any other state."[20] In addition, Iraq accepted the presence of an American military mission to discharge the agreement, while the State Department announced that it would not make deliveries if there were any signs that United States military equipment might be used against Israel.

The possibility that Iraq would adhere to the evolving Northern Tier defense system quickly drew the whole question of Arab membership in a non-Arab, Western-oriented defense grouping into the tumult of Arab nationalist polemics and intra-regional rivalries. Even before the formation of the non-Arab Turco-Pakistani Pact, Egypt had reaffirmed the Arab League policy that called on the

Arabs to present a united front against such pacts until they had solved their own problems. The reason, according to official Egyptian comments, was that such groupings only isolated the Arab world from the region as a whole.

Egypt informed the American leadership that it would combat these pacts by all available means.[21] After the Turco-Pakistani agreement was signed, Nasser issued a further warning that "any Arab state which thinks of acceding to the Turco-Pakistani Pact would not only shake the Arab League but would also bind itself with Anglo-American imperialism."[22]

The Egyptian press stressed the internal danger of communist subversion as opposed to a "nonexistent" Soviet threat of invasion. American insistence on concluding military agreements with the Arab countries was viewed as a means of increasing American influence within the area: "The Arab states, which have not yet got rid of British or French influence, cannot involve themselves in new agreements with any Western power."[23] The commentary pointed out that Arab confidence in the West was undermined by Western support of Israel and the Western powers' ingrained colonialist habits. Turkey, too, came under attack because of its historical imperial position in the region and its moderate attitude toward Israel.[24]

Egyptian criticism was surely foreseen by the Iraqi leaders when they agreed to closer ties with the United States. These leaders must have counted on the internal power struggle that weakened the Egyptian leadership at the time and on the fact that Nasser had offered to allow Britain to re-enter the canal base in case of an attack on Turkey. But the Iraqi leadership greatly underestimated the strength of nationalist opposition at home as well as that of the Egyptian broadside. The Iraqi government under Fadil Jamali was forced to resign immediately after concluding its agreement with the United States and the National Front soon organized resistance groups for the purpose of opposing future Iraqi membership in cold war blocs.[25]

Meanwhile, the Egyptian leadership was careful not to reject every possibility of future collaboration with the West despite Egypt's aversion to the Iraqi agreement with the United States. Instead Egypt maintained that the Arab Collective Defense Pact was the only acceptable basis for future collaboration while refraining from any precise definition of the nature of this cooperation. This caution was dictated by the advanced state of the negotiations for British withdrawal and Egypt's concomitant need for American support. Egypt also feared that an outright refusal to collaborate might have induced the West, and especially America, so to strengthen Iraq's position in the Arab region that Iraq would be able to lure other Arab states out of the Egyptian-dominated Arab League into the Northern defense grouping.

The combined pressures brought to bear on Iraq caused it to mark time on the question of adhering to the Turco-Pakistani axis and to give fresh assurances that it would avoid commitments outside the framework of the Arab League. At the same time, Egypt's reaction induced the American leadership to defer attempts to solicit the Arab states until Egypt's dispute with Britain had been resolved. Washington thus sought to avoid alienating Egypt in the belief that, once Egypt achieved independence, its resistance to Western defense pacts would cease. An arrangement could then be found that would facilitate Arab collaboration with the West without endangering Israel.

America's expectations began to founder on the shoals of Egypt's domestic political situation soon after Egypt signed the draft agreement with Britain at the end of July 1954. Even though Nasser had succeeded in defeating his major rival, General Naguib, by April of that year, he had yet to defeat the Moslem Brotherhood and the communists. Both groups vehemently criticized the Anglo-Egyptian Agreement, and both now demonstrated the dangers to be faced by any leader who dared to pursue a policy that implied further commitments to great powers at that time.

The Moslem Brotherhood sought to discredit the regime by contending that the agreement was a treacherous act in that too many concessions had been made to Britain at the expense of national interests. This group pointed to the similarity between the reactivation clause in the new agreement and that of the 1936 Anglo-Egyptian Treaty of Alliance.[26] The communists criticized the agreement from a different angle. They feared that it contained an implied promise of closer relations with the West and that Egypt might even adhere to a Western defense pact against the Soviet Union. Both groups drew considerable support from those Egyptian nationalists who also feared that the agreement overcommitted Egypt to the great powers and from Naguib's supporters who sought any grounds for discrediting Nasser.

The strength of this opposition was quickly manifested. One author gives this account of the dramatic events that occurred just after the conclusion of the draft agreement.

> The following morning soon after Naguib's arrival at Abdin Palace, a crowd began to gather outside his office. . . .As its chants grew louder, Hassan Ibrahim, the Minister of State for Presidential Affairs. . .closed the windows: the crowd was cheering Naguib. Later in the day, the official Moslem Brotherhood position was announced: the new agreement bound Egypt to unfavorable conditions at a time when the 1936 Anglo-Egyptian Agreement had almost expired. July 28, originally meant to be a festive holiday to celebrate the departure of the British, was fast becoming a day of violence.[27]

As the internal situation in Egypt deteriorated, public demonstrations were banned. Nasser and his Minister of National Guidance, Salah Salem, emphasized that the draft agreement with Britain contained no new military commitments.[28]

By November Nasser appeared to have the domestic situation under control once again. The outlawed Communist Party had become the object of severe governmental repression.[29] The Moslem Brotherhood, because of its popular support, proved more difficult to deal with, but an abortive attempt by this group to assassinate Nasser in November supplied the occasion for a confrontation. Mass arrests of principal Brotherhood members and the execution of six of its high-ranking leaders greatly reduced the threat from this quarter. Because of Naguib's association with this group and alleged implication in the assassination attempt, Nasser was provided with a strong reason to remove him from the political scene.

Popular aversion to new Egyptian commitments to the great powers colored Nasser's approach to the question of regional defense long afterward. The Egyptians must be left alone, he declared, because they needed time

> to overcome their residual suspicion of Western imperialist intentions. After the Suez settlement nothing stands in the way of good relations between Egypt and the West. But this hammering, hammering, hammering for pacts will only keep alive the old suspicions in the minds of the people, and the communists know well how to exploit these suspicions.[30]

Nevertheless, the idea of cooperation for the defense of the Middle East was not altogether discarded. In private discussions with unnamed Western diplomats, Nasser is said to have considered such cooperation on an informal basis and to have implied that indirect links between Egypt and a NATO country might be acceptable.[31] Apparently his reasoning was that the West held a monopoly on military supplies to the region and that any regional defense system needed to cooperate with the West in order to acquire arms.[32]

Cooperation, however, had to be on conditions acceptable to Egypt, which meant that the presence of a great power in the region was no longer needed or acceptable. If the British feared a "power vacuum", Nasser feared that a great power presence would be exploited by extremists, especially the communists, as a heritage of the "master-servant" relationship of the past.[33]

A sharp distinction was therefore drawn between the concept of a pact with formal ties to a great power and that of a purely regional defense structure developed from within that could be linked informally to the West. More formal commitments were conceivable once the Arab-Israeli problem had been resolved and once sufficient time had elapsed for Egypt to forget its colonial past.

Now Egyptian policy became increasingly oriented toward two interrelated goals: that of unifying the Arab world behind the Arab Collective Security Organization as the only valid answer to the problem of regional defense, and that of winning Western support for this Egyptian-backed organization.[34] If successful, such a policy would reinforce Egyptian hegemony and provide for integrated Arab military planning against aggression from any side. Egypt also claimed that its object was to provide an Arab solution to Arab problems.

In the months following the Anglo-Egyptian settlement Iraq and Egypt competed for influence in the Arab world. In August 1954 Nasser dramatized his campaign to reassert Egyptian leadership in regional affairs by leaving his country for the first time ever in order to attend an Islamic conference in Mecca.[35] From August through November Egypt's representative, Salah Salem, visited Iraq, Jordan, and Saudi Arabia in an attempt to rally these countries to the Egyptian cause. The same aim was pursued when Egyptian leaders met with other high-ranking Arab officials during the September Arab League Conference in Cairo.[36]

Of particular interest during this period were the three-way exchanges between Iraq, Turkey, and Egypt. Relations between Iraq and Turkey had grown cordial since early 1954, when both countries perceived a common interest in collaborating on the defense of the region despite the conflict occasioned by traditional Turkish designs on Mosel and Iraq's problems with a Turkish irredentist minority.

Now Iraq believed that the Anglo-Egyptian agreement had removed the grounds for Egypt's opposition to Arab cooperation with the West. The stipulation in this agreement permitting reactivation of the Suez Canal Base in case of an attack on Turkey, a NATO member, especially seemed to provide Iraqi leaders with strong ammunition against further Egyptian criticism if Iraq persevered in collaborating with Turkey and other countries that had entered a Western-oriented defense system.

The Anglo-Egyptian agreement also seemed to offer Iraq a model for its own relations with Britain. Iraqi leaders hoped to avoid fire from local nationalists at a time when Britain's reverses in Egypt and its concern for Iraqi petroleum led Britain to support Iraq's claim to leadership in the Arab region.[37]

Egypt's response was to try to draw Iraq back into the Arab fold while seeking to counter the Iraqi lead with Turkey by persuading and encouraging Turkey to cooperate with the Arab Collective Security System. Relations between Iraq and Egypt during August and September accordingly hinged on Egyptian attempts to coax Iraq into agreeing that a remodeled and strengthened Arab League was the appropriate fulcrum for regional defense. This principle was reportedly accepted during Salah Salem's visit to Iraq in August 1954 and reiterated during Nuri El Said's return visit to Cairo in September.[38]

However, the two countries seriously disagreed on the extent to which they should cooperate with Britain and the United States. In the course of his visit to Iraq, Egypt's Salem, who may have exceeded his mandate, agreed to immediate contacts with the United States and Britain for the purpose of coordinating Arab defense policy with that of the Western great powers. This incurred Nasser's displeasure and is held to be the reason for Salem's suspension from office in September.[39]

Salem's error is understandable when it is recalled that Egypt had already established close contacts with the United States for the purpose of securing arms. After Nasser's request for American military assistance in August, arms talks reportedly began late in the same month.[40] In September an Egyptian military mission visited the United States, and the Pentagon dispatched experts to Cairo reportedly to discuss future Egyptian military cooperation.[41]

But Egypt's leaders found it impossible to collaborate with the West on the same terms that Iraq had accepted. One big problem was the requirement that an American military mission be posted to Egypt to survey the use of military supplies sent there. As Ambassador Byroade later testified, Nasser refused the military aid offer because he believed that acceptance of this and other American conditions might be interpreted as a sell-out to another great power even before the total British withdrawal scheduled for June 1956.[42] Nasser feared that such a charge would have strengthened the hand of the very opposition groups, including the communists, that the aid was designed to check.

The disagreement with Iraq, and the twists in Egypt's policy at this time, indicate the dilemma of the Egyptian leadership and the extent to which firm decisions had yet to be taken. For example, an official "background paper" distributed in early September by the Egyptian Revolutionary Command Council stated that "there seems to be no doubt that Egypt today stands in every respect with the West" and that the only possible danger to the Middle East on a global scale was an invasion by the Soviet Union.[43] Yet Nasser soon emphasized that future military collaboration with the West would have to be based on the Arab Collective Security Pact. Besides stressing the view that the communist problem in Egypt was internal rather than external and that great power alliances would merely bolster the forces opposed to his leadership, Nasser insisted that Israel was the immediate external enemy rather than the Soviet Union.

> They [the Arabs] know that if they show any intention of fighting their enemy, you would quickly stop all aid. Any regional military agreement which did not take this attitude into account would be a fraud.[44]

Another facet of Nasser's position may be seen in the following statement:

> It is only by a period of complete independence during which mutual trust is built up between Egypt and the Western powers that the Egyptians will be able to look without suspicion on any closer ties between this country [Egypt] and other powers. Cooperation based on trust and friendship, even though it is not specified by any written agreement, is better than a treaty that is regarded suspiciously by the average Egyptian.

He concluded this statement with a plea that the West should understand Egypt's domestic political situation and leave the Arabs to themselves for a while so that they could build their own defense system against possible communist aggression.[45]

Despite the conflicting views Iraq and Egypt held concerning the form that cooperation with the West should take, cordiality was maintained. Meanwhile, the Iraqi leadership marked time as Egypt's relations with Turkey began to warm up.

If Turkey's motives for hoping to draw Egypt closer to the Western defense scheme seem clear, Egypt's motives in canvassing Turkey's support for Egypt's own defense scheme are less apparent. A convincing hypothesis is that Egypt was exploring the possibilities for a pan-Islamic regional pact centered on the Arab defense system and that it was also aiming to overtake the Iraqi lead in the development of a broad regional system.

At the Mecca Islamic Congress in August 1954, Nasser reportedly discussed regional defense problems with Pakistani Prime Minister Mohammed Ali, who was also bidding for the leadership of the Middle East Islamic Community.[46] Soon after, Anwar El Sadat, then Secretary-General of the Islamic Congress, announced a charter for Arab-Moslem cooperation that in part aimed at encouraging cooperation between the Arab League and Moslem organizations. Welcoming this charter, Nasser announced that Egypt would seek to strengthen its position as a leader in the struggle of other Arab and Moslem peoples for full independence.[47]

Egypt's receptivity to Turkish overtures calling for better Arab-Islamic relations must be viewed against this same background.[48] An October statement by the Egyptian Ambassador to Turkey indicated the official Egyptian attitude:

> The necessary ground had been prepared for the establishment of close cooperation between Turkey and Egypt as the two great Republics of the Middle East and Near East. The opening of official negotiations in this connection in the near future has been agreed upon. . . .Close cooperation between Turkey and Egypt, as well as becoming a great source of strength for the Egyptians, will also constitute a support for the Arab world. . . .To put it briefly, the Turkish-Egyptian alliance will constitute a tremendous force in the Near East with a total population of fifty million.[49]

In an article published in the Egyptian press, Nasser personally drew attention to the common interests of the two countries:

> No matter what has happened between us and Turkey in the past or the present, we belong to each other. Its father and our father were brothers in history. . . .If Turkey is secure, we Egyptians are likewise secure. Turkey and Egypt are members of the same family. Today the two countries are brothers as they were in the past.[50]

Plans for the exchange of high-level visits to discuss a treaty of friendship between Egypt and Turkey were announced in November.

Until late December Turco-Egyptian relations remained exceedingly cordial, as each sought to persuade the other of the benefits of close collaboration. As will be seen, however, neither was willing to give ground on its own plan in order to accomodate the other's, while each sought to bolster its position as the central leader from which a regional defense system could evolve.

If one of Egypt's objectives in courting Turkey in this period had been to limit the scope for Iraq's own initiative, Egypt's policy fell short of the goal. Rather than blocking Iraq, Egypt's friendly advances toward Turkey and the possibility of close Turco-Egyptian relations only made Iraq less hesitant to deepen its own understanding with Turkey.[51]

The Iraqi leaders may even have felt the need to reassert their own primacy with Turkey. Far more willing than Egypt's leaders to accept Western conditions, the Iraqi leaders, following the final Anglo-Egyptian agreement in October 1954, embarked upon a new initiative directed toward Turkey and the Northern Tier countries. Nuri El Said announced that Iraq was greatly concerned over the security of Turkey and Iran and that neutrality was "not possible". With the resolution of the Suez problem, collaboration with the West had at last become feasible.[52]

Iraq moved rapidly not only to solidify its relations with the northern, non-Arab grouping but also to coax other Arab states into joining the projected Western defense system. This quickly dispelled all semblance of cordiality between Egypt and Iraq, and a new phase opened in their traditional rivalry.

In the ensuing struggle for influence—which centered on Jordan, Syria, and Lebanon—Iraq seemed to hold a number of early advantages over Egypt. The Syrian government was at the time dominated by the pro-Iraqi National Socialist Party. Moreover, the internal dissension that troubled the Egyptian regime after its agreement with Britain harmed Egypt's relations with Syria, which had become the refuge for extremist members of the Moslem Brotherhood. So strongly had the Syrian regime backed this major opposition group in Egypt that the Egyptian government finally recalled its Ambassador to Damascus and lodged a series of firm protests.

Iraq could count on at least the benevolent neutrality of both Jordan and Lebanon as long as Egyptian resistance was weak. The brother Hashemite Kingom of Jordan, heavily supported by Britain, was naturally prone to side with pro-British Iraq. However, its freedom to collaborate with a grouping outside the Arab League was affected by Egypt's attitude since two-thirds of Jordan's population consisted of pro-Egyptian Palestinians.

The pro-Western leanings of Lebanon's dominant Christian community were noted by Dulles in a personal memorandum: "Lebanese consider themselves a possible bridge between U.S. and Arab states because of their greater Western orientation and Christian population."[53] But the Moslem community, which made up the remaining 50 percent of the population, sympathized with the Arab Nationalists. Iraq therefore needed to persuade Syria and Jordan to follow its lead in order to gain Lebanese acquiescence in the bargain.

In an effort to solicit all these countries, King Feisal of Iraq, accompanied by high-ranking government officials, visited Jordan and Lebanon in November 1954, where they were joined by Syrian Prime Minister Fares El Khouri. Following these exchanges, the Iraqi leaders greatly embarrassed Egypt by announcing their intention to replace the 1930 Anglo-Iraqi Treaty of Alliance with a new agreement similar to that recently signed by Britain and Egypt. The Iraqi version would allow British troops to re-enter Iraq in the event of an attack on Iran.[54]

This treaty, to be signed on 4 April 1955, was the outcome of Britain's policy of reinforcing its position in Iraq once Egypt had proved itself a force that could no longer be dealt with by traditional colonialist methods. As a major source of British petroleum, Iraq had always been a primary regional concern for Britain. By supporting Iraq's leadership pretensions in the Arab world, Britain now hoped its own regional influence would indirectly be enhanced. Indeed, America's success in wooing Iraq, evidenced by the April 1954 Military and Economic Agreement, was probably viewed by Britain with some misgivings.

In the meantime Iraq, while still leaving open the possibility of collaboration within the framework of the Arab League, called upon the League to admit Iran as a member.[55] Calculated or not, this move embarrassed Egypt still further, since Egypt had previously indicated its willingness to draw Turkey within the Arab orbit. Besides, the Iraqi proposal was sure to be rejected, which gave Iraq an additional excuse for acting in its own interest outside the Arab League.

The initial receptivity of Jordan, Syria, and Lebanon to the Iraqi plan prompted Egypt to call upon the Western powers to assist the Arab world within the framework of the Arab League. At the December 1954 conference of Arab League Foreign Ministers, it was decided that no alliance should be concluded outside the Arab Collective Security Pact; that cooperation with the West was possible provided that Arab problems were solved first; and that the Arabs should be allowed to build their own military strength.[56] This showed that Egypt still retained its traditional hold on the Arab League as such.

However, Egypt suffered a setback at the end of December when Premier Menderes of Turkey made it quite clear that future Arab-Turkish cooperation would have to be on Turkish terms, i.e., based on the principle of close collaboration with the "free world".[57] By rejecting any plan for Turkey's integration within the Arab system he hastened the formation of a Turco-Iraqi axis, and the two countries became more determined than ever to incorporate the Arab region into the northern grouping.

The battle for the Arab states was announced in a joint Turco-Iraqi communique on 12 January during Premier Menderes's visit to Baghdad. Proclaiming its independence from the Egyptian-dominated Arab League, Iraq disclosed its intention to conclude a defense pact with Turkey. The two countries urged "other like-minded states" to join them and declared that they would "make every endeavor to persuade those states to sign the treaty simultaneously with them."[58]

Afterward, Premier Menderes set out on a tour of Syria and Lebanon, where he was joined by the Prime Minister of Jordan.[59] The apparent purpose of their visits was to persuade these countries to become members of the future pact.

In Egypt this development was viewed in the following terms:

> It was clear that the battle between our policy and Iraq's would be joined over   Syria. The issue was quite simply this: If Turkey and Iraq got Syria on

their side, Jordan and Lebanon would soon follow and Egypt would be completely isolated.[60]

To block this initiative, Egypt summoned an emergency meeting of the Arab League Prime Ministers to discuss the Iraqi position. At this meeting, which lasted from 22 January to 6 February 1955, Egypt apparently hoped to rally sufficient opposition to dissuade Iraq from continuing its independent line and to prevent other Arab states from following the Iraqi example. Instead, Egypt found that it was not master of the situation. A twelve-point Egyptian proposal against the pact was tacitly defeated, with only Saudi Arabia and Yemen indicating their support. A few days later a second, more compromising Egyptian resolution likewise failed to secure Syrian, Lebanese, and Iraqi assent.[61]

Another Egyptian move during this meeting was to address a final plea to the United States for greater understanding of Egypt's position.[62] The Egyptian Ambassador in Washington flatly stated that Egypt was "naturally opposed to communist doctrines of atheism and collective materialism." He added that a "sound defense system must logically emerge from within" and that his country could then call for "appropriate external assistance from friendly powers. . .equally opposed to aggression."[63] The Egyptian press echoed these sentiments by calling on the West to support and strengthen the Arab bloc as the way to "ensure the security of the Middle East."[64]

Its failure to prod the Arab League into censuring Iraq induced Egypt to tone down the overt hostility that characterized its position at the start of the meeting and to invite Iraq instead to postpone its agreement with Turkey.

The Egyptian leaders probably hoped to muster sufficient pressure to forestall the pact if Iraq could be persuaded to delay its decision. To this end, the Egyptian press unleashed a barrage of attacks against the Iraqi leadership, accusing it of trying to destroy Arab unity and of attempting to draw the Arab world into the "Turkish-Israeli orbit."[65] Radio Cairo joined in by inaugurating the Radio Free Iraq program.

Although the precise impact of this propaganda campaign cannot be measured, Egypt's tactics seemed to pay off. In Syria, where the leadership supported the Iraqi position, there were riots against the pact; the strength of the opposition was such that the government could not openly endorse the policy of which it approved.[66] Even the decision to remain outside the pact without censuring Iraq was not enough to save the Syrian government, which collapsed on 6 February because of this very issue.[67] It was succeeded by a new government under the leadership of the pro-Egyptian Syrian National Party. Although the position of this government was far from secure, it aligned itself with Egypt, and on 22 February Syria officially condemned the Turco-Iraqi pact.[68] Jordan and Lebanon, which had been tempted to support Iraq, now assumed the role of neutral mediators.[69]

The Arab League Conference had represented a diplomatic failure for Egypt because Iraq was neither forced to yield nor censured for its position. Egypt nonetheless succeeded in preventing other Arab League members from following the Iraqi example. When Turkey and Iraq signed the Baghdad Pact on 26

February 1955,[70] it ushered in still another phase in the battle for hegemony in the Arab world.

The role of the Western great powers in the formation of the Baghdad Pact has been subjected to varying and often conflicting interpretations. Whether, as official Western sources contended, this defense organization arose from a purely local initiative or whether, as it is widely held, a direct great power involvement was a principal factor, cannot be established with certainty until confidential government documents are declassified. Nevertheless, by a comparative analysis of private interviews with then responsible government officials, of unofficial reports by these same persons, and of the great power interests that were actually at stake, it seems possible to sort out the different versions that have been advanced and to arrive at certain broad inferences concerning this controversial subject.

One such inference is that it was definitely in the interest of the Western great powers to remain behind the scenes during the negotiating stage in order to minimize local nationalist resistance. Hence, if abundant evidence may be marshalled to show that these powers were deeply involved, it is likely that the degree of involvement was purposely made to appear small.

The extent to which America, Britain, or both powers acting in concert, took the initiative in fathering the pact is a more debatable issue. One group of specialists contends that the United States was a prime mover and that even the initial suggestion came from Dulles, with Turkey merely the instrument by which the project was carried into effect.[71] Others, equally authoritative, claim that the Baghdad Pact came as a surprise to the American leadership, that the United States had been kept in the dark as regards the final negotiations, and even that it was really the fruit of a British initiative undertaken in collusion with Turkey and Iraq.[72]

When these conflicting opinions are appraised in terms of the respective interests of the powers concerned, it appears that Britain stood to gain far more direct and immediate benefits from this pact than the United States. Once its dispute with Egypt was settled, Britain quickly made Iraq and the Persian Gulf the center of its attention.[73] In this context the pact not only enabled Britain to shore up its weakened position in the Middle East, but also offered it a means of retaining its influence in Iraq with a minimum of nationalist resistance.

As then American Ambassador to Iraq Gallman has pointed out, Britain's interest in the evolution of Turco-Iraqi relations was "more than casual."[74] If so, it hardly seems coincidental that Iraq began its vigorous campaign to build up relations with Turkey and certain Arab countries shortly after visits by King Feisal and Prime Minister Nuri El Said to London.[75] As previously observed, the very inroads made by the United States upon Iraq while Britain quarrelled with Egypt were probably viewed with concern by the British government.

Soon after Turkey and Iraq signed the pact, Britain hastened to join, even though its bilateral agreement of 4 April 1955, which superseded the 1930

Alliance, otherwise secured Britain's "special" position in Iraq.[76] In defending British policy before the House of Commons, Prime Minister Eden elaborated on his government's position as follows:

> Our purpose in acceding to this pact was a simple one. I think that by doing so we have strengthened our influence and our voice throughout the Middle East. . . .I am in favour of any arrangement which has the result of increasing the influence of my country.[77]

From this time until the 1956 Suez Crisis, the Baghdad Pact was to remain the major instrument of British policy in the Middle East.[78]

In contrast, the United States, which had already secured many of its regional interest through a system of bilateral arrangements, had little reason to push for the inclusion of the Arab states in a formal multilateral defense system at this particular juncture. True, the avowed purpose of the Baghdad Pact was to structure the region's defenses against potential Soviet encroachment, a policy that furthered America's global interests. Yet, many factors, including the strong Egyptian reaction to the April 1954 Iraqi-American Military and Economic Agreement and the pro-Israeli internal pressures being exerted on the administration, had made the American leadership wary of the problems that would be stirred up by the formal adherence of Arab Iraq to such a system.

This reasoning helps to explain what the weight of the evidence suggests, namely, that the American administration maintained a "wait and see" attitude during the negotiations that led to the creation of the Baghdad Pact. Loy Henderson, former Under-Secretary of State, even contends that the United States would have preferred to exclude Arab states from the pact at the time: ". . .I don't think our government was really comfortable about Iraq's being in the pact; we had doubts about an Arab country being included in it."[79] But whether or not the desire to exclude Iraq had been expressed to the negotiating parties still remains to be demonstrated.

To argue that the American leadership was unaware that serious negotiations were in progress seems farfetched given the close relations between the United States and Britain. Nevertheless, those who uncritically accept the view that America was the prime mover often fail to distinguish between the early American initiatives in the Northern Tier and the different circumstances from which this later development emerged. They also tend to overlook or to play down the fact that Britain, though fast declining, was still the major great power in the Arab world of 1955. On balance it would seem that America preferred to remain aloof while Britain took the initiative that resulted in the creation of the Baghdad Pact and that this pact in turn largely superseded the earlier American initiative in the Northern Tier.

The reasons for America's refusal to become a full-fledged member of the Baghdad Pact, which are well documented, acquire added significance in light of the thesis developed above. High on the list were the "very strong feelings in some of the [Arab] countries against the Baghdad Pact" which, as Secretary Dulles recognized at a 1957 Senate hearing, made the pact "a divisive force."[80]

Any hopes that Arab opposition would be appeased if the pact appeared to arise from within the region were nullified when Britain became a member in April 1955.

American policymakers were particularly concerned about the effects of the pact on Egypt, Saudi Arabia, and Israel. The United States was still trying to persuade Egypt to draw closer to the West, a goal that would not be furthered by Arab nationalist claims that the Baghdad Pact was nothing more than a neo-colonialist manifestation.[81] Nor could the hostility of Saudi Arabia be ignored in view of the important American petroleum interests and military base in that country. Dulles expressed these fears in the following terms:

[T]he Baghdad Pact is not a unifying force as among the Arab countries. There are problems of a somewhat complicated character to us perhaps relating to dynastic situations, the Hashemite dynasty and so forth, as a result of which there is a very large degree of question about the Pact in the Arab world.

[I]t was too controversial as among Arab countries, and we had friendly countries like Saudi Arabia with whom we had long had very close associations where the United States has an air base.

The situation never seemed to be one where the purposes which we had in mind could best be served by joining the Baghdad Pact.[82]

The Arab-Israeli feud must also be considered an important obstacle to American adherence. The Baghdad Pact, which implied an eventual arming of the Arab world, was one of a number of issues involving the security of Israel that were bound to produce strong domestic repercussions. There are definite indications that America's political leaders desired to avoid the congressional debate that would have ensued if American membership had been seriously contemplated at this time:

[T]o get. . .ratification [for American membership] takes a two-thirds vote of the Senate, and we would have difficulty. . .getting such a vote — unless there was some comparable security arrangement made with Israel. And if we tried to get a comparable agreement with Israel, you would find objection from the Senate to that. So we are stymied.[83]

Ambassador Gallman, speaking to delegates at the November 1955 Baghdad Pact Conference, held that full United States membership might elicit Israeli counterdemands for a mutual defense treaty, which could become an issue in the 1956 elections.[84]

Another serious obstacle to American membership was the fear of provoking a Soviet countermove.[85] Although American policy sought to contain Soviet expansion, the American leadership had concluded that a low-profile approach of bilateral agreements was a less dangerous strategy for the Middle East at that time than premature American membership, with all it implied, in a multilateral defense system flanking the Soviet Union's southern border.

For these and other reasons, the United States chose to abstain from membership in the Baghdad Pact despite pressure from Britain and the recommendation of its own Ambassador to Iraq.[86] Instead, the United States was represented by an observer until 1956, when it agreed to join both the Economic Council and the Counter-Subversion Committee.[87] A permanent American liaison was finally established with the Military Committee, and America became a full member of the same committee in June 1957.[88]

Nevertheless, the United States provided constant moral and financial support to the Baghdad grouping,[89] and its relations with the pact members remained close. As will be seen in a later chapter, the further strengthening of these countries was definitely a goal of the American policymakers who formulated the Eisenhower Doctrine in 1957.[90] In this way a special American relationship with the Baghdad group evolved that has been characterized as follows: "It [the United States] was in the Pact but not of it, a participant for all practical purposes but without the legal commitments."[91]

Although the creation of the Baghdad Pact did not directly affect American-Egyptian relations, it caused certain major regional problems to resurface that did harm this relationship. For example, Western support through the pact for Iraq's traditional leadership pretensions in the Arab Middle East conflicted with deep-rooted Egyptian ambitions. The mere decision by Iraq to join this non-Arab grouping was a defeat for Egyptian policy, which aimed at maintaining a united Arab front to convince the West that it should accept an Arab solution for regional defense. Iraq, in offering the West an alternative, had broken this front and threatened to carry other Arab states with it.

The prospect that its oil-rich rival, now to be endowed with Western arms, might isolate Egypt from the Arab Middle East or force it to accept Iraq's leadership intensified Egypt's efforts to block the Western-backed Iraqi attempts to win further Arab adherence to the pact. Nasser, in a posterior evaluation, even went so far as to claim that, with the conclusion of the Baghdad Pact, "the ill-feelings began between us and Nuri [El Said, the Iraqi leader] and between us and America."[92]

Egypt's hostility toward Iraq was in turn bound to be resented by the United States. Whatever initial doubts the American leadership may have entertained concerning the wisdom of Iraq's joining the Baghdad grouping, Egyptian criticism of Iraq necessarily struck at the entire Middle East defense structure and its objectives as then conceived by the United States. Moreover, in its verbal attacks on Iraq, Egypt made little distinction between Baghdad's British backer and the United States.

The Baghdad Pact also contributed to the tension between Israel and Egypt that began to boil over in this period. The Anglo-Egyptian Agreement of October 1954, which provided for the phased withdrawal of those British troops that constituted a buffer between Egypt and Israel, had already been viewed by the latter with serious misgivings. Now, with the conclusion of the Baghdad Pact and its projected extension to Israel's Arab neighbors, the possibility that its enemies might be armed with the blessing of the Western powers greatly strengthened the more militant circles in Israel. Four days after Iraq signed the document making it a member of the pact, Israeli forces raided the Egyptian-controlled Gaza Strip and the Egyptian-Israeli border erupted with unprecedented violence.

The concatenation of unfavorable events—from the American point of view—that were linked to the Baghdad Pact may be extended still further. Egypt's quest for support against both Iraq and Israel ultimately led it to form an anti-Baghdad Arab grouping, to accept the aid and backing of the Soviet Union, and to canvass the nonaligned countries for support. As will be seen in the following chapters, Egypt's recourse to all these solutions enabled it to avoid isolation and to assert its leadership in both the Arab region and the international political arena despite American intransigence over matters Egypt considered of vital importance. Yet, for obvious reasons, these same solutions interfered with the basic, global cold war strategy of the United States. The actions and reactions that followed soon dragged American-Egyptian relations into an abyss of misunderstanding, inflexibility and, finally, outright hostility.

Far from eliminating or mitigating regional instability, the Baghdad Pact proved to be a disruptive force, especially in the Arab world. Whatever the benefits to the countries of the Northern Tier, where long-standing friction was assuaged in the name of unity,[93] the pact directly intensified pre-existing Arab regional rivalries and indirectly led to new Israeli activism, a situation from which only the Soviet Union stood to gain. The regional bipolarization between Egypt and Iraq, intensified by the latter's membership in the pact, soon reverberated with global cold war implications as each antagonist chose one of the rival great power blocs to back its local ambitions.

Whether a full American commitment to the Baghdad grouping could have forestalled these developments remains the object of speculation. British Prime Minister Anthony Eden, among others, charged that American aloofness only served to harden Egypt's resistance and that "an ounce of [U.S.] membership would have been worth all the wavering and saved a ton of trouble later on."[94] Yet, with a neutralist force already beginning to coalesce and the Soviet Union willing to foster its growth, Eden's notion that Egyptian resistance would have melted before a wholehearted American commitment to the pact seems wishful thinking.

What cannot be denied is that America's half-hearted support for the pact proved unsatisfactory to all concerned.[95] Anti-pact forces continued to accuse the United States of neo-colonialist leanings despite its refusal to become a full member. Member states accused it of deception for having let them down. And Israel levelled the politically dangerous charge that the American government had aided and abetted the creation of a situation that threatened Israel's very survival.

Notes

1. J. F. Dulles, "Policy for Security and Peace," U.S. Department of State, *Bulletin*, 16 March 1954. See also ibid., 12 January 1954.

2. P. M. A. Linebarger, "Air Power in the Modern Middle East," *Annals*, May 1953, pp. 109-17. See also J. S. Raleigh, "The West and the Defense of the Middle East," *Middle Eastern Affairs*, June/July 1955, p. 178.

3. The Atlas missile developed in 1953 was capable of carrying a thermonuclear head. With such massive destruction capacity, accuracy was no longer necessary. Nor had the anti-missile missile been developed. Because of the limited range of the Atlas, however, close proximity of delivery bases was necessary. Note that it was only after 1959, with the development of long-range bombers, that dependence on overseas bases was greatly diminished. Leonard Beaton, *The Struggle for Peace* (London: George Allen and Unwin, 1966), p. 27.

4. According to American Ambassador Wadsworth, the Northern Tier concept involved the following strategy: "If Russia is to be stopped by force from entering the Near East, strategically the best line is the line of the Caucasus, and then the Zagros Mountains down through Persia" (U.S. Cong., *Hearings, 1957*, p. 637).

5. *Egyptian Gazette*, 4 June 1953.

6. Ibid., 18 June 1953.

7. Dulles, "Evolution of Foreign Policy," U.S. Department of State, *Bulletin*, 12 January 1954.

8. For example, the Iranian government, following the fall of the leftist Mossadegh regime in August 1953, needed American aid to consolidate its position against remaining opposition elements. Pakistan's need to reinforce its position against India was urgent. Campbell, *Defense of the Middle East*, pp. 49-62. The cases of Turkey and Iraq are considered at length in the text.

9. *New York Times*, 13 November 1953.

10. Ibid., 8 and 23 February 1954; see also Eisenhower's statement, 25 February 1954, *Documents on American Foreign Relations, 1954*, pp. 373-74. Note that Pakistani-Indian hostilities were a major problem. Probably the American insistence on Pakistan's collaboration with Turkey was a device to reorient Pakistan toward the Middle East. In an effort to allay Indian fears, the nonoffensive nature of the agreement was stressed. U.S. Department of State, *Bulletin*, 15 March 1954, p. 401; see also ibid., p. 400, for letter from Eisenhower to President Nehru. Britain remained aloof in order not to mar its relations with India.

11. E.g., the February meeting between Eisenhower and President Bayer of Turkey. *New York Times*, 15 February 1954.

12. For text see *Documents on American Foreign Relations, 1954*, pp. 376-79. See also June statement by Pakistani Prime Minister Mohammed Ali emphasizing that this agreement was to be the first step and that other Middle East states could aspire to the aims it embodied. *New York Times*, 13 June 1954. For all practical purposes, the agreement was later to be superseded by the Turco-Iraqi Pact in February 1955. See *Diplomacy in the Near and Middle East*, 2:345.

13. On 8 September 1954. U.S. Department of State, *Bulletin*, 1 November 1954, pp. 639-40. Following the agreement, the United States gave additional military aid to Pakistan.

14. After the fall of Mossadegh, additional American assistance was made available. U.S. Department of State, *Bulletin*, 14 September 1953, p. 350. See also Eisenhower, *Mandate for Change*, p. 164. Eisenhower holds that $85 million had been made available to Iran in fiscal year 1954.

15. "Evidence indicates Iraq more willing to consider defensive arrangements than other Arab states, U.S. military equipment and training mission urgently desired." Dulles, "Important Points of Trip," Unpublished Memorandum, *Dulles Private Papers*.

16. The Fertile Crescent Unity Scheme continued to occupy the Iraqi leaders. See Mansoor, ed., *The Arab World* (3), 13 and 19 January and 18 August 1954 for examples.

17. Iraq, however, was the only Arab country among those that declared war on Israel in 1948 that had yet to conclude an armistice agreement with it.

18. In Syria there was the internal support of prominent pro-Iraqi political factions; Jordan was a

cousin Hashemite state; Lebanon, because of its Western leanings, could follow the Iraqi lead. Saudi Arabia was excluded because of traditional hositility toward the Hashemites. American Ambassador to Iraq Gallman holds that Dulles encouraged an arrangement with Iraq "because of the effect it would have on the other Arab states" (W. J. Gallman, *Iraq under General Nuri* [Baltimore, Md.: The Johns Hopkins Press, 1964], p. xiii).

19. Campbell, *Defense of the Middle East*, p. 52; for text of the 21 April 1954 agreement see *Diplomacy in the Near and Middle East*, 2:346-47. Also note earlier statement by the Iraqi Prime Minister calling for the establishment of "a defense line, similar to that of the West" (*New York Times*, 11 March 1954).

20. *Diplomacy in the Near and Middle East*, 2: 346. *New York Times*, 29 April 1954.

21. Egyptian Foreign Minister Fawzi to Ambassador Caffery, *Egyptian Gazette*, 23 March 1954.

22. *Al Gomhouria*, 15 April 1954. See also ibid., 12 April 1954, for Nasser's comments on the effects of such a pact on Arab unity.

23. *Al Misri*, 3 April 1954, and 5 March 1954.

24. *Al Gomhouria*, 20 February 1954.

25. Mansoor, ed., *The Arab World* (3), 21 April and 26 July 1954. Nuri El Said reportedly admitted to American Ambassador Gallman that 95% of the Iraqi population was against the Israeli enemy, not the Soviet Union. Gallman, *Iraq Under General Nuri*, p. 27.

26. See open letter of Moslem Brotherhood Supreme Guide Hodiby of 2 August 1954 to Nasser. Lacouture, *Egypt in Transition*, p. 237, and Wheelock, *Nasser's New Egypt*, pp. 44-45 quoting a 1958 personal interview with Anwar El Sadat. Note that although the Brotherhood had been officially disbanded in January 1954 (*Al Ahram*, 16 January 1954), it resurfaced during the struggle between Nasser and Naguib in support of the latter.

27. Wheelock, *Nasser's New Egypt*, p. 43.

28. *Al Ahram*, 30 and 31 July 1954.

29. Little, *Modern Egypt*, p. 147.

30. Statement by Nasser, *el Tahrir*, 21 August 1954.

31. Wheelock, *Nasser's New Egypt*, p. 217. Egypt may in fact have accepted the inclusion of Turkey in the Arab Collective Defense Organization.

32. The Soviet Union had not yet begun to supply non-Soviet Bloc countries. Anthony Nutting, a British representative to Egypt during this period, reports that Nasser told him that the soldier in him called for cooperation in a defense agreement for consolidating and strengthening Egypt with modern weaponry. Anthony Nutting, *Nasser (London: Constable, 1972), p. 74.*

33. Nasser, in *US News and World Report*, 1 September 1954. See also statements in the *New York Times*, 23 July and 22 October 1954. He declared that "the Government of Egypt has pointed out that this evacuation [of British troops] will not create a military 'vacuum' in the Middle East but will pave the way for strengthening the area's defenses." See also Abdel Nasser, "The Egyptian Revolution," p. 210.

34. Ibid., p. 210. See also Spain, "Middle East Defense: A New Approach." *Middle East Journal*, Summer 1954, p. 253.

35. *Egyptian Gazette*, August 1954. Prior to the Anglo-Egyptian agreement the Egyptian spokesman, Salah Salem, had visited Saudi Arabia, Lebanon, and Yemen, reportedly to strengthen the Arab League ties of these countries (*Al Ahram*, 12 and 30 June and 11 July 1954). Following his sojourn in Saudi Arabia it was announced that agreement had been reached for a joint Egyptian-Saudi Arabia military resource merger and that efforts were being made to persuade Jordan to join (ibid., 1 July 1954; and Mansoor, ed., *The Arab World* (3), 11 June 1954). This development could still, however, be interpreted in terms of forcing Britain to make further concessions for agreement with Egypt.

36. Iraq's Nuri El Said and Syria's Prime Minister Said Ghazz were present. *Egyptian Gazette*, 18 September 1954.

37. Gallman, *Iraq under General Nuri* (p. 37), holds that fear of Egypt was a heavy constraint on Iraqi policy toward the northern pact. Britain's interest in Iraq was intensified by the approaching expiration of the 1930 Anglo-Iraqi Treaty of Alliance, due to lapse in 1957.

38. *Egyptian Gazette*, 22 and 24 August, and 18 September 1954.

39. Mansoor, ed., *The Arab World* (3), 10 September 1954.

40. *New York Times*, 4 August 1954; *Egyptian Gazette*, 31 August and 1 September 1954.

41. The group sent to Washington included Chief-of-Staff Major General Mohammed Ibrahim and four other high-ranking Egyptian army officers. Mansoor, ed., *The Arab World* (3), 16 September 1954. Former CIA agent Miles Copeland gives an account of the discussions between Nasser and American Colonels Albert Gerhardt and Wilber Eveland. Copeland, *The Game of Nations*, pp. 120-25.

42. U.S. Cong., *Hearings, 1957*, pp. 730-31.

43. *New York Times*, 31 September 1954.

44. Copeland, *The Game of Nations*, pp. 120-25.

45. *Egyptian Gazette*, 20 August 1954.

46. Mansoor, ed., *The Arab World* (3), 21 August 1954; ibid., 9 and 28 April 1954.

47. *Egyptian Gazette*, 17 September 1954 and *New York Times*, 20 October 1954.

48. See Turkish Prime Minister Menderes's statement, *Egyptian Gazette*, 18 September 1954.

49. On 31 October 1954, BBC, no. 515, 5 November 1954, quoted in Seale, *The Struggle for Syria*, p. 209.

50. Mansoor, ed., *The Arab World* (3), 1 December 1954; Seale, *The Struggle for Syria*, p. 209.

51. Nuri El Said, quoted in Gallman, *Iraq under General Nuri*, p. 30.

52. *Egyptian Gazette*, 19 October 1954.

53. Dulles, "Important Points of Trip," Unpublished Memorandum, *Dulles Private Papers*.

54. Mansoor, ed., *The Arab World* (3), 18 and 21 November and 1, 4, and 18 December 1954; also 1 January 1955. Since the Egyptian agreement allowed for British re-entry in case of an attack on Turkey, it was felt that Egypt could hardly object to a similar arrangement between Iraq and Britain.

55. Mansoor, ed., *The Arab World* (3), 6 December 1954.

56. Ibid., 16 December 1954; Seale, *The Struggle for Syria*, p. 211.

57. Mansoor, ed., *The Arab World* (3), 27 December 1954.

58. Ibid., 12 January 1955; Nutting, *Nasser*, p. 81.

59. Mansoor, ed., *The Arab World* (3), 13, 14, and 15, January 1955.

60. Salah Salem to Seale, *The Struggle for Syria*, p. 212.

61. Mansoor, ed., *The Arab World* (3), 24 January 1955; ibid., 30 January 1955. Traditional Hashemite-Saudi rivalry made Saudi Arabia a natural ally of Egypt against Iraq. See official Saudi Arabian statements condemning Iraq in *Al Ahram*, 9, 11, and 12 February 1955.

62. See the statement of Foreign Minister Mahmoud Fawzi to U.S. Chargé d'Affaires Jones in *New York Times*, 18 January 1955.

63. Ibid., 31 January 1955.

64. *Al Akhbar*, 1 February 1955.

65. See, for example, *Al Ahram*, 20 and 29 January 1955 and *El Gomhouria*, 14 and 31 January 1955; Seale, *The Struggle for Syria*, pp. 216-17, 223; Gallman, *Iraq under General Nuri*, p. 38.

66. See *Egyptian Gazette*, 16 and 17 January 1955. The Syrian Prime Minister excused the Iraqi move as a result of Arab League weakness. Mansoor, ed., *The Arab World* (3), 1 February 1955.

67. Ibid., 7 February 1955.

68. Ibid., 22 February 1955.

69. Ibid., 14, 20, and 21 February 1955, for example.

70. Britain adhered to the Pact in April, Pakistan in September, and Iran in October 1955.

71. E.g., Copeland, *The Game of Nations*, p. 126; see also former Ambassador to Iraq, Gallman, *Iraq under General Nuri*, p. 29.

72. Former U.S. Ambassador to Egypt Raymond Hare to the author. See the remarks by then Ambassador to Egypt Byroade, quoted in Love, *Suez: The Twice-Fought War*, p. 199, as well as Byroade's comment in U.S. Cong., *Hearings, 1957*, p. 740. See also comments by Raymond Hare and Loy Henderson in *Dulles Oral History Collection*.

73. Eden, *Full Circle*, 3:214-20.

74. Gallman, *Iraq under General Nuri*, p. 61. See also Eden, *Full Circle*, 3:214-20.

75. Mansoor, ed., *The Arab World* (3), 18 September and 16 October 1954.

76. Great Britain, *Treaties Series*, nos. 50 and 9544, London, HMSO 1955. Although its bases legally passed to Iraq, Britain still retained its former privileges (Raouf El Said, "The Baghdad Pact in World Politics," Thesis, Graduate Institute of International Studies, Geneva, 1971, p. 81).

77. Great Britain, House of Commons, *Five Parliamentary Debates*, Doc. 39 (1955), p. 897.

78. El Said, "The Baghdad Pact in World Politics," p. 84 and Harold Macmillan, *Riding the Storm, 1956-1959* (London: Macmillan, 1971), p. 639.

79. Quoted from *Dulles Oral History Collection* and confirmed by Loy Henderson to the author. This is indirectly corroborated by Gallman, who notes that — for unstated reasons — the United States was very slow in responding to Iraqi approaches concerning arms and the pact (*Iraq under General Nuri*, pp. 16 and 33).

80. U.S. Cong., *Hearings, 1957*, p. 334. See also Dulles's comments in Unpublished Background Press Conference, 24 March 1957, *Dulles Private Papers*, where he recognized the extreme sensitivity of Arab countries in general, and of Egypt in particular, to the issue of national sovereignty raised by the pact.

81. Ambassador Gallman to Baghdad Pact delegates at their 12 November 1955 meeting, *New York Times*, 27 November 1955. See Mansoor, ed., *The Arab World* (3), 16 April 1956.

82. U.S. Cong., *Hearings, 1957*, pp. 50, 334, and 107; see also pp. 255-56.

83. Dulles, Unpublished Background Press Conference, 24 March 1957, *Dulles Private Papers*. See also Eisenhower, *Waging Peace* (Garden City, N.Y.: Doubleday, 1965), p. 27; Macmillan's comments on a Dulles note in this regard, Macmillan, *Riding the Storm*, pp. 631 ff.

84. *New York Times*, 27 November 1955. Deputy Under-Secretary J. D. Jernegan had assured Israel that the United States would refrain from membership until Arab-Israeli tensions were resolved. Ibid., 7 March 1955. Dulles reportedly promised that as soon as this issue was settled, the United States would join the pact. Macmillan, *Riding the Storm*, p. 631.

85. Ambassador Gallman admitted this fact. *New York Times*, 27 November 1955.

86. Nuri El Said desired American membership, which would have supported Iraq against Egypt. Gallman, *Iraq under General Nuri*, p. 30. For Britain, see Eden, *Full Circle*, 3:371-75 and Macmillan, *Riding the Storm*, p. 632. Ambassador Gallman later said he had urged U.S. participation on the following grounds: (1) the U.S. was the originator of the Northern Tier concept; (2) U.S. and British adherence would give the Middle East proof of their common cooperation; (3) U.S. adherence would enhance its own influence in the Middle East; (4) no material enlargement of the U.S. commitment was implied; (5) American membership might quell Israeli fears by controlling the use of arms sent to Iraq; (6) it would also reduce Iraqi fears of Turkish irredentist designs on Mosel (*Iraq under General Nuri*, p. 57).

87. Mansoor, ed., *The Arab World* (3), 18 and 19 April 1956.

88. U.S. Department of State, *Bulletin*, 7 May 1956, p. 755 and 17 June 1957, p. 989.

89. For example, see J. D. Jernegan, U.S. Department of State, *Bulletin*, 4 April 1955, p. 564. The United States welcomed Pakistani and Iranian adherence. See ibid., 3 October 1955, p. 534 and 24 October 1955, p. 653. In April 1956 it assumed a share of the Pact's financial burden. Mansoor, ed., *The Arab World* (3), 19 April 1956.

90. Dulles, Unpublished Background Press Conference, 24 March 1957, *Dulles Private Papers*.

91. Campbell, *Defense of the Middle East*, p. 61.

92. Gamal Abdel Nasser, *Where I Stand and Why* (Washington, D.C.: Press Department, Embassy of the U.A.R., 1959), p. 4. See also Nasser's statement, *Al Ahram*, 28 March 1956.

93. See comments by Henry Byroade in U.S. Cong., *Hearings, 1957*, p. 707.

94. Eden, *Full Circle*, 3: 336, 374-75.

95. This was noted by Senator Hubert Humphrey: "For many months we have. . .known that America's participation in the Baghdad Pact is half in and half out — in just enough to cause irritation; out just enough to make us ineffective." *U.S. Congressional Report*, 85th Cong., 2nd sess., 1958, 104, pt. 10, p. 13604; see also Campbell, *Defense of the Middle East*, pp. 61-62.

5

Neutralism: Nasser Trumps the West

In mid-1950, during a Security Council debate on a resolution calling for United Nations assistance to the Republic of South Korea, Mahmoud Fawzi, the representative of a country occupied by British troops, denounced the hypocrisy behind the Western Bloc's concern for "national sovereignty" in the Far East:

> [F]irst, the conflict under considerations is in fact but a new phase in the series of divergencies between the Western and Eastern blocs, divergencies which threaten world peace and security; secondly, there have been several cases of aggression against peoples and violations of the sovereignty and unity of the territories of States members of the United Nations. Such aggressions and violations have been submitted to the United Nations which did not take any action to put an end to them as it has done now in the case of Korea.[1]

By declaring Egypt's abstention on the Korean resolution, Fawzi reminded his listeners not only of the unresolved Palestine issue, but especially that the question of British occupation of Egypt, brought before the Security Council in 1947, was still pending.[2]

More than a year later, this time during the General Assembly's disarmament discussions, Egypt proclaimed its refusal to accept the cold war as the "supreme struggle" "What was wanted," according to Egypt's U.N. Ambassador, Andraos, "was not a *pax britannica, americana or sovietica*, but just peace."[3]

The neutral stance thus taken by exponents of the old regime reflected an attitude already formed during the Second World War, when Egypt's frustrated aspirations for independence led to a generalized disinclination to back Britain's war efforts. The Revolutionary Junta that seized power in 1952 had been formed in the same school. By hinting at the possibility of a neutral stance on carefully chosen occasions,[4] it succeeded in drawing American attention to the unresolved Anglo-Egyptian dispute and its implications for Egypt's future position in the cold war line-up. At the same time, the new regime could not long have survived without playing down at home the very prospects for future cooperation it dangled before the West, lest it be accused of collaboration with the occupying power itself.

"The governments of Britain and the United States are. . .dreaming of a defense agreement with Egypt and the Arab states," railed the former Wafdist mouthpiece, *Al Misri*. ". . .Whoever commits the crime of signing any such agreement will be regarded as a traitor."[5]

Western attempts to convince Egypt of the danger of Soviet encroachment were not persuasive. Britain, not Russia, had been the traditional occupier of Egypt; since 1948, Egypt and the Arab states believed that the immediate danger came from Israel. This was a favorite theme of Nasser, who reportedly told Miles Copeland:

> The Arabs will say, you [the representatives of the Pentagon] are trying to get them to unite to fight *your* enemy, while they know that if they show any intention of fighting *their* enemy you would quickly stop all aid. Any regional military agreement which did not take this attitude into account would be a fraud.[6]

Moreover, an Egyptian commitment to a Western alliance was thought to increase Egypt's vulnerability to attack in the event of any future great power conflagration in which Egypt would become a battleground because of its strategic importance.[7]

In a still broader perspective, Egypt was well aware that, with the Korean conflict, the Afro-Asian nations just emerging from colonial domination had begun to find themselves unified in their abstentions on cold war issues.[8] Searching for an identity in the international political arena, the Egyptian leadership soon discovered that Egypt could not only find needed support for its own cause and that of the Arab nationalists in general, but could even play a leading role among these emerging countries. As early as December 1952, Egypt sponsored an Afro-Asian Conference of twelve nations where it had its first major experience of such support.[9]

Nasser's subsequent encounters with Indian Premier Nehru exposed him to the theoretical aspects of doctrinal neutralism, a philosophy that Nehru had fathered. Nehru frequently visited Cairo and lent his good offices in seeking a settlement of the Anglo-Egyptian dispute. That such meetings made a deep impression on Nasser is reflected in an official statement issued after a June 1953 visit by Nehru and Pakistani Minister Mohammed Ali to Cairo. On this occasion strong hints were given that Egypt would ally itself with the Asian neutralists as a means of terminating British occupation.[10]

As a rule, however, Egypt was far more concerned with the tactical aspects of neutralism than with ideological considerations. It should be remembered in this connection that the terms "neutralism," "noncommitment," and "nonalignment" were for long synonymous in popular usage. Only after 1961 was "neutral" formally abandoned in favor of "noncommitted" and "nonaligned."[11] A neutral stance as a pragmatic approach to the accomplishment of Egypt's political objectives contrasts greatly with the more sophisticated Indian form of doctrinal neutralism.[12]

The link between this pragmatic approach and Egypt's drive for true independence — and the maintenance of that independence once attained — was clear to Nasser:

> One of the fundamental aims of Arab nationalism is independence. . . freedom to make our own decisions, freedom to keep outside anybody's sphere of influence. . . .I am against the alignment of Arab countries with any big powers. Such an alignment could open the door for the big power to become dominant and to bring back imperialism and colonialism to the Arab lands.[13]

Nevertheless, the Egyptian regime did not try to define its position during the early years of the Revolution, in the knowledge that a too overt commitment to neutralism was not expedient. The Soviet Union had yet to present itself as an alternative source of moral and material support; the United States remained the symbol of affluence and democracy. As Heikal himself acknowledged, it was Britain — not yet America — that was held chiefly responsible for Egyptian and Arab problems in this period.[14] Hoping that the United States would help it to obtain a British withdrawal, the Egyptian leadership declined to affront American sensibilities by any outright declaration of neutrality in the cold war.

A clear relation may be traced between the frequency and intensity of early Egyptian neutralist gestures and the state of the Anglo-Egyptian negotiations. A major example was the deadlock that occurred in the spring of 1953. When negotiations bogged down mainly on the issue of Egypt's willingness to commit itself to a Western defense system in exchange for British withdrawal, the Egyptians categorically refused to admit direct American participation in the talks and rejected the British "package deal" outright. This position was reinforced by the success of Egyptian endeavors to form a unified Arab front in opposition to all alliances with the West under existing conditions. Although no Egyptian threat to assume a permanent neutralist stance was officially made, Egypt's refusal to cooperate and its demonstrated ability to rally support for non-cooperation among other Arab states apparently helped to convince Britain that compromise was necessary.

A second major deadlock occurred at the end of the same year, this time over the issues of wartime reactivation of the canal base and the status of British technicians who were to operate the base for a given period. The Egyptian leaders again set out to convince the West that their threat of noncooperation was not a bluff. Nasser is even reported to have informed the American Secretary of State that unless its demands were met, Egypt would "officially announce a policy of complete neutrality between East and West."[15] The Egyptian Ambassadors to Pakistan, India, Britain, the United States, and the Soviet Union were also recalled, allegedly to discuss and reappraise Egypt's position. Still more ominous were the Egyptian government's announced intentions to recognize Communist China, to establish diplomatic relations with East Germany, to increase diplomatic representation in the Eastern Bloc, and to alter its voting pattern in the United Nations.[16]

During a January 1954 exchange between Ambassadors Ahmed Hussein and Caffery, the former reportedly warned that if agreement between Britain and Egypt were not forthcoming, Egypt's only options were to attempt to oust Britain by force and/or to adopt a policy of noncooperation with the West.[17] Caffery answered that Egypt's flirtation with neutralism endangered that country's chances of obtaining American economic and diplomatic assistance.

In February the Egyptian government showed that it was capable of acting on its neutralist threat. Egyptian Ambassador Aziz El Masri held press conferences in Moscow to delineate areas of possible cooperation between Egypt and the Soviet Bloc.[18] Reportedly, he had already informed his government of the Soviets' willingness to aid Egypt economically if it remained outside the Western camp.

Egypt's readiness to work with all nations was stressed by regime spokesman Salah Salem:

> We will not discriminate between one state and another except according to its response to our demands and its support of us in various fields whether economic or political. Egypt has submitted all its principal projects to many countries in the world, including Russia. There are now continuous contacts in this respect. You are aware that a trade delegation has been sent to Russia and to the East European countries. There is a real possibility that Russia may execute some of these projects for Egypt if there should be a final agreement on details.[19]

Egypt thus firmly warned the United States of what it could expect should Egypt's national aspirations remain unfulfilled. Its official position was the following: ". . . Egypt would cooperate with those nations that demonstrated their friendship . . . but would refuse to cooperate with those nations that are unfriendly to its legitimate aspirations."[20]

When the Soviet Union championed the Egyptian and Arab causes in the United Nations in January and again in March 1954, the Egyptian government responded by concluding the most significant trade agreement yet made with that country. Egypt also agreed to raise diplomatic representation between the two countries from legation to embassy level.

It is worth repeating that the Egyptian position during the Anglo-Egyptian dispute was not ideologically oriented. If noncooperation with the West proved a useful tactic to hasten Britain's departure, the Egyptian leadership was still careful not to alienate the United States even during the periods of greatest tension. Nevertheless, official Egyptian utterances, such as Nasser's statement in April 1954, hinted at the growing exasperation:

> The American insistence on creating a pact in the Middle East is going to wreck the Arab world and stand in the way of its unity. There is

duplicity in American policies in this area. They say one thing and do another....It seems clear that the United States is walking with the "wheel of imperialism" so far. The U.S. should hasten in welcoming the Arab hand of friendship which has long been extended toward her; otherwise, she will "miss the boat." We began our relations with the U.S. full of hope for just solutions of the problems of this area, but this hope has now vanished or is on the verge of vanishing.[21]

At the same time Nasser refrained from defining the Egyptian position as neutral: "It is not useful to speak of neutrality because it has no meaning, especially in wartime, unless the country is strong enough to maintain neutrality."[22] The tenets of doctrinal neutralism were similarly absent from the Anglo-Egyptian Agreement as finally concluded, which allowed for the reactivation of the Suez Canal base by Britain in the event of an attack on Turkey, the regional representative of NATO.

Nor did Egypt take any decisive steps in the direction of neutralism immediately after the Anglo-Egyptian Agreement. Rather, the Egyptian leadership attempted to persuade the West to collaborate on an informal basis with the Egyptian-centered Arab Collective Security Organization.[23] The threatening tones temporarily abated: "It is only by a period of complete independence during which mutual trust is built up between Egypt and the Western powers that the Egyptians will be able to look without suspicion on any closer ties between this country and other powers."[24]

This phase ended abruptly with the signing of the Baghdad Pact and the Israeli raid on Gaza that followed it. Now Egypt's reactions began to lead it away from the West toward other willing sources of support, and the possibilities for collaboration with the Western defense scheme progressively diminished.

To interpret America's opposition to neutralism it should be remembered that, for the American leadership, the Western struggle with the Soviet Union was global and total in nature. With no "free" nation immune from Soviet expansionist designs, the vulnerability of the world's "soft spots" was a constant preoccupation. As discussed in the last chapter, the remedy seemed to lie in the creation of a tightly knit defense system capable of deterring potential Soviet encroachment.

An important tenet of the concept of collective security was its indivisibility: each "free" nation was obliged to "stand up and be counted" with the West. By the same token, nations that refused to participate in Western defense efforts weakened the effectiveness of these efforts by creating weak or doubtful links in a single chain.

Moreover, any "free" country that successfully resisted a commitment to the Western system further weakened that system by setting an example for other emerging nations to follow. Dulles, during an off-the-record speech before the Conference Group of National Organizations of the United Nations, worried aloud that neutral nations might be regarded as being in a better bargaining position than allies that were "loyal . . . out of conviction."[25]

With this political outlook, the United States was hardly to remain passive toward the policy of neutralism. Indeed, with the advent of the Eisenhower administration, American opposition to neutralism had become even more stubborn than in the past, despite early post-Stalinist indications of greater Soviet willingness to coexist peacefully with the West. In this respect Senator McCarthy's "reign of terror" may have significantly affected the policy of the Eisenhower administration and induced American leaders to cling to principles that had governed America's relations with Stalinist Russia.[26]

Soon the administration's battle against nonalignment was voiced in moralistic terms, with the cold war depicted as a "holy war" between the "forces of freedom" and the "forces of enslavement". A neutralist approach was deemed immoral, and countries that refused to ally themselves with the West were reminded by no less than Vice-President Nixon that "he who sups with the devil must have a long spoon."[27] In a June 1956 statement at Iowa State College, Secretary Dulles phrased it this way:

> The principal of neutrality. . .pretends that a nation can best gain safety for itself by being indifferent to the fate of others. . . .This has increasingly become an obsolete conception and except under very exceptional circumstances, it is an immoral and shortsighted conception.[28]

In practice, however, the American leadership selectively applied this moral condemnation. For example, Dulles chose to avoid the issue in his 1953 encounter with Prime Minister Nehru, who was a moderating influence during the Anglo-Egyptian dispute at the time. Insisting that differences between American and Indian policy were a question of semantics, he emphasized the Indian commitment to democracy.[29] After his June 1956 statement on the immorality of neutralism, Dulles was asked in a press interview to specify to which nations that statement might apply. He answered that there were very few, if any, immoral nations, an answer consistent with the fact that American aid was continued even to countries that had openly embraced nonalignment.[31]

President Eisenhower showed that he was well aware of this contradiction in a statement on 6 June 1956:

> If you are waging peace, you can't be too particular sometimes about the special attitudes that different countries take. We were a young country once, and our whole policy for the first hundred years was... neutral. We constantly asserted we were neutral in the wars of Europe and [their] antagonisms.
>
> Now, today there are certain nations which say they are neutral. This doesn't necessarily mean what it is so often interpreted to mean, neutral as between right and wrong or decency and indecency.
>
> They are using the term 'neutral' with respect to attachment to military alliances. And may I point out that that is not always to the disadvantage of such a country as ours.[32]

Needless to say, a White House statement purporting to "clarify" the President's remarks showed that Eisenhower had inadvertently strayed from the official line.[33]

American policymakers thus demonstrated their ability to evolve a form of loose cooperation with nonaligned countries that did seem acceptable. Once the cold war rivalry for influence entered the economic domain, which had definitely occurred by 1955, the continuation of aid to certain emerging nations despite their neutralist leanings was even deemed essential in combating the spread of Soviet influence.[34]

It follows that neutralist tendencies as such were not necessarily a serious disruptive factor in a country's relations with the United States. This means that other factors must have combined to render the Egyptian brand of neutralism singularly unpalatable to the American leadership.

Hindsight on to the events of February 1955 clearly suggests that the formation of the Baghdad Pact and the Israeli raid on Gaza had a decisive impact on Egyptian policy. Egypt felt that its hegemony in the Arab world was under attack precisely at a time when its military weakness had been humiliatingly exposed by the Israeli armed forces. It needed to reassert its leadership, regain lost prestige, and secure indispensable military equipment. It found that Iraq, Egypt's main rival, was attempting to draw other Arab states into its orbit with Britain's aid, while the United States was unwilling or unable to meet Egyptian demands for arms. Egypt's response was to take an increasingly anti-Western position and to regard neutralism as the most promising way out of its difficulties.

The Egyptian leadership began to move in three political directions. It tried to form a competing anti-Baghdad grouping under the banner of Arab nationalism; it sought membership in the extra-regional grouping of nonaligned nations; and it further developed its relations with the Soviet Union and other Eastern Bloc countries. At the same time, Egypt's own position on nonalignment was gradually defined, and a distinctly Egyptian brand of neutralism began to emerge.[35]

In seeking to limit Iraqi influence in the Arab world, the Egyptian leadership discovered that Arab nationalism could advantageously be linked with neutralism. The struggle for independence everywhere seemed to dictate the avoidance of further commitments to the traditional colonial masters; pacts with such powers were viewed as a means of perpetuating colonialist dominance under a new guise and were therefore to be rejected. Nonalignment helped to preserve independence by circumscribing colonialist influence.[36]

The anticolonialist side of neutralism also had an application in the Palestine question and the Arab conflict with Israel, since Israel could be depicted as a "colonialist manifestation of Zionist imperialism." The responsibility for its creation was blamed exclusively on the Western powers; the Soviet Union's later

championship of the Arab cause cleared it of guilt in Arab eyes despite initial
Soviet support for Israel.

Nasser discovered that opposition to alignment struck a responsive chord in
the Arab nationalist struggle for complete independence. His ability to rally
and lead the Arab nationalist forces by exploiting pre-existing anti-imperialist
sentiments proved a very effective weapon in his campaign against Iraq and the
extension of the Baghdad Pact. Thus regime spokesman Salah Salem declared:

> Egypt has opposed that pact because it destroys Arab solidarity, dis-
> integrates the united ranks of the Arab Governments and diverts Arab
> efforts from their future objectives and interests; especially so since this
> Arab area has not yet achieved its goals and aspirations in securing com-
> plete freedom and true liberation.[37]

An examination of the reasons for Nasser's widespread popularity helps to
understand this success. His ability to appreciate the frustrations and aspirations
of the masses and to channel popular discontent was enhanced by the fact that
he had risen from the lower middle class. As an ardent nationalist, by the end of
1954 he had not only emerged as the undisputed leader of his country but also
won the admiration of the Egyptian masses both as the symbol of Egypt's successful struggle against British colonialism and as the great reformer.

His popularity was to reach beyond Egypt's borders. Even before the events of
February 1955, Nasser had set out to identify Egypt with the Arab world. This
was evident in Nasser's speech commemorating the second anniversary of the
Egyptian Revolution:

> Compatriots, Egypt has started a new era of relations with the Arabs—
> an era based on true and frank fraternity, facing up to and thinking
> out problems and endeavoring to solve them. The aim of the Revolutionary
> Government is for the Arabs to become one Nation with all its sons
> collaborating for the common welfare....The Revolution also believes
> that the weight of the defense of the Arab states falls first and fore-
> most on the Arabs and they are worthy of undertaking it.[38]

These efforts to identify Egypt with the Arab world were intensified in the
campaign against the Baghdad Pact that was in turn facilitated by the post-
British growth of mass communication and the ability of Radio Cairo broadcasts
to reach Arab masses.[39] Urging the Arabs to unite in the struggle against what
was deemed a manifestation of imperialist colonialism, Nasser renewed his commitment to Arab nationalism and pledged that "I shall never again see the Arab
nation subject to foreign domination if I can help it."[40] However, some authors
contend that Nasser's external concern was an attempt to divert his
countrymen's attention from urgent, unsolved domestic problems.[41]

Nasser was careful to distinguish between the Arab masses and their leaders.
He accused the latter of destroying Arab unity and of collusion with the colonial

masters. Iraq was accused of linking itself with the friend of Israel, Turkey; this was played up by the announcement of an alleged agreement between Turkey and Israel.[42] Iraq and the West, Egypt charged, were trying to draw Arab attention away from the real enemy, Israel.

The Arab masses proved highly receptive to the accusations broadcast by Radio Cairo. Radio Iraq's attempts to counter Eygyptian accusations were less successful. Prime Minister Nuri El Said later admitted to Ambassador Gallman that over 95 percent of Iraq's population saw Israel as the enemy rather than the Soviet Union.[43]

Soon the Arab masses came to look upon Nasser as the symbol of their own struggle for independence and unity. His refusal to yield to Western pressure was interpreted by the nationalists as heroic defiance. His emphasis on Arab unity was well received. His assumption of the role of leader in the Arab cause against Israel after the Gaza Raid strengthened his image as *the* spokesman for the Arab cause in general.

The Arab masses, incited by Radio Cairo, thus turned to Nasser for the fulfillment of their aspirations. His victories represented victories for the Arab nation; his defeats, seen as the work of the great powers, made him a martyr in their eyes.

Confronted with Nasser's charismatic personality, Arab leaders feared the domestic consequences of publicly opposing his interpretation of Arab nationalism. Most of them became convinced that their interests, personal and national, would be damaged by close collaboration with Iraq and the Baghdad Pact. Nasser's fusion of "national pragmatic neutralism"[44] with Arab nationalism had thus helped Egypt to deal with its political problems and to reassert its leadership in the Arab region at one and the same time.[45]

Even before the Baghdad Pact was signed, the Egyptian attempt to block the growth of Iraqi influence in the Arab world had led it to promote the creation of an anti-Baghdad group. During the January-February 1955 Arab League Prime Ministers' Conference, the Egyptian leadership announced its intention to form a military alliance that would exclude Iraq. The Arab Collective Security Organization, which met on the day that the Turkish-Iraqi accord was concluded, was promptly dissolved at Egypt's bidding. A period of diplomatic skirmishing ensued, as a result of which Syria and Saudi Arabia were persuaded to join Egypt in forming a new organization to be known as the Arab Defense and Economic Command.[46] Jordan reserved time to study the plan but expressed opposition to the Baghdad Pact; Lebanon remained neutral.

All this set off an intense diplomatic struggle between the Iraqi-Turkish axis and Egypt, which soon centered on Syria.[47] The Syrian government had voiced its opposition to the Baghdad Pact by the end of February 1955. However, by mid-March this government was in serious difficulty because of the strong external pressures in favor of the pact, including Turkey's massing of troops on the Syrian border.

These pressures aggravated the internal instability that plagued the country and forced Syria to postpone indefinitely its attendance at a conference of the prime ministers of the countries that were to be the future members of the Egyptian-sponsored entity. Only after the Soviet government issued a warning to Turkey, and the United States finally expressed its opposition to the Turkish tactics, did that country desist in its attempt to coerce Syria.[48]

The United States action to restrain Turkey did not erase the impression created by its earlier warnings against a Syrian link with Egypt. An Egyptian statement characterized the American role as follows:

> The United States cannot by supporting Turkey, Iraq, and Israel, isolate Egypt from the rest of the Arab world, nor can she stop Egypt's steady progress toward the salvation of the Arab world from Zionism and Imperialism.[49]

In contrast, the Soviet Union, a supporter of the Arab cause against Israel since 1954, was now portrayed as the protector of the Arab world.[50] The political issue of Arab membership in Western pacts had consequently led to an ugly cold war line-up in the region, with the United States behind Iraq and Turkey and the Soviet Union behind Egypt and Syria.

This cold war tension and the threatening atmosphere that accompanied it contrasted sharply with the Third World's own contribution to the Egyptian-Iraqi clash. The leaders of nonalignment, Tito and Nehru, during their respective visits to Cairo at the height of the struggle, openly backed Egypt. Nehru was particularly sensitive to pacts after Pakistan's adherence to SEATO in September 1954. Fearing that Pakistan's membership in the proposed Baghdad Pact was merely a matter of time, he endorsed Nasser's opposition to Western intervention in regional affairs. The two leaders affirmed that military alliances and power entanglements served only to "increase tension and rivalry in armaments," adding nothing to the security of a country:

> We are fed up with bombs...We are fed up with imperialism, capitalism, and communism. We are fed up with alliances and blocs.[51]

The moral support of these elder statesmen strengthened the young Nasser politically and confirmed his belief that nonalignment was the right course for Egyptian policy. In the end, it was this policy that enabled Egypt to win the first round in its latest contest with Iraq: the new Syrian government, with Egyptian, Soviet, and Third World backing, successfully resisted being pressured into joining the Baghdad Pact.

The victory was fragile because Syria remained exposed to the effects of "crypto-diplomatic" pressures that continued to be exerted by interested foreign powers. Nevertheless, it seemed to demonstrate that neutralism worked precisely because it provided an effective means of counteracting Western pressures without sacrificing Egyptian and Arab independence.

Then, in April 1955, neutralism yielded still another dividend of far-reaching importance: the Bandung Conference recognized Nasser as the leader of the Arab world.

The idea for this conference was suggested at the Colombo Conference held in April-May 1954, and plans were formulated at Bogar in December. Invited by the sponsoring nations, India, Burma, Indonesia, Pakistan, and Ceylon, the leaders of twenty-eight Afro-Asian states, representing 56 percent of the world's population, met to discuss mutual cooperation and the promotion of peaceful coexistence between all nations. As such, the Bandung Conference was by far the largest and most important gathering of emerging nations that had ever been held.

Nasser left for the conference somewhat hesitantly in view of Egypt's still insecure position in the shifting Arab political constellation. His timidity may also have stemmed in part from the fact that his only previous venture outside Egypt was his attendance at the August 1954 Islamic Conference in Saudi Arabia. Nevertheless, he was received as a leading figure along with Nehru, Chou en-Lai, and Sukarno; he was elected to the chairmanship of a subcommittee of twelve nations on coexistence; and he even saw his proposed resolutions on French colonialism in North Africa and on the Palestine issue adopted by the Conference.[52] In his public statements Nasser condemned *all* colonialist manifestations, including the communist brand: "In our opinion there is a sort of colonialism on the Communist side and we thought it should be recognized."[53]

One observer wrote that Nasser "came to the Bandung Conference known only by name to the great majority of the delegates and left as an accepted leader in Afro-Asian affairs."[54] The Egyptian press extolled his performance as a personal and national triumph:

> All the representatives of the African and Asian countries, as well as all of those who attended the conference, have paid tribute to Premier Abdel Nasser in view of his sound proposals, his wisdom and his proper understanding of the role which his country should undertake for the sake of world peace.

The Arabs were urged to follow Nasser's example:

> Arab rights and interests can only be safeguarded if the Arab states adopt Egypt's independent foreign policy, which has enabled Premier Abdel Nasser to win the admiration and respect of all the peoples of the world and has enabled this country to restore her national dignity in full.[55]

Nasser himself viewed the Bandung Conference as a major formative experience. En route to the conference he had spent five days conferring with Nehru, which he later described as "a turning point in my political understanding. I learned and realized that the only wise policy for us would be [one] of positive neutralism and nonalignment."[56] Traveling with Nehru, Nasser met Chou en-Lai in Burma, who invited him to visit China.[57]

After Nasser's success at Bandung, Egypt's neutralist leanings became a full-fledged commitment. This greatly bolstered Nasser's position as the leading Arab nationalist spokesman and enhanced Egypt's own prestige and influence in Arab politics. "Coming back home," he said, "I found out from the response . . . that it [neutralism] is the only possible policy which could get the broadest support from the Arab people."[58]

As a new and prestigious member of the leaders who spoke for the Afro-Asian bloc,[59] Nasser found that the support of these nations augmented his capacity to bargain with the great powers. He became increasingly bold and dynamic in both his regional and international dealings.

By the end of May 1955, an Egyptian-Syrian-Saudi Arabian grouping against the Baghdad Pact had begun to take shape. On the global scene, Nasser soon assumed the role of mediator in the Pakistani-Afghan dispute, and a cultural accord between Egypt and Communist China was concluded.[60] With his diplomatic position thus significantly strengthened, Nasser then embarked on the quest for arms that had become imperative after Israel's raid on Gaza in February 1955.

The United States had broadly hinted that military aid would be forthcoming once Britain and Egypt settled their differences. Eisenhower himself, in July 1953, reportedly assured Naguib of the American willingness to enter into "firm commitments for economic and military assistance following the conclusion of the Anglo-Egyptian dispute."[61]

When the Egyptians invoked this promise after the Anglo-Egyptian Agreement, the Pentagon insisted, as in the past, that Egypt should either commit itself to the Middle East defense system or that it should accept an American military mission to monitor the use of American arms.[62] At the same time pro-Israeli forces in America stepped up their lobbying against a policy of arming the Arabs.

The conditions set by the United States were unacceptable to the Egyptian leadership. Nasser explained his view on the matter in a September interview:

> Because of our history we have complexes in this country about some words—especially those which imply that we are being tied to another country. Words like 'joint command,' 'joint pact,' and 'mission' are not beloved in our country because we have suffered from them....
> I think your men who deal with this area should understand the

psychology of the area. You send military aid, but if you send ten officers along with it nobody will thank you for your aid but instead will turn it against you.[63]

Colonel Anwar El Sadat, reportedly infuriated at American conditions for arms aid, exclaimed that Egypt would never accept aid with strings. He said that, by strings, he meant any conditions that the United States would not set for aid to Britain or France.[64]

After the Gaza Raid Egypt's military weakness led to increased pressure for arms from the army officers on whose support Nasser depended. One member of the Junta described the situation as follows:

> We were desperately weak. Our armed forces were short of every-thing. At the time of the Gaza raid, Egypt had six serviceable planes, about thirty others were grounded for lack of spare parts: Britain had stopped deliveries. We estimated that our tank ammunition would last for a one-hour battle. Nearly sixty percent of our tanks were in need of major repairs. Our artillery was in the same deplorable state. We were even short of small arms.[65]

Nasser became increasingly pessimistic about Western sources of supply. Even if Pentagon conditions were accepted, American arms would be embargoed in a conflict with Israel and could not therefore be relied on in defending Egypt against Israel. Any hope that Britain might satisfy Egypt's needs was also quickly dispelled. The cordial atmosphere fostered by the Anglo-Egyptian Agreement led Britain to lift its own embargo on arms to Egypt. By the summer of 1955, however, relations had again cooled because of Egyptian hostility toward Iraq and the Baghdad Pact and its opposition to Britain's remaining colonial interests in the Middle East. Only a small part of the arms purchased from Britain were consequently delivered, and subsequent consignments were made to depend on a more cooperative attitude.[66]

As for France, the only other Western source of real significance, Egyptian support for North African forces resisting French colonialism ruled out fulfill-ment of a July 1955 arms agreement. Indeed, France went on to become the principal supplier of Israel despite the early Tripartite Declaration, which had in theory excluded this possibility.

Nevertheless, Nasser continued to press for American arms during the first half of 1955. One reason, according to available evidence, is that the Egyptian Army was accustomed to Western arms. A certain wariness about the political repercussions of arms purchases from the Eastern Bloc was no doubt another consideration, if allegations by former CIA agent Miles Copeland are to be believed. Copeland reported that he had been informally approached by the Egyptian Ambassador to Washington in an attempt to secure at least $2 million worth of "parade items" to take the pressure for arms off the Egyptian leader-ship.[67]

According to Eisenhower, Nasser officially requested $27 million worth of military aid.[68] This time Egypt was informed of still another condition: it would be required to pay with the hard currency that America knew was in short supply. Thus the Americans imposed terms that were too stringent to be accepted without rejecting the sale of arms to Egypt outright.

Nasser therefore turned to the alternative source of supply—the Eastern Bloc. Already at the Bandung Conference, Nasser had reportedly sounded out Chou en-Lai on the possibility of Egypt's securing Chinese arms. Because of China's own dependence on Soviet sources, Chou en-Lai agreed to relay the Egyptian demand to the Soviet authorities. According to Egyptian Minister of Guidance Salah Salem, the Soviet Ambassador to Cairo, Daniel Solod, conveyed a positive response to him in early May 1955.[69]

The Soviet answer was not unexpected. Despite some Soviet irritation over the terms of the Anglo-Egyptian Agreement, relations with Egypt had continued to grow and flourish since early 1954. The conclusion of the Baghdad Pact in February 1955 brought the two countries even closer together, as each felt threatened by "pactomania" and its implications.

Still, the Egyptian leadership was reluctant to exercise this option. At a meeting of the Revolutionary Command Council in June 1955 , it was reportedly decided to make a last attempt to secure Western arms. Nasser then informed the American Ambassador that, if the West continued to refuse to satisfy Egyptian needs, Egypt would obtain arms from the Soviet Union.[70] But the American leadership again chose to leave Nasser with no firm commitment, partly in the conviction that Nasser was bluffing and trying to blackmail the United States, a tactic that was not new.[71]

Confronted by the tacit American refusal, Nasser set out in earnest to negotiate an agreement with the Soviet Union. Technical details were worked out between the Soviet Military Attaché, Colonel Nimoskinka, and the Egyptian leadership in June and July. The remaining points were settled during the July visit of the high-ranking Soviet official, Shepilov.[72] However, the Soviets were reluctant to figure as a direct party to the agreement, perhaps because they did not want to disrupt the "spirit" of the Geneva Summit of July 1955.[73] Egypt's negotiators were accordingly referred to Czechoslovakia, from which Israel had purchased arms during the Stalinist period, and the final agreement was signed.

On 27 September Nasser publicly announced that an Arms Deal with Czechoslovakia had been concluded:

> We refused to sign any mutual security pact, any form of alliance; and so. . .we were unable to obtain arms from America. . . .Last week, Egypt signed a commercial agreement with Czechoslovakia for a supply of weapons to her. This agreement stipulates that Egypt shall pay for these weapons with products such as cotton and rice.[74]

Later, elaborating on the deal to an American audience, Nasser argued as follows:

We look at things a lot differently from you Americans. We don't spend our time worrying about a world war, or Russian aggression, or the struggle between East and West. We are interested in Egypt's security, and Egypt's security today means protection against Israel.[75]

The announcement of Egypt's Arms Deal with Czechoslovakia was tantamount to a declaration of political independence from the West.

On 21 September 1955, the American Ambassador to Cairo was informed of the Egyptian-Czechoslovakian Arms Agreement. The American leadership's immediate reaction was to waive its previous conditions and to offer arms to Egypt on credit in a belated attempt to counter the Soviet move.[76] Nasser chose to announce the deal officially on 27 September, reportedly to forestall further discussion.[77]

The American leadership, however, did not consider the matter closed. Dulles immediately lodged a protest with Molotov, and the United States joined Britain in expressing concern over the affair.[78] A few days later Assistant Secretary of State George V. Allen was dispatched to Cairo, presumably for the purpose of dissuading Nasser from going through with the deal. Futile from the start, the Allen Mission was badly received and portrayed as an American attempt to interfere with Egyptian internal affairs.

Rumors spread that Nasser contemplated breaking off relations with the United States.[79] The effect this had on the mission can only be conjectured. Some claim that Allen originally carried an ultimatum to Nasser;[80] others state that Allen's message was extensively altered by the time he conferred with Nasser.[81] In any event, the mission was quickly made to assume the character of an official routine American visit to exchange views with the Egyptian leadership.

This apparent failure soon induced Dulles to change his tone. At a news conference on 4 October he rejected the notion of an ultimatum and explained that the purpose of the Allen visit had been to enable the two sides to clarify their positions. He continued:

[T]he Arab countries were independent governments and free to do whatever they wished in the matter. . .It is difficult to be critical of countries which, feeling themselves endangered, seek the arms which they sincerely believe they need for defense.[82]

In retrospect, the whole issue of arming Egypt aptly illustrates the American tendency to make ad hoc adjustments to situations as they developed in the Middle East. Dulles had received ample warning of the pending Arms Deal. Byroade claimed he had advised the State Department as early as 9 June to come to terms with Egypt in order to forestall an agreement with the Soviet Union.[83] Dulles himself admitted having got wind of the deal in June 1955.[84] The CIA reportedly informed him in August that the deal was finalized.[85] Yet Dulles's only response had been to attempt to infuse new life into Arab-Israeli peace projects.[86]

Later, a multitude of excuses were offered for the Americans' refusal to supply Egypt with military equipment. The United States was not "a market for arms," declared Dulles at a 1957 congressional hearing, and "our prices were too high." Caffery gave yet another reason — Nasser wanted military assistance without conditions and the United States had imposed conditions. For Admiral Radford, the reason was that "what they [Egypt] wanted to buy, as I recall them, were types of weapons we did not want them to buy."[87]

If the United States had really wished to supply Egypt with arms, the matter would hardly have been allowed to bog down over questions such as Egypt's ability to pay in hard currency. Nor would the American administration really have been hindered by its commitment to the 1950 Tripartite Agreement if any policy involving the arming of the Arab states had not been highly controversial and likely to cause political embarrassment when brought to congressional attention.

Egypt's neutralist stance was a key factor in the American position. Still acting on the premise that the West was the only feasible supplier of arms for the Middle East, the American leadership continued to withhold the arms it knew Egypt needed, apparently in the belief that Egypt would sooner or later "stand up and be counted." The United States seemingly discounted the possibility that any regional leader would dare confront the West with an agreement such as that which Egypt finally concluded with the Soviet Union.

Once the Arms Deal with Czechoslovakia finally drove home the fact that a policy of severity with Egypt had been counterproductive, moderation was quickly manifested. Playing down the significance of Egypt's move, the American leadership devised a new policy of inducements to ensure that the deal remained a "one-shot affair."

The Arms Deal was a dramatic demonstration of Egypt's ability to defend its national interests in a political arena conditioned by cold war pressures. As such, it was the culmination of Egypt's three-pronged response to the events of February 1955 and to the difficult position in which it had then been placed. This response enabled Egypt to continue the struggle against the Baghdad grouping under the banner of Arab nationalism; to prove that neutralism was a force capable of limiting Western influence in the Arab world; and to develop relations with the Eastern Bloc to the point where Egypt's own interests stood to gain from cold war rivalries.

These developments, as viewed from Egypt and the Middle East, contrasted with the view from Washington and the West. Nasser's popularity and prestige in Arab political circles now allowed him to assume the role of defiant hero and "mystical savior" of Arabism.[88] Unlike the Iraqi leadership, which had bowed to Western demands, he had secured arms without humiliating conditions.

Arab jubilation was widespread:

The Syrian, Lebanese, and Jordanian Chambers of Deputies at once voted resolutions of congratulations to Colonel Nasser, and almost the entire Arab press greeted the news with rapturous acclamation. . . .Even Nuri El Said felt constrained to send a message of congratulations and approval to the Egyptian leader. This response was not due to any special love of Russia, nor to any desire to see either communism or Soviet power extended in the Middle East; it was due rather to a lively appreciation of the quality of Colonel Nasser's act as a slap in the face of the West.[89]

Nasser's bargaining position in his struggle for leadership within the Arab community was greatly strengthened. This was to pay handsome dividends in the next round of the political battle against Iraq and the Baghdad Pact.

In terms of cold war politics, Egypt ran a calculated risk that its willingness to deal with the Soviet Union would actually enhance its ability to assume a neutral posture. By the same token, the Arms Deal proved that the American concept of "deterrence" was short-sighted. The possibility that a local power would invite the Soviet Union to intervene had not been taken into consideration by American strategists. "Brinkmanship," when such a situation did occur, was hardly a feasible approach.

Moreover, at Egypt's invitation, the Soviet Union found the means to leapfrog over the Baghdad configuration into the heart of the Arab world. By this move the Soviets checked the Baghdad system, scored a major psychological victory, and became from then on a major force to be reckoned with in Middle East politics.

The lesson to be drawn from the whole affair was that the global bipolar balance could hinge on attitudes and decisions of local governments and political forces. The new situation has been described as follows:

The disposition of outside military forces and the possession of bases continued to have some significance, but the crucial aspects in what was primarily a political competition lay in the standing of each of the competitors on the local scene. The interlocking of global and local cold wars, moreover, was not without risks for the great powers, for they could become the captives of the policies of their smaller partners.[90]

The new dynamism in Egyptian foreign policy was bound to conflict with Western interests in the region. Now more was at stake than Egypt's refusal to commit itself to a Western defense structure. On the contrary, the Egyptian brand of neutralism, coupled with Egypt's ability to unite the forces of Arab nationalism against all remaining colonialist manifestations including the "neocolonialist" Baghdad Pact, seemed a threat to the status quo and, by extension, to continued Western influence in the region.

For the United States in particular, Nasser's prominent role at the Bandung Conference alongside some of America's arch enemies—Communist China, North Vietnam, and North Korea—had already been viewed with dismay. Now Egypt's expanding relations with the Eastern Bloc was seen as a move toward the

Soviet camp rather than as a shift toward neutralism. Given the American preoccupation with the Middle East theatre in its global efforts to contain the Soviet Union, an Egyptian move that actually opened the door to a Soviet presence constituted a major setback for American policy.

The repercussions of the Arms Deal on Egyptian-Israeli relations were also to affect future American-Egyptian relations. Pro-Israeli groups in America intensified their pressure on the American leadership in order to secure arms for Israel and to prevent the United States from establishing closer relations with Egypt before that country made peace with the Jewish state.

The Western powers thus gradually came to see Nasser-led Arab nationalism as their chief regional antagonist, a phenomenon they disparagingly labeled *Nasserism*. Pretending to ignore the existence of an authentic nationalist movement among the Arab peoples, Britain and the United States were quick to place the blame for the failure of their regional policies on Nasser and his "agents". Their use of the term Nasserism was meant to drive a wedge between the Arab world and its leading spokesman, Nasser.[91] By playing on Arab fears of Egyptian hegemony, the Western opponents of Arab nationalism apparently hoped to convince the Arab world that Egypt's Arab policy was motivated by visions of an empire headed by Nasser.

Paradoxically, these efforts to weaken Arab opposition to Western policy merely added to Nasser's stature and strengthened both his role and Arab nationalist resistance at one and the same time. An attack on Nasser was viewed as an attack on Arab nationalism itself:

> Nasserism does not refer to a single individual, and does not refer to a specific government. . . .It refers clearly and precisely to the national revolutionary force — in its ideological position, its principles, its goals, in whatsoever it has realized in the way of victories in the spheres of nationalism, liberation, unity, and in the economic and social spheres of life.[92]

By September 1955 it had become evident to the American leadership that further deterioration in relations with Egypt was not in the best interests of the United States. In response to congressional pressure for cutting off all aid to Egypt, the administration hinted that only outdated weapons were involved and sought to shift the blame for the Arms Deal from Egypt to the Soviet Union.[93] A new American willingness to improve relations was relayed to Cairo, where fears about increased dependence on the Eastern Bloc were already being voiced.

The United States' next step was to try to counter Soviet gains in influence and prestige by offering to finance the construction of Egypt's highest priority development project — the Aswan High Dam.

Notes

1. U.N. Security Council, *Official Records*, 5th sess., no. 17, 475th meeting, 1950.
2. *Egypt and the United Nations*, ed. The Egyptian Society of International Law (New York: Manhattan Publishing Co., 1957), pp. 62-63.

3. U.N. General Assembly, *Official Records*, 6th sess., 1st Committee, 450th meeting, 22 November 1951, pp. 15-16.

4. Malcolm Kerr, "Egyptian Foreign Policy and the Revolution," in *Egypt Since the Revolution*, ed. P. J. Vatikiotis (London: George Allen and Unwin, Ltd., 1968), p. 114.

5. *Al Misri*, 14 April 1953. In explaining the regime's position to the American public, Nasser maintained that military pacts with great powers would give rise to local discontent that could only benefit political extremist groups, including the communists. *US News and World Report*, 4 September 1954.

6. Copeland, *The Game of Nations*, pp. 124-25.

7. Nasser, *US News and World Report*, 4 September 1954.

8. S. Yin'am, "The Middle East in 1953: Annual Political Survey," *Middle Eastern Affairs*, January 1954, p. 2.

9. Wheelock, *Nasser's New Egypt*, p. 215. Within the U.N., Afro-Asian support for Arab problems was frequently expressed.

10. *New York Times*, 25 June 1953.

11. Fayez A. Sayegh, "Anatomy of Neutralism—A Typical Analysis," in *The Dynamics of Neutralism in the Arab World*, ed. Fayez A. Sayegh (San Francisco: Chandler, 1964), p. 1.

12. Ibid., pp. 28-29 and 42-43.

13. Abdel Nasser, *Where I Stand and Why*, (Washington, D.C.: Embassy of the U.A.R, Press Department, 1959), p. 2

14. M. H. Heikal, *Nahnu wa Amrika*, pp. 55-5?

15. *Akhbar Al Yaum*, 5 December 1953.

16. *New York Times*, 28 December 1953.

17. Ibid., 7 January 1954.

18. Ibid., 14 February and 4 January 1954.

19. Ibid., 14 February 1954.

20. Statement by Abul Assoud, Under-Secretary of the Ministry of National Guidance. Ibid., 18 February 1954.

21. *Al Ahram*, 16 April 1954.

22. *New York Times*, 20 April 1954.

23. See statement by Salah Salem, *Egyptian Gazette*, 20 December 1954. "Why does not the West assist the Arab Alliance by supplying arms and economic aid so that they may be able to check any aggression? I assure you that such a step would remove many of the complications which have arisen between the Arabs and the West."

24. "Background Paper" of the Revolutionary Command Council, *New York Times*, 3 September 1954.

25. Unpublished record, 2 January 1956, Sills Reporting Service, *Dulles' Private Papers*.

26. This seems a fair inference from a study of the *Dulles Oral History Collection*.

27. U.S. Department of State, *Bulletin*, 16 July 1956, p. 95.

28. U.S. Department of State, Press Release 307, 9 June 1956.

29. *New York Times*, 23 May 1953.

30. Ibid., 12 July 1956.

31. For India, see Dulles, "Free World Unity," U.S. Department of State, *Bulletin*, 4 June 1953. For the general situation, see Dulles, U.S. Department of State, Press Conference, Press Release 380, 11 July 1956.

32. *New York Times*, 7 June 1956. See also Nixon's 7 June 1956 statement, which warned that nonaligned nations were not going to be "frightened into alliance with the West by military power." Ibid., 8 June 1956.

33. U.S. Department of State, *Bulletin*, 18 June 1956, pp. 1004-1005.

34. C. V. Crabb, "The United States and the Neutralists: A Decade in Perspective," *Annals*, November 1965, p. 92.

35. For the various brands, see Sayegh, "Anatomy of Neutralism", pp. 27-37. Nasser's brand has been labeled "national pragmatic neutralism" (p. ??)

36. Don Peretz, "Nonalignment in the Arab World," *Annals*, November 1965, p. 36. Note that

Afro-Asian support was lent to the struggle for independence of the Maghreb countries.

37. *Egyptian Gazette*, 23 January 1955.

38. BBC no. 486, 21 July 1954, quoted in Seale, *The Struggle for Syria*, p. 198. See also Copeland, *The Game of Nations*, p. 165.

39. Wheelock, *Nasser's New Egypt*, p. 224.

40. *Al Ahram*, 1 April 1955.

41. Wheelock, *Nasser's New Egypt*, p. 223.

42. *Al Ahram*, 27 January 1955 and *Al Gomhouria*, 27 January 1955.

43. Gallman, *Iraq under General Nuri*, p. 27.

44. Sayegh, "Anatomy of Neutralism," (*The Dynamics of Neutralism in the Arab World*), p. 35.

45. Malcolm Kerr, *The Arab Cold War* (New York: Oxford University Press, 1967) p.118.

46. *Egyptian Gazette*, 3, 7, and 14 March 1955.

47. Salah Salem to Seale, *The Struggle for Syria*, p. 212.

48. *New York Times*, 30 and 31 March 1955.

49. Ibid., 10 March 1955.

50. Ibid., 8, 10, and 28 March 1955.

51. *Egyptian Gazette*, 17 February 1955.

52. U.A.R., Ministry of National Guidance, *The UAR and the Policy of Nonalignment* (Cairo: State Information Service, n.d.), p. 15; *Egyptian Gazette*, 22 April 1955.

53. *New York Times*, 26 April 1955.

54. Tom Little, quoted in the *Egyptian Gazette*, 26 April 1955.

55. *Al Gomhouria*, 25 April 1955.

56. R. K. Karanjia, *Arab Dawn* (Bombay: Blitz, 1958), p. 187.

57. *New York Times*, 16 April 1955.

58. Karanjia, *Arab Dawn*, p. 187.

59. In the Afro-Asian group, Egypt does not represent herself only, but also a pattern of cultural history and thinking which has its own importance" (*Al Akhbar*, 30 April 1955).

60. *Egyptian Gazette*, 15 and 31 May 1955.

61. *New York Times*, 31 July 1954.

62. Lacouture, *Egypt in Transition*, p. 216; See also Copeland, *The Game of Nations*, pp. 123-26.

63. *US News and World Report*, 4 September 1954.

64. Wilton Wynn, *Nasser of Egypt: The Search for Dignity* (Cambridge, Mass.: Arlington Books, Inc., 1959), p. 70.

65. Salem to Seal, *The Struggle for Syria*, p. 234.

66. Heikal holds that Britain had delivered only sixteen of eighty centurion tanks purchased by Egypt. Heikal, *The Cairo Documents*, p. 46; see also Childers, *The Road to Suez*, p. 133.

67. Copeland, *The Game of Nations*, p. 132.

68. Eisenhower, *Waging Peace*, p. 24; U.S. Cong., *Hearings, 1957*, p. 714.

69. See Salah Salem's comments to Seale, *The Struggle for Syria*, pp. 235-36. See also Heikal, *The Cairo Documents*, p. 48.

70. Byroade, U.S. Cong., *Hearings, 1957*, p. 714.

71. Copeland, *The Game of Nations*, p. 132. Copeland reports that American Assistant Secretary of State, George V. Allen, informed him that a decision on the project was officially held up for "administrative reasons."

72. Salem to Seale, *The Struggle for Syria*, p. 236. It is impossible to verify the exact date; Salem indicated that the agreement was concluded by end-July, to be announced later (September).

73. Heikal, *The Cairo Documents*, p. 49. This conflicts with Copeland's version that the use of Czechoslovakia was suggested by Kermit Roosevelt at the last moment to take some of the "sting" out of the agreement. Copeland, *The Game of Nations*, p. 135. Heikal's version was confirmed by Salah Salem, Seale, *The Struggle for Syria*, p. 236, and also by a former Czech officer — interviewed by the author — who was dispatched with the arms to Egypt.

74. Nasser's 27 September 1955 speech at opening of Armed Forces Exhibition, *Documents on International Affairs, 1955*, pp. 370-73.

75. Interview with *US News and World Report*, 4 November 1955.

76. *New York Times*, 26 September 1955. This offer was confirmed by White House spokesman Lincoln White. Ibid., 27 September 1955. After Nasser's 27 September announcement, the United States denied having made any such offer. Ibid., 28 September 1955.

77. Nasser in an interview with Kennett Love, in *Suez: The Twice-Fought War*, p. 283.

78. *New York Times*, 28 September 1955; see "Policy on Supplying Arms to Countries of the Middle East," Joint United States-Britain Statement. U.S. Department of State, *Bulletin*, 10 October 1955, p. 560.

79. *New York Times*, 19 October 1955.

80. Ellis, *Challenge in the Middle East*, p. 42.

81. Copeland, *The Game of Nations*, p. 140-43. See also Love's account in *Suez: The Twice-Fought War*, pp. 284-89.

82. U.S. Department of State, *Bulletin*, 17 October 1955, p. 604.

83. U.S. Cong., *Hearings, 1957*, p. 728; *New York Times*, 14 November 1955.

84. U.S. Cong., *Hearings, 1957*, p. 16.

85. Love, *Suez: The Twice-Fought War*, p. 283.

86. Ibid.

87. U.S. Cong., *Hearings, 1957*, pp. 17, 183, and 483.

88. Hussein, *Uneasy Lies the Head*, p. 88.

89. Bernard Lewis, *The Middle East and the West* (Bloomington: Indiana University Press, 1954), p. 132.

90. J. C. Campbell: "American Search for Partners," *Soviet-American Rivalry in the Middle East*, ed. J. C. Hurewitz (New York: Praeger, 1969), p. 200.

91. Leonard Binder, *The Ideological Revolution in the Middle East* (New York: John Wiley and Sons, 1964), p. 198.

92. Ibid., p. 199, quoting Abu Allah Al Rimawi, *Al Mantig Al Thawri* [The Revolutionary Logic] (Cairo, 1961), p. 95.

93. For example, see Dulles's statement about "discarding the old types [of weapons]" at an 18 October 1955 press conference (U.S. Department of State, *Bulletin*, 31 October 1955, pp. 688-89). In another statement (*Documents on International Affairs, 1955*, p. 383), the Soviet willingness to supply arms to Egypt was described as a "move to gain popularity at the expense of the restraint shown by the West."

6

The Dam that Ivan Built

The Aswan High Dam was the keystone of the Egyptian government's ten-year economic development plan, and few projects—at least in theory—could exert a greater impact on the life of a nation. It was estimated, for example, that this project would permit 1.3 million feddans[1] of land to be reclaimed and 700,000 feddans to be converted to perennial irrigation, while another 700,000 feddans would be used for the yearly rice crop.[2]

The hydroelectric power to be generated by the dam would vastly increase industrial potential and enable Egypt to modernize its predominantly agricultural economy. New jobs would thus be created in both sectors; domestic production of many goods previously imported would rise; and exports of agricultural produce could be boosted by as much as 50 percent. A 30 percent projected increase in total national income—worth about £E 255 million—after the first 10 years was to reach £E 355 million annually in the course of another 15 years.[3]

The construction of the Aswan High Dam also offered a means of preventing the extreme fluctuations between low-water years and the flood years that devastated Egyptian villages. By regularizing the flow of the Nile, utilization of its precious waters could be maximized and their loss into the Mediterranean reduced.

The political and economic repercussions of projected development on a scale as vast as this readily explains why plans that had begun to be formulated as early as 1949 came to be viewed as one of the Egyptian Revolution's principal aspirations. To attain their goal, the Free Officers had to resolve four basic problems. A feasible technical plan had to be devised; the construction site had to be chosen; the distribution of the Nile waters had to be negotiated with the Sudan; and, condition sine qua non, hard currency had to be found.

On 8 October 1952 the Egyptian Council of National Production issued a decree authorizing preliminary steps toward construction of the High Dam.[4] Groups commissioned to undertake appropriate studies included Dr. H. E. Hurst and his associates who explored the hydrological aspects; Egyptian technical missions that surveyed possible sites for the dam; and the West German group, Hochtief and Dortmund, which drew up a preliminary plan on the basis of which the dam was finally built.[5] A committee of Egyptian engineers from the

National Production Council was granted authority over the project, and a board of international consultants was set up at the suggestion of the World Bank.[6] By late 1954 the projected site at Aswan had been approved and the feasibility of the project verified.[7]

The Free Officers had been led to expect that, once the Anglo-Egyptian dispute was settled, American aid would be forthcoming. Former World Bank head Eugene Black, after discussing the High Dam with Egyptian President Naguib in mid-1953, reportedly contacted President Eisenhower concerning the project. Eisenhower, who strongly favored improving relations with Egypt, agreed to look into the High Dam project "at the appropriate time."[8]

Shortly after the conclusion of the July 1954 Anglo-Egyptian draft agreement, a number of articles on the High Dam and its importance appeared in the Egyptian press. Apparently, this was intended to fan interest among potential sources of finance. In summer 1954 American participation in a new feasibility study[9] further encouraged the Egyptian government to hope that the United States, in fulfillment of its promises to aid Egypt, would in fact offer to finance this project. Instead, the United States chose to grant $40 million for secondary projects, while allocating only limited funds for another engineering survey related to the dam.

The notion that this tactic was to induce Egypt to yield to Western defense demands is supported by a memorandum of 23 April 1953 in which President Eisenhower stressed that American aid for the Aswan High Dam should be specifically given in compensation for Egypt's backing of Western policy in the area.[10] Meanwhile, the World Bank had investigated the possibility of investing in the scheme, and a favorable preliminary report entitled "The Economic Development of Egypt" was issued in August 1955.[11] Egypt, acting on its own initiative, allocated $8 million in order to extend roads and railway tracks to the future construction site.[12]

The American leadership renewed its interest in the High Dam project after the Arms Deal of September 1955 had produced a surge in Soviet popularity all over the Middle East. It was argued in the United States that if Egypt committed its economic resources to this gigantic project, it would be less able to buy additional arms from the Eastern Bloc. Internal development efforts would also divert Egyptian energy from its conflict with Israel and from rivalry with Iraq.

Once the World Bank's study mission issued its favorable report on the Egyptian project, Bank President Eugene Black claims he contacted the American government and suggested that the United States and Great Britain join the Bank in helping to finance the hard currency Egypt required for the project.[13] This time Black's suggestion was well received, not only because of the Arms Deal but also because of reports that the Soviet Union had now expressed its willingness to aid Egypt in this project.

Hints of this offer appeared in an October 1955 statement by Soviet Ambassador Solod and were echoed by the Egyptian Minister of Production. Ambassador Ahmed Hussein reportedly mentioned to Dulles that the Soviets might offer $200 million at 2 percent interest, to be repaid over a 30-year period. In November Solod was said to have framed the deal on a barter basis with repayment in cotton over a 25-year period; a much later report spoke of $600 million at 2 percent interest over a 50-year spread.[14]

The validity of these reports could never be verified, and the Soviet Union was shrewd enough to exploit their propaganda value without confirming or denying them. Salah Salem claimed the reports were true and that the "Soviet government had expressed an interest in this project" in May 1955. Heikal, who was probably one of the best placed Egyptians to know the truth, holds that a firm Soviet offer was never pending during the period in question.[15] The events discussed in the next chapter seem to bear out Heikal's view, which, however, was delivered ex post facto. Whether true or false, the sense of urgency these reports created on both sides of the Atlantic is a matter of record. According to Anthony Eden:

> The Soviet Government then made tempting overtures for the construction. They offered to build the High Dam on terms which were uneconomical and all the more attractive for being so. I did not want to see Soviet influence expand in Africa, and in November 1955 we discussed the threat of this with the United States Government and determined to persist.[16]

Back in October 1953, when the High Dam project had been discussed between American leaders and Egyptian Minister of Finance Abdel Galil El Umari, the latter reported:

> I have made contacts with the United States Government for the purpose of assistance in financing various Egyptian industrial projects; chief among them was the Aswan High Dam. All American circles have shown a positive response in this regard.[17]

However, the above statement was made shortly after a major breakthrough in Anglo-Egyptian negotiations. When these negotiations bogged down again during the winter of 1953 and the spring of 1954, Western European bankers were also sounded out.[18]

For its part, the Egyptian leadership indicated that it preferred Western aid despite the allegedly generous offer from the Soviet Union in October 1955. Nasser reportedly told Ambassadors Trevelyan and Byroade that his priorities for finance were first the World Bank, second the Western governments, third the Egyptian government alone, and fourth the Russians.[19]

A mission headed by the Egyptian Minister of Economy, Abdel Monein El Kaissouni, opened negotiations with World Bank President Eugene Black in Washington on 15 November 1955.[20] By early December, when American Under-Secretary of State Herbert Hoover, Jr., joined in the discussions, the estimated total cost of the High Dam project was $1.3 billion. Of the $400 million needed in convertible currency, Egypt requested $200 million from the United States and Britain together, plus $200 million from the World Bank; Egypt itself was to finance the remaining $900 million.[21]

Finally, on 17 December the United States and Britain jointly agreed in principle to aid in financing the Aswan High Dam:

> The United States and British Governments assured the Egyptian Government through Mr. Kaissouni of their support for this project. . .[and] would, subject to legislative authority, be prepared to consider sympathetically in the light of then existing circumstances further support toward financing the later stages to supplement World Bank financing. . . .Final understanding with the British and American Governments and the World Bank will await Mr. Kaissouni's consultation with the Egyptian Government.[22]

Grants of $54.6 million and $15.4 million were offered by the United States and Britain respectively[23] for the first stage of the High Dam construction, which was estimated to take 4 years and cost $70 million. These grants wre made on condition that the World Bank would lend Egypt $200 million, repayable over 40 years at 5.5 percent interest, to cover expenses during the second stage. The completion of the High Dam was estimated to require 8 to 10 years and the entire project between 15 and 18 years.[24]

Britain and the United States further promised to consider helping to find the balance of $130 million required in convertible currency for later stages of the project, although they were unwilling or unable to make a firm commitment at the time.[25] Since the World Bank loan was itself to be contingent on the availability of the total sum of foreign exchange required for the project, this reservation bred complications from the outset and raised the possibility that any one of the three parties—the World Bank, Britain, or the United States—could have the loan automatically canceled by withholding its assent to a final agreement.

It was clear that serious obstacles lay ahead. For the Egyptian leadership, which was ultra-sensitive to anything that could be interpreted as foreign interference in Egypt's internal affairs, acceptance of the terms of the World Bank's loan posed a thorny problem. As early as the October 1955 report by Eugene Black, the Bank had stressed that Egypt would have to adopt "sound methods of financing the project and rigorously adhere to sound fiscal and economic policy" in order to mobilize the necessary funds at home and abroad.[26]

One condition had the effect of limiting Egypt's power to conclude other economic agreements during the period of the loan, since it was reportedly stipulated that the Bank could proportionately reduce its own loan if Egypt secured another foreign loan or substantial suppliers' credit. Such a condition, if accepted, could also have been invoked to restrict Egypt's capacity to conclude further arms deals involving substantial loans.[27] Furthermore, the World Bank seemingly insisted on the right to supervise Egypt's economic policy. Each credit installment under the loan agreement was reportedly subject to the Bank's satisfaction with Egypt's economic situation in general and with progress on the construction work in particular.[28] These conditions, which in some respects resembled those set by the International Debt Commission in the 1870s, were seen by Egypt as constraints on its economic and even political independence.[29]

When Eugene Black returned to Cairo in February 1956 to discuss the matter personally with Nasser, the reasons for Egypt's reluctance to accept these terms were made explicit, and Black was told that the Bank's conditions appeared to impinge upon Egypt's sovereign rights. Moreover, Egypt wanted an absolute and irrevocable undertaking from the Bank, whereas the Bank's offer of a mere letter of intent apparently led Nasser to fear that the loan might be withdrawn half-way through the project.[30]

Nasser also declared his aversion to the conditions set by Great Britain and the United States. He preferred that these countries should turn over their quotas to the Bank, which would then be the sole party to deal directly with Egypt. In this way, the Bank, from which a loan was necessary for the second phase, would have been involved from the start, a factor that Nasser felt would have modified the political implications of the agreement.[31]

By 9 February a compromise had been reached concerning the degree of "control" the Bank was to exercise over the Egyptian economy. Black ceased to insist on "supervision" and agreed that the Bank should act in an "advisory" capacity; Egypt in turn was to keep the Bank informed of its economic situation. Black also agreed to lower the interest rate from 5.5 to 5 percent, and the idea of a letter of commitment was reportedly substituted for that of a letter of intent.[32] In addition Egypt accepted that:

> The Government's own contribution to the project will be provided in such a way as to avoid inflation and impairment of Egypt's credit worthiness. To this end, the Government and the Bank will reach an understanding on, and will periodically revise, an investment program which will recognize the priority of the High Dam Project and the need for adjusting total public expenditures to the financial resources which can be mobilized.[33]

A joint statement by the government of Egypt and the World Bank was issued on 9 February 1956 announcing that "substantial agreement had been reached concerning the basis of the Bank's participation. . .in the financing of the foreign exchange cost of the High Dam project, in an amount equivalent to $200 million."[34]

Other problems had still to be resolved. The conditions set by the United Staes and Britain required discussion, and Egypt duly responded in a *contre mémoire*.[35] Moreover, the requirement that Egypt reach an understanding with Sudan on the latter's rights to the Nile waters was becoming a highly delicate issue. Since the Sudanese elections in the spring of 1955, relations between the two countries had cooled and negotiations on the distribution of the Nile waters had bogged down on political and technical issues.[36] Both Sudan and Egypt insisted on their respective formulas, and when the Egyptian authorities charged that Sudan was injecting political factors into the discussions, the negotiations collapsed. At this point the Egyptian leadership apparently chose to leave matters as they stood until they had resolved still other seemingly intractable problems.

Meanwhile, the American administration was having troubles of its own. Although the necessary funds for the first phase of the High Dam project were already available under Mutual Security allotments for 1956, no executive authority existed at the time to earmark funds for later phases of the project.[37] Since American aid for the High Dam project called for a long-term financial commitment, the executive power to allocate these funds thus depended in part on congressional approval for future appropriations.

Efforts to convince a reluctant Congress of the need for long-term American commitments began soon after the announcement of the Anglo-American offer. In his State of the Union message to Congress on 5 January 1956, President Eisenhower asked to be granted "limited authority to make longer-term commitments for assistance to such projects, to be fulfilled from appropriations to be made in future fiscal years."[38] In defending this request before the Senate Committee on Appropriations, Under-Secretary Hoover asserted that "our help will largely fail in its appeal and effectiveness if it cannot be expressed in terms of major projects which can catch the imagination of the people." He assured the committee that "this project is taking no more aid than would otherwise be available for Egypt. That. . .is a very fundamental point."[39]

The debate occurred in a presidential election year, which rendered the administration especially susceptible to pressure groups opposed to the project. During the 26 January 1956 Senate Appropriations Committee hearing on the subject, the Southern cotton growers' lobby led the opposition of these groups, whose interests often overlapped. Since United States cotton met with difficulty in competing with superior quality, long-staple Egyptian cotton, this lobby feared that Egypt's cotton output would expand at the expense of American growers if the dam was built.[40] Despite government efforts to allay its fears, this group was to remain a major opposition force.

Also highly influential were the pro-Israeli groups that believed the United States should withhold aid from Egypt so long as Egypt refused to make peace with Israel.[41] This lobby apparently dismissed arguments concerning the long-term benefits of the High Dam project and the possibility that these would turn Egyptian attention inward to problems of economic development. Stressing the recent escalation in hostilities between Egypt and Israel, these groups echoed Israeli feelings that American aid for the dam would only bolster Nasser's prestige. According to Abba Eban, first Nasser had succeeded in concluding the Arms Deal; now, there was the dam: "He would dominate Jordan, Lebanon and everybody else. . . .Israeli influence, I will say quite frankly, was exercised against American support of the Dam."[42]

Strong opposition also came from the highly conservative, anti-neutralist members of Congress. Apart from professing a policy of "trade, not aid", this group interpreted developments in Egyptian foreign policy as pro-Soviet oriented. Led by Senator Knowland, these congressmen voiced the opinion of a large segment of the American population as well as that of the Pentagon.

The administration supported its proposal both publicy and behind the scenes. To convince the reluctant Senatorial Committee to grant the aid requested, Hoover warned that "the Egyptians are going ahead with this project. . .there is no question about that. If they do not do it with us, they are going to do it with somebody else."[43] This certainly referred to Soviet aid. Hoover also stressed the potentially stabilizing effects of the dam on Egypt.

Off-the-record discussions undoubtedly stressed the advantages that would accrue to the West if Egypt accepted the proposed terms. Quite apart from the popularity that aid for a project of this magnitude was certain to bring, the conditions on which it was to be granted made it possible to exercise indirect pressures on Egyptian policy during the lengthy period required for construction of the High Dam. Not only had the Western negotiators reserved the right to withhold any portion of the promised grants in "exceptional circumstances", but the definition of "exceptional circumstances" was virtually left to Anglo-American discretion. This was in addition to the Egyptian government's obligation to accept certain general conditions pertaining to the management of its economy.[44]

The implications were that Egypt would have to maintain its "best behavior" — according to Anglo-American interpretation — for the duration of the project, so that aid for the dam was in fact a means of curbing Egyptian activity hostile to Western interests in the Middle East. Should Egypt fail to "toe the line" despite these pressures, it could not count on obtaining the $130 million that the United States and Britain would still have to appropriate at a later date.

In short, the administration could easily have argued that Egypt's acceptance of the terms as proposed would have guaranteed a kind of cooperation between Egypt and the West that would significantly have benefited Anglo-American interests. Yet, the American Congress remained hesitant, as reflected in the Senate hearings on the issue, and was slow to recognize that aid of this kind had become a cold war exigency.

Had these congressional deliberations occurred in a vacuum, this reluctance to endorse a project about which Secretary of State Dulles was still enthusiastic as late as February 1956 might have been overcome. In reality, events in the Middle East and the global political arena were unfolding that would soon strain American-Egyptian relations as never before.

Any illusion the United States and Britain may have entertained that Egypt would adopt a more moderate attitude toward Western interests as a result of the loan offer were quickly dispelled during the Jordanian crisis of December 1955—January 1956. This crisis was precipitated when Britain, in conjunction with Turkey and Iraq, again set out to solicit Jordanian membership in the Baghdad Pact despite Britain's agreement with Egypt that no further attempt would be made to secure the adherence of other Arab states to that treaty.[45]

Among the voices raised against this move was that of British diplomat Humphrey Trevelyan. He holds that attempts to convince Jordan began in October 1955 against his advice. The Foreign Office reportedly informed him that Britain was not about to change its policy because of Nasser's objections.[46]

The British maneuver was prepared by a gift to Jordan of ten jet fighters, coupled with an offer of economic aid and of £11 million for the Arab Legion.[47] Turkey's President Bayar made a state visit to Amman in November reportedly to urge Jordan to consider joining the pact.[48] Iraq played its part by agreeing to aid Jordan in its development plans.[49]

British Chief of Staff General Gerald Templer was dispatched to Jordan in conjunction with the jet fighters. Despite official British denials that the purpose of Templer's visit was to pressure Jordan to adhere to the Baghdad Pact, it is a fact that Jordan's Prime Minister and four cabinet members resigned in protest against British attempt to do just that.[50]

The Templer Mission set off an internal crisis marked by the fall of three successive governments, widespread anti-pact demonstrations, and riots.[51] Shortly after his resignation Prime Minister El Mufti declared:

> I told General Templer as he arrived that the Jordanian people were against the Baghdad Pact. He answered me in English 'Don't worry'. I told him I would not consent to any forceful measures in this regard. . .I must state that the people of Jordan have every reason to be proud of their King, Hussein. For he too, . . .like me, was under British pressure to join.[52]

The turbulence subsided only after the Jordanian government pledged that it would not join the Baghdad Pact.[53]

The precise extent of Egypt's responsibility for the events in Jordan remains a highly controversial issue, even if Egypt's reasons for opposing Jordan's adherence to the Iraqi nucleus seem clear.[54] Radio Cairo broadcasts beamed at the Palestinians, who accounted for two-thirds of the Jordanian population, could easily have stirred up pre-existing hostility toward Britain and Iraq—the former blamed for the creation of Israel and the latter accused of treachery toward the Arab cause.[55]

Apart from the Palestinians, many government leaders and high-placed army officers were also opposed to the pact.[56] So were those segments of the non-Palestinian population that were receptive to the tenets of Arab nationalism.[57] Some of these elements may also have been influenced by Saudi Arabia, which had its own reasons for opposing Hashemite cooperation with the Baghdad Pact and which was even accused of massing troops on its border with Jordan.[58]

If the British leaders sought to placate Nasser's ire by making the High Dam offer in the midst of the Jordanian crisis, the tactic fell far short of its goal. Ten days after the Anglo-American announcement, Egypt and its Saudi ally offered to replace the British subsidy to the Jordanian army, then virtually headed by Lieutenant General Glubb Pasha, a British officer.[59] This offer, which was not to be accepted until 1957, further demonstrated the Egyptian desire to undermine British influence on Arab politics.

The two months that followed the initial Jordanian crisis proved to be a lull before the storm. On 1 March 1956 Jordan dismissed Lieutenant General Glubb Pasha and three other British officers from the Arab Legion. Although there is evidence that Glubb's dismissal was largely an internal decision,[60] Britain again insisted that Nasser was the principal instigator of the Jordanian action.[61]

Moreover, insult was added to injury because Foreign Minister Selwyn Lloyd happened to be in Cairo to confer with Nasser at the time of Glubb's dismissal. Lloyd was thus confronted by the jubilation of the Egyptian Press, which lauded "Nasser's victory over British imperialism." A few days later, in Bahrain, he was the object of anti-British demonstrations.

All this abruptly ended any modus vivendi with Egypt. Smarting from the loss of prestige and position it had suffered at the hands of the Arab nationalists, the British leadership regarded Nasser as the number one enemy of its Middle East interests. According to then Minister of State for Foreign Affairs, Anthony Nutting, these events—especially the dismissal of Glubb—were deemed intolerable by Prime Minister Eden.[62] From this point on the question of British aid for the Egyptian High Dam project became a dead issue, and most certainly, Britain's attitude influenced Secretary Dulles's own position.[63]

It has been seen that the American offer to aid Egypt was largely motivated by the desire to curb communist bloc influence in the region as part of America's global cold war strategy. A corollary of this thinking was that the large-scale aid at stake would induce Nasser to cooperate or at least not to interfere with United States policy. But these expectations were frustrated as Egypt grew even bolder in its attempt to exert itself as an independent neutralist leader.

According to Eugene Black, for example, Secretary Dulles hoped that the American offer of aid for the Aswan Dam would prod Nasser into using his influence to resolve the Arab-Israeli problem.[64] Robert Anderson was dispatched on a secret mission to both Egypt and Israel for the purpose of convincing the two countries to accept an American formula for terminating hostilities. Apparently, it was felt that if Egypt agreed to take the initiative, other Arab states would follow its example.

Nasser, despite his great popularity, declined to move in the desired direction. Perhaps he feared to undermine his leadership by making an unpopular decision of this magnitude, especially on a major rallying point for the Arab cause.[65] This and subsequent American attempts to defuse the Arab-Israeli crisis met with failure, in part because of America's own reluctance to commit its troops to guarantee the Arab-Israeli borders. Violence along these borders, especially on the Israeli-Egyptian border in April 1956,[66] kept increasing. This in turn strengthened the hand of pro-Israeli groups in America who opposed the Aswan Dam project[67] precisely at a time when Dulles's new policy of inducements had produced no visible impact on Egypt's attitude toward Israel.

Nasser's independent line was in no way confined to the Arab-Israeli question. Apart from his unrelenting attacks on the Baghdad Pact and Iraq, and his insistence that "the danger threatening the Middle East is not communism but Western colonialism,"[68] Nasser's dealings with communist countries expanded steadily.[69] Nor were these dealings limited to trade. In February 1956 it was announced that the Soviet Union had agreed to assist Egypt in establishing an atomic research program. By March a large number of Egyptian officers were being trained by the Soviet Union in Poland. Various Eastern Bloc delegations visited the High Dam site, reportedly for the purpose of assessing the feasibility of other projects that could be coordinated with the dam.[70] On 2 April Nasser claimed he was still holding a Soviet offer to aid in the construction of the dam itself.[71]

Of even greater significance for its relations with America was Egypt's attitude toward the People's Republic of China. China, the most populous country in the world, had entered the communist camp in 1949 despite United States support for the Chiang Kai-shek regime. The bitterness this produced was heightened by the Korean conflict, after which America did everything in its power to isolate this colossus. The American leadership was therefore dismayed to see that its offer of large-scale aid in no way diminished the growing Egyptian-Chinese cordiality that followed the Bandung Conference. Exchanges of all kinds became more frequent, a trade agreement was signed, and a Chinese trade fair opened in Cairo on 1 April 1956.[72]

Then on 16 May, Egypt became the first nation to recognize the People's Republic of China since the Korean War.[73] The Egyptian leadership offered the explanation that the possibility of an arms embargo by Britain, the United States and the Soviet Union had led it to recognize Communist China as an alternative source of arms.[74] In a speech on 19 May Nasser vowed that he would resist with all his force any foreign effort to limit the quantity of arms to Egypt; a Polish-Egyptian arms deal was announced the very next day.[75]

Nasser's recognition of Communist China shocked American public opinion and may well have been decisive in bringing about a reversal of American policy. The official reaction was given in Secretary Dulles's press conference on 22 May. It sounded the growing American weariness with Nasser and his policies:

> I expressed a regret of his action extending recognition to Communist China. I have also indicated that we are sympathetic with whatever action he

reasonably takes to emphasize the genuine independence of Egypt, and to the extent that he is a spokesman for Egyptian independence, we have sympathy with his point of view. . . .*But* to the extent that he takes action which seems to promote the interests of the Soviet Union and Communist China, we do not look with favor upon such action.[76]

But Dulles's warning had so little effect that Shepilov, then head of *Pravda* and subsequently Foreign Minister, was guest of honor at the Egyptian national celebration of the departure of the British troops in June.

This series of moves was bound to elicit a stern response from the United States. Conservative elements in Congress, headed by Senator Knowland, took the lead in stoking oppositin to the Egyptian High Dam offer.[77] The question now was no longer *if* the Western offer to aid Egypt would be maintained, but *how* the offer would be withdrawn.

In view of the final outcome, it is pertinent to consider why Egypt did not modify its approach toward the West despite its warm reception of the Western offer to finance the High Dam. As noted earlier, the terms of this offer did not bind the United States and Britain to finance the later stages of the High Dam construction. Since Egypt could have been exposed to discretionary decisions by these powers during the course of the construction, outright acceptance of the offer as made was extremely difficult. Indeed, Heikal reports that from the beginning:

> Nasser got the feeling that the Americans, through the size and expense of the project, thought that they could get a firm grip on Egypt and that the very duration of the project would give them time either to offset the growth of Soviet influence in Egypt or to topple him from power.[78]

The Egyptian leadership bargained for guarantees and may have intended to apply indirect pressure to obtain them. Egypt wanted the World Bank to serve as the direct administrator of the loans, which would be paid into the Bank by the United States and Britain. Nasser also wanted the financing of the project to be considered in its entirety, with the World Bank involved from the beginning and a minimum of risk that the fund would be discontinued.[79] In effect, Egypt was seeking a full and binding commitment to the project that would at the same time limit great power influence on Egyptian policy.

The Western powers were disinclined to accept the Egyptian formula and showed little understanding of Egypt's sensitivity to terms and conditions affecting its independence. Instead, America's leaders viewed Egypt's hesitation only as a Nasserian tactic in the game of playing one superpower off against the other in order to up the stakes. Secretary of the Treasury George Humphrey reflected the opinion of many American leaders by reportedly affirming that Egypt was holding the Western offer as an option while looking for a better one from the Soviet Union.[80]

Objective grounds did exist to support this interpretation. Nasser, inflated by his success in dealing with both the East and the West, may actually have thought that the United States and Britain would finally accept his terms. Besides, Nasser's very popularity had resulted from his independent stance toward the great powers and the need to maintain his image may have strengthened his resistance to the Western conditions.

The Egyptian attitude was also colored by the realization that Western enthusiasm for the project was waning. It was evident that the United States and Britain were stalling, especially since these countries had never responded to the Egyptian *contre mémoire* of February 1956.[81] If Nasser's own conduct contributed to this waning of interest, the tendency to dangle aid with no firm commitment certainly increased Egypt's reluctance to modify its approach to Middle East politics.[82] As the West appeared less and less likely to modify its demands on Egypt, Nasser became more determined than ever to prove that he would not yield to the dictates of any power concerning the direction of Egyptian policy. In short, the Aswan High Dam issue was lodged in a vicious circle of political actions and reactions that finally destroyed all hope that the promised aid would in fact be delivered.

As early as February 1956, the United States had begun to reconsider its offer of aid to Egypt.[83] By the end of May, according to Ambassador Henry Byroade, a decision was taken to reprogram the funds earmarked for the Egyptian project because they would not be needed during fiscal 1956.[84] While this decision was undoubtedly based on a review of Egyptian policy as a whole,[85] the timing suggests that Egypt's recognition of Communist China had settled the matter.

Even then, the decision was tentative, not final. It meant that Egypt's chances of receiving aid for the project in the immediate future were virtually nil. If the American leadership were to reverse its decision, the funds would depend on a fiscal year 1957 appropriation by a Congress that had grown very hostile toward Egypt. Loy Henderson states that the Chairman of the House Committee on Appropriations had emphasized to Dulles during a closed session that not a cent would be approved for the dam in Egypt.[86]

Moreover, during a private conversation between Dulles and Senator Knowland, as reported by then Under-Secretary George V. Allen, Dulles was reminded of the strength not only of anti-neutralist and pro-Israeli sentiments, but also of American cotton interests. Knowland allegedly declared that "we were forbidden under the aid program to go into projects which were primarily for the purpose of adding to the world supply of commodities already in very great over-supply." According to Allen, this conversation made an impression on the Secretary.[87]

In late June the Senate Appropriations Committee unanimously passed a resolution prohibiting the use of fiscal year 1957 funds for the Aswan High Dam. Dulles did not contest the right of the committee to take such a decision. On the contrary, he had notified the committee on 19 June that funds were no longer reserved for this purpose.[88]

Since this and other evidence suggests that Dulles had already decided to reprogram the funds by end May, it may be inferred that adverse congressional pressure was not his primary concern. Under-Secretary of State Herbert Hoover, Jr., and Ambassador Raymond Hare agree that Dulles had reached his own conclusion, namely, that "Egypt had disqualified itself."[89] Dulles then deferred to congressional pressures until presented with an appropriate occasion to make the American refusal known.

As will be seen, Nasser also appeared to have been searching for the proper moment to bring the issue to a head. In mid-July 1956, while attending a high-level neutralist conference in Yugoslavia, Nasser dispatched Ambassador Ahmed Hussein to Washington with instructions to convey Egyptian acceptance of the American offer.[90] Ambassador Hussein called on the Secretary of State on 19 July to deliver Egypt's message. This encounter was described by George V. Allen in the following terms:

> There was some preliminary chitchat. Then Hussein began by saying he was greatly concerned by the Russian offers and the expectations they raised. He eulogized the High Dam, emphasized Nasser's strength of vision, and said how he, Hussein, wanted the U.S. to do it. He showed that he realized we had problems. But he touched his pocket and said 'We've got the Soviet offer right in our pocket!'[91]

One reliable Egyptian source claimed that Hussein exceeded his mandate on this point. At any rate, it gave Dulles the cue he was waiting for, since Eisenhower had often declared that "the first person to say such a thing, he'd tell him to go to Moscow."[92]

Dulles is said to have replied in a kindly tone. He acknowledged that the United States had seriously considered the project and understood its importance. "But frankly," he said, "the economic situation makes it not feasible for the U.S. to take part. We have to withdraw our offer."[93]

The following official statement was immediately released to the press:

> Developments. . .in [recent] months have not been favorable to the success of the project, and the United States Government has concluded that it is not feasible in present circumstances to participate in the project. Agreement by the riparian states has not been achieved, and the ability of Egypt to devote adequate resources to assure the project's success has become more uncertain than at the time the offer was made. This decision in no way reflects or involves any alteration in the friendly relations of the Government and people of the United States toward the Government and people of Egypt. . . .[T]he United States remains ready to assist Egypt in its effort to improve the economic condition of its people and is prepared, through its appropriate agencies, to discuss these matters within the context of funds appropriated by the Congress.[94]

America's revocation of its offer voided the complementary undertakings by Britain and the World Bank according to the terms of the original agreement in principle. Britain chose to formalize this by announcing its own withdrawal the next day; the World Bank followed suit on 23 July.[95]

The abrupt manner with which Dulles revoked the American offer reflected a new approach toward Egypt. This was the "big stick" tactic, designed to punish the Egyptian leadership for its refusal to cooperate with the West. In the words of Dulles's biographer, J. K. Beal:

> The choice was between letting him [Nasser] down easily, through pro-tracted renegotiation that came to nothing, or letting him have it straight. Since the issue involved was more than simply denying Nasser money for a dam, a polite and concealed rebuff would fail to make the really important point. It had to be forthright, carrying its own built-in moral for neutrals in a way that the formula of applied propaganda would not cheapen.[96]

If Beal's explanation is valid, the notion that Dulles's abruptness was a spontaneous reaction to the Egyptian threat to accept a Soviet offer hardly stands up. On the contrary, the plain inference is that Secretary Dulles's reaction was a well-calculated riposte designed to set a "moral" example to any other country with leanings similar to those of Egypt.

The method chosen for the withdrawal may also be viewed as an act of political brinkmanship. The frequent reports that the Soviet offer to aid in the High Dam project was still valid seem to have prompted Dulles to call the Russian hand.[97] Dulles was aware of the large Soviet expenditures to quell growing unrest in Eastern Europe.[98] He also knew the cost of the High Dam project and was apparently skeptical of the Soviet Union's capacity, at least at that time, to grant a loan of the size required. Apart from the damage it would inflict on Nasser, Dulles's withdrawal of the American offer could thus have the added effect of placing the Soviet Union in a highly embarrassing position.

Of the many reasons put forward to justify the American move, two were mentioned in the official communiqué of 19 July 1956: the absence of agreement between Egypt and riparian states, and the uncertainty of Egypt's ability to "devote adequate resources to assure the project's success." Concerning the first, the American leadership reportedly maintained that Nasser had been using the lack of agreement with the Sudan as an excuse for delaying his answer on the Western offer.[99] But this was a specious argument in view of the new cordiality that characterized Egyptian-Sudanese relations after the Sudan became fully independent in December 1955. Indeed, Sudanese Minister of Communications Tewfiq, during a May visit to Cairo, spoke of a "new phase of mutual cooperation between Egypt and the Sudan." He ascertained that progress in negotiations between the two countries on the Nile waters heralded a favorable settlement.[100]

In querying Egypt's ability to sustain a project of such vast dimensions, the Americans implied that the economic situation in Egypt had deteriorated in the

period since the Western offer had been advanced. The fact that Egyptian indebtedness under the Czechoslovakian Arms Deal was finally valued at $280
million instead of the $80 million that had been incorrectly estimated by
American policymakers[101] was cited to support this argument. Eisenhower afterward revealed that, in his mind,

> the Egyptians could not simultaneously build up unwarranted defensive
> forces because if they did then the economy of Egypt which had to be dedi-
> cated almost entirely to this one project, could not support a strong military
> force. It was clear that if the Egyptians tried to re-arm extensively, out-
> siders would have to do the entire job of building the dam.[102]

In reality, Egyptian repayments for the Arms Deal were scheduled over a
twelve-year period at the rate of £E7 million annually.[103] Despite the size of these
figures, Eugene Black, after his June 1956 visit to Cairo, held that "there was no
deterioration in the Egyptian economy between November and the time that
Dulles called the deal off." Since this opinion was conveyed by Black to Dulles
during a conversation in June,[104] American allegations that Egypt had been
obliged to mortgage its cotton crop for the arms purchases also appear specious.

If Egypt's ability to finance its share of the High Dam project had in fact been
impaired since the original undertaking, much of the blame could have been
ascribed to America's own cotton policy. Less than two months after the initial
American offer was extended, a provisional lower quota on cotton imports to the
United States went into effect. This reduced the volume of American imports of
Egypt's main hard currency earner and made it expedient to assure that country
that the United States would avoid upsetting the world cotton market.[105] Yet this
did not stop Secretary of Agriculture Benson from announcing shortly afterward
that the United States intended to put (dump?) the federal surplus cotton on the
world market as of August.[106] The resulting fall in the world market price for
cotton cut deeply into Egyptian hard currency earnings, since Egypt could com-
pete with price-supported American surplus cotton only at a substantial loss in
income. This provoked an official Egyptian protest to the United States.[107]

Finally, in early July 1956, a drastic new American cotton quota lowered cotton imports to the level of 1939.[108] These restrictions seriously compromised
Egypt's ability to market its cotton, and by extension, that country's ability to
finance its part of the Aswan project. In ignoring America's own role in this sequence, the least that can be said is that the American policymakers lost sight of
cause and effect.

A further reason adduced for rescinding the offer was that the Aswan project
was too great an undertaking for Egypt to cope with. In discussing this aspect of
the matter with the press, Dulles drew attention to the fact that the project
called for twelve to fifteen years of austerity, that popular discontent was likely
to develop, and that the West would be blamed for the burdens that had to be
shouldered.[109] However, Dulles disregarded the fact that the huge scale of the

project had already been made known by Hoover during the January hearings.[110]

It was also objected that once the United States became involved in the project, it would probably be called upon to provide large, supplementary financial grants for other projects that would be needed to render the High Dam fully effective. In this vein Secretary of the Treasury George Humphrey pointed out that "the Aswan Dam in and of itself, while an expensive thing, would do nothing for the economy of Egypt, unless a lot more was also done."[111] Concerning the financing of ancillary projects, he pointed out that the United States was likely to find itself again competing with the Eastern Bloc and caught in a never-ending cold war competition.

President Eisenhower offered yet another explanation. He reported that the counterproposals Nasser had earlier submitted to Eugene Black indicated to Eisenhower that Nasser was not seriously interested in the project.[112] Whether this had in fact been a reason for American hesitation is difficult to ascertain, since the Western powers never replied to Nasser's *contre mémoire*. However, Nasser's July acceptance of the original terms of both the American and the British *aide mémoires* before the offer was withdrawn would seem to parry this argument. It, too, looks more like a pretext after the fact than a valid reason for the action.

If the declared justifications for the American move thus seem unconvincing, there is no doubt that the American leadership did have strong reasons for rescinding its offer. Of these, the single factor that most profoundly influenced Dulles's reasoning was Egypt's refusal to curb its relations with communist bloc countries. This is strikingly evident in the hardening of the American attitude toward a certain kind of neutrality that is "indifferent to the fate of others," an attitude that was singled out for reproach in statements by Secretary Dulles during June and July 1956.

Given the cold war global context, in other words, Egypt could hardly have expected the West to applaud its growing relations with the Eastern Bloc, its recognition of Red China, and its continued attacks on the Baghdad Pact and other Western regional interests. If aid on a huge scale was nonetheless to be bestowed upon such a "renegade", the American leadership could justifiably fear that America's loyal regional allies, which had committed themselves to the West, would perhaps reconsider their position.[113] Eden spelled this out with reference to Iraq:

> Already at the beginning of the year the Iraqi Government was complaining that the Egyptians had done better out of the West by bullying than they had by cooperating. . . .If there was to be charity, then friendly Arab countries had the right to apply. They could hardly be expected to view with enthusiasm the advance of large sums for an Egyptian project, while that country was becoming even more closely linked with Soviet Russia and while Egyptian propaganda was viciously attacking them and the United States.[114]

Dulles himself later put it this way: "Do nations which play both sides get better treatment than nations which are stalwart and work with us?"[115]

In this perspective Egypt's frequent insinuations that a Soviet offer of aid for the High Dam was still being considered seem especially to have influenced Dulles's choice of methods for revoking the American offer. For Dulles, this represented blackmail.[116] His abrupt withdrawal of the offer was probably intended to warn other nations besides Egypt that the United States would refuse to submit to the neutralists' tactic of playing off cold war rivalries to their own advantage.

The tenor of Egypt's immediate reaction suggests that it was not so much the canceled offer that stung as the manner in which it was accomplished. Indeed, there are strong grounds for believing that Nasser expected the offer to be withdrawn.[117] But the method chosen by Dulles was odious to Nasser and Egypt, especially the pointed and public questioning of the stability of the Egyptian economy by an American leadership that was guilty, in Egyptian eyes, of rendering its economic difficulties even more acute.[118]

On 24 July 1956 Nasser expressed his resentment in terms that vividly revealed the depth to which American-Egyptian relations had sunk:

> If an uproar in Washington creates false and misleading announcements, without shame and with disregard for the principles of international relations, implying that the Egyptian economy is unsound and casting shadows of doubt on Egypt's economy, then I look at Americans and say: May you choke to death on your fury.[119]

On 26 July, at the celebration of the fourth anniversary of King Farouk's abdication, Nasser responded to the "slap in the face" received from the West.[120] In a dramatic two hour and forty minute speech, he announced the nationalization of the Suez Canal Company, the revenue from which would henceforth be used to construct the Aswan High Dam.[121]

Notes

1. One feddan = 1.038 acres.

2. National Production Council, *Permanent Council for the Development of National Production*, (Cairo: 1955), p. 137, quoted in Wheelock, *Nasser's New Egypt*, p. 181.

3. *Sadd El Aali Report* of February 1955, pp. 12 and 20-21, quoted in Wheelock, *Nasser's New Egypt*, pp. 181-82; *Middle East News Agency*, 26 March 1955.

4. UAR, Ministry of Power, *The High Dam*. High Dam Public Relations Department, n.d., p. 17.

5. Wheelock, *Nasser's New Egypt*, p. 179; Love, *Suez: The Twice-Fought War*, p. 301.

6. This board was composed of five Americans, one Frenchman and one German. UAR, State Information Service. *Egypt's High Dam*, (Cairo, n.d.) p. 8. By April 1953 it had prepared the guidelines for the entire project. Wheelock, *Nasser's New Egypt*, p. 180. See *Report by the Board of Consultants on the Sadd El Aali Project*, November 1954 (Cairo: Misr Press, 1955) for construction

features. For World Bank President Eugene Black's comments, see *Dulles Oral History Collection*.

7. UAR, Ministry of Power, *The High Dam*, p. 20; the soundness of the project was verified by the Board of International Consultants. UAR, State Information Service, *Egypt's High Dam*, p. 8.

8. Black, *Dulles Oral History Collection*.

9. *Al Ahram*, 31 July and 25 August 1954.

10. See Memorandum by the President, 23 April 1953, quoted by Hugh Thomas, *Suez* (New York: Harper and Row, 1966), pp. 17-18.

11. Black, *Dulles Oral History Collection*.

12. Love, *Suez: The Twice-Fought War*, p. 301.

13. This contention diverged from that of Under-Secretary Herbert Hoover, Jr., who held that the idea of financing the project originated in Britain, *Dulles Oral History Collection*. However, George V. Allen, Under-Secretary for the Near East, South Asia and Africa, supported Black's allegation (ibid.).

14. *Le Journal d'Egpyte*, 11, 14, 18, 21 October and 21 November 1955; Salah Salem to Seale, *The Struggle for Syria*, p. 336.

15. Ibid.; Heikal, *The Cairo Documents*, p. 67.

16. Eden, *Full Circle*, 3: 468.

17. *Al Ahram*, 7 October 1953. See also Ali Sabri's comments, ibid., 20 June 1953.

18. Wheelock, *Nasser's New Egypt*, pp. 186-87.

19. Trevelyan, *The Middle East in Revolution*, p. 50. See also Ambassador Ahmed Hussein's comment to Dulles, New York Times, 18 October 1955.

20. *Egyptian Gazette*, 19 November 1955.

21. U.S. Cong., *Financing the Aswan*, p. 4.

22. U.S. Department of State, *Bulletin*, 26 December 1955, pp. 1050-51.

23. International Bank of Reconstruction and Development, *Loans, United Arab Republic (Egypt)*, September 1951-December 1959, Unpublished Board Reports. Love points out that Britain was offering to release blocked Egyptian sterling, which Britain had owed Egypt since World War II. *Suez: The Twice-Fought War*, pp. 302-3.

24. U.S. Cong., *Financing of Aswan*, p. 19.

25. See Hoover's statement that there was no existing authority to commit United States funds for later stages. *Financing of Aswan*, p. 7; Trevelyan, *The Middle East in Revolution*, pp. 50-51. According to Trevelyan, the Bank did receive secret letters from the United States and Britain promising that they would *find* the foreign exchange requirement for later stages.

26. Quoted in M. L. Cooke, *Narrer's Aswan Dam: Panacea or Politics?* (Washington D.C.: Public Affairs Institute, 1956), p. 13.

27. Trevelyan, *The Middle East in Revolution*, p. 50. The Egyptian press demonstrated awareness of this fact. See *Al Ahram*, 21 June 1956.

28. Trevelyan, *The Middle East in Revolution*, pp. 50-51.

29. According to Trevelyan, Nasser considered this condition political, practically calling for World Bank control of Egyptian finances. Ibid., p. 51.

30. Black, *Dulles Oral History Collection*; Heikal, *The Cairo Documents*, p. 60. For its own assurance in this matter, Egypt reportedly also expressed the desire that its agreement with the Bank be kept separate from the others. Trevelyan, *The Middle East in Revolution*, pp. 52-53. See also Wheelock, *Nasser's New Egypt*, p. 188.

31. Black, *Dulles Oral History Collection*; Trevelyan, *The Middle East in Revolution*, pp. 52-53.

32. Heikal, *The Cairo Documents*, p. 61.

33. Quoted in Love, *Suez: The Twice-Fought War*, p. 313.

34. International Bank of Reconstruction and Development, *Loans, United Arab Republic, September 1951-December 1959.* Unpublished Board Reports.

35. Black, *Dulles Oral History Collection*.

36. Wheelock, *Nasser's New Egypt*, p. 189. Mansoor, ed., *The Arab World*(3), 7 April 1955. See also Wheelock, *Nasser's New Egypt*, pp. 183-86.

37. See Hoover, in U.S. Cong., *Financing of Aswan*, pp. 7, 16. Also see Dulles's statement of 11

January, U.S. Department of State, *Bulletin*, 23 January 1956, p. 120.

38. U.S. Department of State, *Bulletin*, 16 January 1956, p. 82. See also Dulles's reference at a 11 January press conference, ibid., 23 January 1956, p. 119. He asserted that long-term projects offered the United States the chance to do things that have "a more permanent value."

39. U.S. Cong., *Financing of Aswan*, p. 2.

40. Ibid., pp. 10-14, 21-22. American cotton was protected by quotas and governmental purchases of surplus stock.

February 1956.

42. Eban, *Dulles Oral History Collection*. See also U.S. Cong., *Financing of Aswan*, p. 10; Adams, *Firsthand Report*, p. 246.

43. U.S. Cong., *Financing of Aswan*, pp. 5 and 16.

44. Trevelyan, *The Middle East in Revolution*, p. 50.

45. Trevelyan, *The Middle East in Revolution*, p. 56.

46. Ibid., p. 57.

47. Mansoor, ed., *The Arab World* (3), 5 November and 14 December 1955.

48. H. G. Martin, "The Soviet Union and the Middle East," *Middle Eastern Affairs*, February 1956, p. 53.

49. Mansoor, ed., *The Arab World* (3), 11 December 1955.

50. Ibid., 9 January 1956 and 14 December 1955. That the reason for the Templer Mission was to convince Jordan to join the Baghdad Pact is implied by Eden in *Full Circle*, 3: 341.

51. Mansoor, ed., *The Arab World* (3), 14, 16, 18, 19, and 20 December 1955 and 7 January 1956.

52. *Al Ahram*, 23 December 1955.

53. Mansoor, ed., *The Arab World* (3), 9 January 1955.

54. King Hussein insists that Nasser had agreed to Jordanian adherence and then turned against it (*Uneasy Lies the Head*, pp. 91-94). If this was the case, Nasser probably counted on internal Jordanian opposition to prevent Hussein from bringing his country into the pact.

55. Jordan's Prime Minister Samir El Rifai accused both Egypt and Saudi Arabia of using broadcasts to undermine the Jordanian internal situation. Mansoor, ed., *The Arab World* (3), 10 and 12 January 1956.

56. Ibid., 25 December 1955.

57. Benjamin Shwadran, *Jordan, A State of Tension* (New York: Council of Middle East Affairs Press, 1959), pp. 324-34.

58. Saudi Arabia was also accused of giving money to the opposition forces. M. Perlmann: "Egypt Versus the Baghdad Pact," *Middle Eastern Affairs*, March 1956, p. 25. For the charge of massing troops on its borders with Jordan, see Mansoor, ed., *The Arab World* (3), 27 January 1956.

59. Ibid., 26 December 1955 for reports of the initial offer. See also ibid., 23 January and 2 February 1956 for repeated offers.

60. King Hussein insists that he dismissed Glubb Pasha for the following reasons: Britain dominated Jordan through him; there was a question of double loyalties; a personal conflict between Glubb and King Hussein existed; his presence supplied the "communists" with a blatant example of colonialist imperialism; and, with the earlier crisis, King Hussein had become aware of the strength of the opposition. *Uneasy Lies the Head*, pp. 107-14.

61. See Eden's 7 March 1956 speech before the House of Commons quoted in *The Times*, 8 March 1956, and Eden, *Full Circle* 3: 347-50. Trevelyan reports that Foreign Minister Selwyn Lloyd was also of this opinion, and further recalls the full-scale attacks on Glubb by Radio Cairo (*The Middle East in Revolution*, pp. 65, 63).

62. Anthony Nutting, *No End of a Lesson* (New York: Clarkson N. Potter, 1956). Note that Radio Cairo was also attacking Britain over its positions in Kenya and Aden. Trevelyan, *The Middle East in Revolution*, p. 74.

63. France also began to view Egypt as a major regional antagonist. Not only had Cairo become the center of Maghrebi nationalist resistance forces, but Egypt was accused of supplying and training these forces. France's anti-Egyptian attitude certainly reinforced the argument of those opposed to American support for the High Dam project.

64. Black, *Dulles Oral History Collection.* See also Heikal, *The Cairo Documents*, p. 63.

65. Black, *Dulles Oral History Collection.*

66. Note that the Gaza Raid had been only the first of five major retaliatory raids on Egypt in 1955. See *Jewish Observer and Middle East Review*, 23 December 1955; reports in the *Egyptian Gazette*, 22 May 1955, 1 June 1955, 24 and 30 August 1955, 22 September 1955.

67. Eban, *Dulles Oral History Collection*; Adams, *Firsthand Report*, pp. 247-48.

68. Quoted by Pierre Rondot, *Orient*, no. 4, 1957, p. 94.

69. Washington reported that 33 delegations from communist countries had visited Egypt in 1955 and that already in the first three months of 1956, this figure had reached 30. Mansoor, ed., *The Arab World* (3), 3 June 1956.

70. *Le Journal d'Egypte*, 10 February 1956; the report about troops was made by the British Foreign Office and was confirmed by Egypt on 24 March. Mansoor, ed., *The Arab World* (3), 23 and 24 March 1956.

71. *Le Journal d'Egypte*, 2 April 1956.

72. See Egyptian-Chinese Trade Agreement, *Le Journal d'Egypte*, 2 March and 16 and 17 April 1956. Ibid., 2 April 1956.

73. Ibid., 17 May 1956.

74. See British-Soviet Joint Communiqué, *New York Times*, 27 April 1956. See also text of Soviet 17 April 1956 statement, *Middle Eastern Affairs*, May 1956, p. 193. See *Al Ahram*, 22 April 1956 and Nasser's 18 May speech, *Le Journal d'Egypte*, 19 May 1956.

75. Ibid., 20 and 21 May 1956.

76. U.S. Department of State, *Bulletin*, 4 June 1956, p. 920.

77. See Senator Knowland's comments during the January 1956 hearings. U.S. Cong., *Financing of Aswan*, p. 18.

78. Heikal, *The Cairo Documents*, pp. 59-60.

79. Trevelyan, *The Middle East in Revolution*, pp. 52-53.

80. Eisenhower, *Waging Peace*, p. 31.

81. Black, *Dulles Oral History Collection.*

82. Heikal claims that Nasser had been informed of the coming United States withdrawal of its offer by a high-level Iraqi delegate to the Baghdad Pact meeting of foreign ministers in April. Heikal, *The Cairo Documents*, p. 64.

83. Black, *Dulles Oral History Collection.*

84. U.S. Cong., *Hearings, 1957.* Note also the American decision in April to join the Economic Committee of the Baghdad Pact after having refused in February (*New York Times*, 19 April 1956).

85. Raymond Hare to the author.

86. Henderson, *Dulles Oral History Collection.*

87. Allen, *Dulles Oral History Collection.*

88. U.S. Cong., *Hearings, 1957*, pp. 23-34.

89. Herbert Hoover, Jr., *Dulles Oral History Collection*; Raymond Hare to the author.

90. *New York Times*, 18 July 1956; Love, *Suez: The Twice-Fought War*, p. 315.

91. Allen, *Dulles Oral History Collection.*

92. Ibid.

93. Ibid.

94. For complete text, see *Middle Eastern Affairs*, August/September 1956, pp. 198-99.

95. *New York Times*, 21 July 1956; Mansoor, ed., *The Arab World* (3), 23 July 1956.

96. J. K. Beal, *John Foster Dulles* (New York: Harper & Brothers, 1957), p. 260.

97. Ibid., p. 258.

98. Following Khrushchev's February 1956 anti-Stalinist speech, certain "revisionist" tendencies began to appear in Eastern Europe. This more nationalistic movement toward liberalization was brutally arrested by Soviet intervention to crush the October/November 1956 Hungarian uprising.

99. *L'Orient*, 8 July 1956.

100. Mansoor, ed., *The Arab World* (3), 9 May 1956.

101. *New York Times*, 21 July 1956.

102. Eisenhower, *Dulles Oral History Collection*.

103. Heikal, *The Cairo Documents*, p. 63.

104. Black, *Dulles Oral History Collection*.

105. U.S. Department of State, *Bulletin*, 16 July 1956, p. 114.

106. Mansoor, ed., *The Arab World* (3), 17 and 28 February 1956.

107. Ibid., 28 February 1956.

108. U.S. Department of State, *Bulletin*, 16 July 1956, p. 114. Cotton law signed by Eisenhower 6 July 1956, to take effect 1 August 1956.

109. U.S. Department of State, Press Release 184, 2 April 1957.

110. U.S. Cong., *Financing of Aswan*.

111. Humphrey, *Dulles Oral History Collection*.

112. Eisenhower, *Waging Peace*, p. 32. He seems to have been confused on the date, which was February.

113. Beal, *John Foster Dulles*, p. 257. Wheelock holds that Turkey, Pakistan, Iran, and Ethiopia were opposed to American aid to Egypt (*Nasser's New Egypt*, p. 195).

114. Eden, *Full Circle*, 3:421.

115. *New York Times*, 3 April 1957.

116. U.S. Cong., *Hearings, 1957*, p. 465.

117. In an interview with Kennett Love, Nasser held that he had informed Ahmed Hussein that "I am 100 percent sure that there will be no financing." Love, *Suez: The Twice Fought War*, p. 321.

118. Egyptian Minister of Interior Zachariya Mohieddin is quoted by Trevelyan as replying: "It is not so much the withdrawal of the money which we mind. We can find other ways of financing the High Dam. It is the way in which it was done" (*The Middle East in Revolution*, p. 55).

119. *Le Journal d'Egypte*, 25 July 1956.

120. See Nasser's statement to Love: ". . .What hurt me was the part in the statement about our economy. I regarded that as a slap in the face. Of course, they are at liberty to say Yes or No, but it must be said politely." Love, *Suez: The Twice-Fought War*, p. 334.

121. For text, see Foreign Broadcast Information Service, *Daily Report*, Foreign Radio Broadcasts, 27 July 1956. For an interesting account of the take-over procedures, see Love, *Suez: The Twice-Fought War*, p. 338-44.

7

Suez: The Hot and Cold Wars

The failure of the West to anticipate that Nasser, the "defiant and heroic leader of Arabism," might eventually respond in kind to the big stick used against him was a serious error of judgment. Dulles had, however, correctly foreseen one of the major problems that revocation of the Western offer would create for Nasser. This was the latter's need to seek an immediate agreement with the Soviet Union, whose ambiguous promises of aid both Egypt and the Soviets—for reasons of their own—had previously been reluctant to clarify.

It may never be known with certainty whether Nasser or his spokesmen had indulged in wishful thinking when they waved the red flag to soften Western conditions for financing the Aswan project. Even if they had, the propaganda value the Soviet Union had obtained by allowing this ploy to be used was so great that Nasser may well have reckoned the Soviets had reached a point of no return. In this case, any retreat by the West might have elicited a compensatory proposal from the Soviet Union.

The contradictory signals emitted by the Soviet Union in this period suggest that the Soviet leadership was embarrassed by the sudden earnestness of Egypt's plea. In December 1955 Soviet Ambassador Daniel Solod had actually singled out the Aswan Dam project;[1] but since the Western offer had already been made, this now appears to have been propagandistic bravado. In early April 1956 the Soviet offer, according to Nasser, was still "very general"; he added that "really we have not studied it."[2]

After Dulles reneged on the Western offer on 19 July 1956, Nasser's hopes were dashed when *Pravda* head (and future Foreign Minister) Shepilov announced on 21 July that the Soviet Union was not considering aid to Egypt for the construction of the High Dam.[3] On 24 July, Soviet Ambassador to Egypt Kiselev corrected the Shepilov denial and stated that the Soviet Union stood ready to aid Egypt in the project. Later that same day, however, the Kiselev statement was in turn denied by an attachè of the Soviet Embassy.[4]

Whether problems in Eastern Europe had brought about a reappraisal of the Soviet attitude toward the Egyptian project or whether a firm Soviet intention to help Egypt build the dam had not yet matured remains unknown. What seems clear is that Shepilov's announcement, besides embarrassing Egypt's leaders,[5] pushed them toward exercising a second option — that of financing the High Dam project from Egypt's own resources.

Among these resources, the Suez Canal stood out — potentially — as Egypt's single most important asset. The canal was operated by the Universal Maritime Suez Canal Company in which the British government owned a 44 percent controlling interest and private French citizens more than 50 percent. In 1955 the Company's revenue from the canal amounted to $100 million, of which Egypt received a mere 3 percent.[6] This alone shows that the Canal Company was a relic of Egypt's colonial past.

Even before the West revoked its Aswan offer, there was little question that the Company's concession to operate the canal, due to expire in 1968, would not be renewed.[7] In the meantime, so long as Egypt could count on Western aid for development, its leadership seemed disposed to accept a certain Egyptianization of the Company. Egypt had therefore requested more posts for its nationals, both as pilots and in management; a larger percentage of the Company's earnings; and a program under which the Company would reinvest part of its profits in Egyptian development projects. After much haggling, the Company merely agreed to invest £21 million in Egypt within the next few years on condition that it would continue to remain exempt from Egyptian exchange controls.[8]

This background suggests that the possibility of nationalizing the Suez Canal Company may well have been contemplated at a much earlier date, an hypothesis corroborated by the fact that preliminary feasibility studies were apparently undertaken some weeks before the final decision.[9] If so, nationalization may have been inevitable the moment it became clear that the West was no longer willing to aid Egypt in realizing the High Dam project: "We had been thinking about the Company for two and a half years," declared Nasser on 12 August 1956, "but the decision was taken after the announcement regarding the High Dam and financial aid."[10]

America's key NATO allies, Britain and France, considered Egypt's nationalization of the Suez Canal Company intolerable. At that time nearly one-fourth of Britain's imports passed through the canal; one-third of the total traffic through the canal was of British registry; and by far the most important consideration, a large percentage of the country's oil requirements depended on the canal.[11] Without British troops in the canal zone, the nationalization seemed to place British interests at the mercy of Egyptian whims.[12]

The psychological impact that nationalization produced on both the leadership and public opinion in Britain was all the stronger because of past clashes with Egypt and the successes of Nasser's anticolonialist policy. The June 1956 final withdrawal of British troops from the Suez Canal Zone had epitomized not only the waning of British influence in the region but even the very decline of the British Empire.[13] For many, including Prime Minister Eden and the conservative "Suez Group", Nasser's nationalization went too far. Accordingly, the major short-term objective of British policy in the ensuing crisis was to force Nasser to relinquish his control over the Canal Company. The long-term objective was apparently either to bring about Nasser's downfall or at least to limit his options in the future.[14]

As regards France, the protection of substantial French investments in the Canal Company was obviously a primary concern. That country's leaders also wanted Nasser to be dealt a severe lesson in the belief that this would undermine and demoralize the Algerian nationalist rebellion, which drew inspiration from Egypt's example. Indeed, France was even more ardently committed to a showdown with Nasser than Britain, and from the outset of the crisis the French leadership excluded no means to attain this end.[15]

Both Britain and France thus determined that Nasser's blow to their interests could not go unanswered. Eden made this clear to the American leadership right after the Egyptian nationalization:

> My colleagues and I are convinced that we must be ready, in the last resort, to use force to bring Nasser to his senses. For our part, we are prepared to do so. I have this morning instructed our Chief of Staff to prepare a military plan accordingly.[16]

Prime Minister Guy Mollet stated on 1 August 1956 that the French government had decided on an energetic and severe response.[17] France immediately made contact with Britain to coordinate plans for action.[18]

Two important considerations, however, prevented an immediate resort to force. The first was that military intervention would take time to prepare.[19] The second was the impact this move would have on the United States. Eden hoped that if Britain and France resorted to force to settle their score with Egypt, the United States would provide a nuclear umbrella balancing off the Soviet Union.[20] Their dependence on Middle Eastern oil also required the allies to ensure that America would provide alternative supplies in case of emergency.[21]

If the role the United States was to play during the crisis was of pivotal importance to Britain and France, it was to prove no less crucial to the interests of Egypt, their common antagonist. In order to understand this role and its effects on the evolution of American-Egyptian relations, it is first necessary to identify some of the principal factors that American decision-makers took into consideration.

One major worry was the presidential elections to be held in November 1956, which heightened sensitivity to the domestic political repercussions of Middle East issues. In stressing President Eisenhower's dedication to peace, the Republican platform exploited the fact that the Eisenhower administration had been credited with ending the Korean War. Hence expediency now dictated the avoidance of a commitment to any policy that threatened the use of military means, such as that proposed by Britain and France. The American posture throughout the first stage of the crisis was thus largely determined by the desire to defer the use of force by its allies, at least until after the elections. That the allies would comply with these desires was a conviction reportedly held at the highest State Department levels.[22]

A closely related factor was the American leadership's desire to keep the Anglo-French-Egyptian dispute over Suez sharply separated from the Arab-Israeli conflict. Fears that Britain and France would find a willing partner in Israel for a military solution to their problem only increased the administration's pre-election anxieties.

Apart from these domestic considerations, however, the American leadership apparently held that the direct interests of the United States were not greatly affected by Egypt's nationalization so long as the Suez Canal continued to function properly. American investments in the Canal Company were negligible, and this fact was mentioned by Secretary Dulles himself.[23] The United States had never deemed it necessary even to sign the 1888 Constantinople Convention, which set up the international regime of free navigation through the canal. If the Suez route shortened the distance from the Persian Gulf around the Cape to Europe by two-thirds, it cut merely two-fifths of the distance to the United States. In 1956, finally, a small percentage of domestically consumed oil originated in the Middle East, and an even smaller percentage was dependent on access to the canal.[24]

For all these reasons, the United States was "a bit astonished" but "not so alarmed as others were," to use President Eisenhower's own words. And the same theme was echoed in Secretary Dulles's statement of 28 August 1956: "The United States is not dependent to any appreciable degree at all upon the Suez Canal."[25]

Of greater concern to the American leadership were the parallels that could be drawn between the status of the Suez Canal and that of the Panama Canal.[26] The very fact that the issue of sovereignty in the one case had triggered a worldwide debate drew unwanted attention to the other and raised embarrassing questions about the colonialist type of control implicit in the traditional position of the United States in Panama. Every solution proposed for Suez had its drawbacks when viewed in relation to Panama. Should Egypt succeed in seizing the Suez Canal Company, this could incite the Panamanian government to attempt a similar action. Should Egypt allow an international control board to govern the operation of its canal, this could serve as a precedent for the Panama Canal. Moreover, if the idea of such a board were ever taken seriously, whether in Egypt or in Panama, the participation of the Soviet Union could hardly have been excluded.

Another external factor that was to influence the American leadership was a fear of the effects that its policy might have on world public opinion, and especially on the newly emerging Afro-Asian Bloc. Should the United States endorse its NATO allies in taking strong action against Egypt, it could appear that the Western powers were ganging up against a small nation. Many believed that only the Soviet Union stood to gain from the bad image this would foster. By the same token, the American leadership queried whether such action would not in fact enhance Nasser's international prestige as the martyr hero of strongarmed colonialist methods rather than weaken his charismatic appeal, as Britain and France intended.[27]

The American leadership nonetheless seemed to believe that Britain and France would be more prone to yield to its pressures for a negotiated settlement[28] if they felt that the American government did not rule out the use of force should all else fail. Besides, the possibility that force might be used gave America's allies added leverage in seeking concessions from Egypt through negotiations. Dulles is reliably reported to have endorsed this tactic despite his protestations about Egyptian blackmail at the time he withdrew the Aswan offer.[29]

All this helps to explain why the United States carefully refrained from taking an unequivocal stand against the use of force. But this reticence only increased the ambiguity of the American position and allowed those who had opted for military intervention to indulge in false hopes about what that position would ultimately be.

The many heterogeneous factors the American leadership felt it had to reconcile made it less likely than ever that a well-defined and coherent policy would be formulated. As usual in its dealings with the Middle East, the want of a policy inclined the same leadership to respond with ad hoc adjustments to each new situation that arose. This time the primary tactic was to draw the issue out so that tempers and tensions might be calmed — at least until election day — without appearing either to condone Egypt's action or to abandon America's allies.[30] The means chosen were a series of proposals for bringing the issue before a specially created international forum where Britain, France, and Egypt could hopefully be persuaded to accept some form of compromise.

During the early weeks of the crisis, official American declarations stressed United States opposition to Nasser's action. Ringing with apprehension, a State Department announcement on 27 July 1956 proclaimed America's intention to work with other affected nations to remedy the situation. In a display of unity with his allies, Dulles attended the London Foreign Ministers' Conference, at which a joint Anglo-French-American declaration was issued on 2 August that spoke of an identity of interests. This declaration deplored the potentially disruptive nature of Egypt's action and drew attention to the "freedom and security of the canal" as guaranteed by the 1888 Constantinople Convention. Insisting that the "operating arrangements under an international system" should be re-established, the United States joined its allies in convoking an international conference of the canal users to take the appropriate action.[31]

However, in other declarations made during this period the United States began to differentiate its position from that of its allies. For example, the latter had argued that the Suez Canal Company was either a French corporation or a transnational entity, whereas the American leadership did not question Egypt's legal right to nationalize the Company as such. This was later recognized by Eisenhower, who declared that Egypt possessed such a right because the Canal Company was privately owned,[32] even if the problem of compensation had yet to be settled. Eden dismissed this view in a telegram to Eisenhower on 27 July: "We shall not allow ourselves to become involved in legal quibbles."[33]

For Dulles, the principal legal question was Egypt's ability or willingness to maintain free passage through the canal as guaranteed by the 1888 Constantinople Convention. He declared that if the nationalization of the Company "affected the operation of the canal itself, that would be a matter of deep concern to the United States. . . ." A strong case could then be made to justify enforcement action by the canal users.[34]

President Eisenhower made the following statement at a meeting of the National Security Council on 9 August:

> If Nasser were to prove (1) that Egypt could operate the canal and (2) would indicate an intention to abide by the treaty of 1888, then it would be nearly impossible for the United States ever to find real justification, legally or morally, for the use of force.[35]

To maintain his leadership in the situation, Dulles tried to coordinate the American position with that of Britain and France despite the differences below the surface. The common posture called for placing the operation of the Suez Canal under an international authority that would be insulated from the politics of any one country. To this end the allies had been persuaded to join the United States in calling an international conference to establish a control board for the canal.[36] The United States also followed its allies in freezing Egyptian and Canal Company assets.[37]

In comments to American congressmen, Dulles took credit for having convinced the allies to follow his lead.[38] This fits in with the strategy of "buying time" attributed to Dulles by Under-Secretary Robert D. Murphy:

> Alternatives, with the delay, buying time, during which you could hope that, well, the government [in Britain, France and Egypt] might fall, a new government might come in, you might have a totally different constellation to deal with. . . .He [Dulles] was maneuvering to produce a peaceful solution. . . .[39]

In reality, Britain and France may have seconded the idea in order to buy time for their own military preparations. These were estimated to require about six weeks for Britain and perhaps even longer for France, whose forces were tied up in the Algerian conflict.[40]

Paralleling Dulles's attempt to find a peaceful solution that might be satisfactory to America's allies, an intense effort was made to convince Britain and France of the "unwisdom even of contemplating the use of military force at the moment."[41] This opposition to the use of force was conveyed through various channels. In exchanges with Eden the American leadership pointed out that world public opinion would be more favorable if the Suez issue was aired before an appropriate international forum; the need to exhaust all peaceful means of reaching a settlement was stressed.[42]

"Initial military success might be easy, but the eventual price may become far too heavy," warned Eisenhower. "We do not want to meet violence with violence", declared Dulles after the London meeting. And he officially denied having given any "commitments at any time as to what the United States would do should the proposed international conference fail."[43]

In view of these and numerous other official and unofficial statements of the same tenor, the assertions by then leading British officials that the United States had led its allies to believe that it would support, or be benevolently neutral to, a military venture against Egypt if peaceful methods failed must be evaluated with caution. Anthony Eden bases this charge on a comment allegedly made to him by Dulles at a private meeting during the Foreign Ministers' Conference in London. According to Eden, Dulles said that "a way had to be found to make Nasser disgorge what he was attempting to swallow."[44] Eden later commented that these words "rang in my ears for months." Although he had recognized the cool and hesitant reception the State Department gave to the British case for force, he nonetheless insisted that Dulles had led him in this way to believe that Britain could count on the United States if force became necessary as a last resort.[45]

It may be argued that Eden misinterpreted Dulles's words to suit his own purpose and thereby chose to ignore the numerous American statements clearly opposing the use of force. But it seems just as likely that Dulles did in fact hold out the possibility that the United States *might* accept force under certain conditions in order to persuade Eden to approve the idea of an international conference and thus to gain precious pre-election time. In either case, Eden's contention and evidence points to the deeper—and probably desired—ambiguity that shrouded America's real intentions despite the surface clarity of its position.

This ambiguity, which followed from the American leadership's inability to arrive at a well-defined policy, may be said to have served its purpose at this early stage of the crisis. By securing the agreement of Britain and France to bring the issue before a carefully contrived international forum, Dulles apparently succeeded in postponing the use of force while gaining the time he needed. It also increased the chances that the crisis would gradually subside. As he himself stated, ". . . the more time that there is, the more people will be thinking of alternatives."[46] In the bargain he had also issued a stern warning to Nasser that Egypt would be held responsible for any disruption of the canal operations whether through inefficiency or arbitrary acts.

In short, the ambiguity that was an integral part of the ad hoc approach to the crisis seemed to give the United States exactly what it desired: a measure of control over all the parties that needed American support. But the Egyptians, who watched this maneuvering from the wings, were the first to warn that these calculated risks might in the end cause the American leadership to lose altogether control of the situation.[47]

The First London Conference convened on 16 August 1956 with the declared purpose of fostering an agreement by the major users of the Suez Canal to a system of international control that would withstand the political pressures of single nations. For the United States, this Conference appeared to offer a means of internationalizing the Suez dispute that would limit the scope for independent action by its allies against Egypt. Besides allowing the American leadership to gain time, it led to the formation of a group of nations whose common interests strengthened the pressure brought to bear on Nasser.

However, the formula adopted by the United States, Britain, and France for selecting the countries to participate in the Conference was based only in part on the 1888 Constantinople Convention, even though this treaty was the basic legal document to be discussed. A review of the list of invitees as tabulated below suggests that the selection criteria were instead biased in favor of countries identified with the Western Defense System:

Signatories to Constantinople Convention	Main users (by tonnage)	Dependent users
United Kingdom[D]	Norway[D]	Australia[D]
The Netherlands[D]	Germany, Fed. Rep.[D]	Iran[D]
Spain[D]	Denmark[D]	Ethiopia*
France[D]	Sweden*	India[N]
Italy[D]	United States[D]	Indonesia[N]
U.S.S.R.[E]	Greece[D + R]	Ceylon[N]
Egypt[R + N]	Japan*	New Zealand[D]
Turkey[D]	Portugal[D]	Pakistan[D]

D   Western Defense.
E   Eastern Bloc.
N   Afro-Asian Neutralists.
R   Refused to attend.
*   Other.

Source: Based on U.S. Department of State, Bulletin, 13 August 1956, p. 263.

If all the signatories to the original Convention had been invited to attend, other Eastern Bloc countries besides the Soviet Union would have been on the list. As it was, the chosen formula[48] included eight signatories to the Convention; eight principal users of the canal (in terms of tonnage) that were not part of the first group; and eight nations with "special dependence" on the canal that did not fall within the other two categories. Given the global political configuration at the time, it is clear that an automatic majority in favor of the Western powers was assured.

Nasser, in declining Egypt's invitation to participate, explicitly objected to this bias:

> The Egyptian Government is most surprised that Britain decided to call a conference in order to discuss the Suez Canal, which is an inseparable part of Egypt, without consulting the Egyptian Government, who is directly concerned in the canal. The British Government alone decided to invite the twenty-four governments to attend this conference, fully aware that forty-five countries used the canal during 1955. Therefore, the Egyptian Government is convinced that this conference and the circumstances in which it was called cannot be regarded in any way as international and it is not entitled to take decisions.[49]

Nasser proposed that Egypt join with *all* the signatories to the 1888 Constantinople Convention (which excluded the United States) in sponsoring a conference to which *all* the nations then using the canal would be invited. The declared purpose of this conference would have been to conclude a new treaty that would reaffirm and guarantee freedom of navigation through the canal.[50]

The treaty proposed by Nasser would thus have covered, at least in principle, the very legal point that Dulles himself had insisted the Egyptians should observe. As to the question of sovereignty, Nasser's proposal, like the American *obiter dicta* on the subject, took the right to nationalize the Canal Company for granted. Despite these parallels, the United States joined Britain and France in refusing either to compromise on, or to make use of, the Egyptian formula in devising their own. This reinforces the inference that the chief interest of these nations was to bring together a group likely to favor their own solution to the problem.

The role of the American Secretary of State was paramount at the London Conference. His proposals served as the basis of discussion and a resolution substantially incorporating them was adopted on 23 August 1956 by an 18-nation majority. It called for the creation of an international board that would operate the Suez Canal and guarantee the respect of Egyptian sovereignty at one and the same time. A committee of five nations—Australia, Ethiopia, Iran, Sweden, and the United States—was formally dispatched to Cairo to induce Nasser to negotiate on the basis of this resolution.[51]

Later revelations indicate that in submitting these proposals Dulles was motivated more by the aim of keeping his allies under American control than by any conviction that an international control board was imperative. In exchanges between Dulles and Eisenhower during the conference, the latter pointed out that acceptance of the proposals under discussion would be impossible for Nasser. Eisenhower was then probably aware of Nasser's own statement on 12

August 1956 that the system under consideration amounted to a form of "collective colonialism."[52]

In a cable to Dulles on 19 August, Eisenhower suggested in effect that the Indian proposal, which called for an international board to *supervise* rather than to *operate* the canal, would be a more acceptable solution. The minority Indian plan was supported by the Soviet Union, Indonesia, and Ceylon.[53] Dulles's reply the next day stressed the importance of British and French agreement and disclosed the real intentions behind his proposals: "I doubt whether we should make at this stage concessions which we might be willing to make as a matter of last resort in order to obtain Egypt's concurrence."[54]

Once Britain and France were persuaded to negotiate, Dulles had in fact begun to weaken the force of the conference decisions even before the conference started. For example, on 6 August Dulles indicated that, should the participants fail to restore international control over the canal, the United States intended to resort only to further economic pressure on Egypt — not armed methods.[55] In this way, Dulles showed how anxious he was to avoid giving his allies a pretext for resorting to force if Nasser rejected a resolution adopted by the London Conference. This attitude, which begged the key question of enforcing any such resolution, became still more evident later on when Dulles further retreated by acknowledging that decisions should not be imposed "on those who do not agree" nor should an ultimatum be delivered to Egypt.[56]

So reluctant was Dulles to give the impression that the Western powers had joined forces against Egypt that he refused even to participate in the five-nation committee dispatched to Cairo by the London Conference.[57] Loy Henderson was sent in his place, and the mission was headed by Australian Prime Minister Robert Menzies.

On the eve of the mission's departure to Cairo in the first days of September 1956, statements by both Eisenhower and Dulles forestalled any attempt by Britain and France to present the conference proposals as a final offer to Egypt. In this vein, Eisenhower declared on 30 August:

> For ourselves, we are determined to exhaust every possible, every feasible method of peaceful settlement. . . . I am very hopeful that this particular proposal will be accepted *but*, in any event. . .even if we do run into other obstacles, we are committed to a peaceful settlement of this dispute, nothing else.[58]

Dulles, at a press conference a few days earlier, had reiterated the secondary importance of the canal to the United States:

> Now, the question of what arrangements about operations would be satisfactory is not primarily a question for the United States to answer. The United States is not dependent to any appreciable degree at all upon the Suez Canal.[59]

The Menzies Mission held a series of meetings with Nasser between 3 and 9 September 1956. To Menzies's credit, it must be said that this mission had neither inducements to offer Egypt nor a mandate to negotiate on the terms of the resolution as they stood. These terms could hardly have been accepted by Egypt without loss of face.

On the debit side, Menzies's own conduct, as described by Heikal, was anything but diplomatic. According to Heikal, the discussion broke down when Menzies threatened Nasser: "Mr. President, your refusal of an international administration will be the beginning of trouble."[60] Nasser refused to negotiate further, the discussions broke down on 9 September, and the committee left Cairo.[61]

Loy Henderson relates that Washington had not wanted the mission to be used to threaten Egypt. Henderson claims that he frequently counseled Menzies against making harsh statements lest the negotiations break down.[62]

Menzies later blamed the failure of his mission on Eisenhower's statement of 30 August.[63] Nasser was perfectly aware of the American leadership's statements excluding the use of force. According to Heikal, Nasser even greeted one of Eisenhower's declarations of this kind with the remark: "That man puzzles me; which side is he on?"[64] Heikal agrees with Menzies in holding that the mission was "doomed" to fail because of these and related statements.

As soon as the failure of the mission became known, the American leadership set out to deter its allies from using this failure as a *casus belli*. Commenting on the Egyptian rejection of the conference proposals in a September statement, Dulles carefully noted that the rights of the canal users should continue to be pursued in a manner consistent "with the spirit of the United Nations' Charter."[65]

The next day the Suez Canal Company announced that it would withdraw British and French pilots as from 15 September.[66] By then Britain and France were presumably prepared for enforcement action should Egypt have proved unable to manage the canal as they expected.

Eisenhower replied by stressing the American aversion to force more firmly than ever:

> This country will not go to war ever while I am occupying my present post unless the Congress is called into session and Congress declares such a war. . . .We established the United Nations to abolish aggression and I am not going to be party to aggression if it is humanly possible. . .to avoid [it] or I can detect it before it occurs.[67]

This statement clearly indicated that the United States would, at that time, regard armed action by its allies as "aggression". The same message was implicit in the fact that the United States was the only NATO country that declined to send its Foreign Secretary to a 5 September NATO meeting in Paris called to discuss the Suez crisis. Reportedly, the reason given was that America wished to avoid creating the impression that the Tripartite powers were "ganging up" against Egypt.[68]

As for the allies, even before the Menzies Mission left for Cairo, Eden had contemplated its failure and what this would entail. Loy Henderson declared that before setting out on the mission he was told by Eden: "I would prefer. . .to see the British Empire go down fighting, than to sit quietly by and watch us disintegrate."[69]

Eden informed the American leadership of the Anglo-French intention to bring the Suez issue before the United Nations. The meaning of such a move was evident to the American leaders.[70] In the United Nations Security Council, a Soviet veto of any Anglo-French draft resolution on this matter was a foregone conclusion, which would mean that the Security Council could not take action on the matter. France and Britain, having fulfilled their obligations under the United Nations Charter, would then have been able to plead that all pacific means to resolve the crisis had been exhausted.

Dulles's immediate reaction was to formulate another plan designed to keep negotiations going between the parties to the dispute. The new plan, as finally evolved, called for the formation of an international association of canal users that would maintain and manage the canal, hire the pilots, and thus control its operation.[71] This group was to be known as the Suez Canal Users Association (SCUA).

Britain and France, divided between recourse to the United Nations in opposition to American wishes and acceptance of the new proposal, yielded to American pressure on 10 September. Britain, according to its Chancellor of the Exchequer, put off going to the United Nations because "American support is so important—especially in the financial field."[72] In compensation, SCUA could have been used to justify taking control of the canal in order to maintain free passage should that prove expedient.[73]

As soon as the American leadership obtained the allies' acceptance of its second scheme, the administration once again began to dispel any idea that it envisaged forcing Egypt to submit to this proposal. At a 13 September press conference, Dulles described the projected association as a "prudent precaution". He rejected the notion that, should Egypt refuse to accept SCUA, the latter intended to boycott the canal; and he asserted that "we do not intend to shoot our way through [the canal]." Nevertheless, he added ambiguously that "each nation had to decide for itself what action it will have to take to defend and, if possible, realize its rights which it believes it has as a matter of treaty."[74]

That Dulles's chief objective was again to prolong the negotiations is evident in his comment to Administrative Assistant Emmet Hughes that he "did not know anything to do except keep improvising."[75] Since there was little doubt that Nasser would refuse to cooperate with SCUA unless forced to do so—and force was ruled out by the American leaders—the projected new scheme seemed another makeshift adjustment to avoid a dangerous impasse. This inference is supported by Under-Secretary Robert D. Murphy's later comment:

If John Foster Dulles ever was actually convinced of the possibility of organizing a Canal Users Association to operate the Suez Canal, I was not aware of it.[76]

On 15 September Nasser duly announced Egypt's refusal to cooperate with SCUA:

We shall not allow the Western-proposed Canal Users Association to function through the canal. We Egyptians shall run the canal smoothly and efficiently and if, despite this, the Canal Users Association forces its way through the Suez Canal then it would mean aggression and would be treated as such.[77]

Once British and French pilots were withdrawn, Egypt proved that it could keep the canal operating effectively. Grounds for enforcement action under the 1888 Convention were thus removed. From this point on it became obvious that the real issue for Britain and France was Nasser and not the Suez Canal.

The Second Plenary Session of the Suez Canal Conference gathered in London on 19 September to discuss the SCUA proposal, with the eighteen supporters of the earlier resolution in attendance. Now differences between the American perspective and that of its allies came increasingly into the open. One revealing problem was the American reluctance to oblige its ships to pay tolls to SCUA, chiefly because Dulles wished to avoid an incident should Egypt refuse passage to nonpaying vessels. Such an incident would have offered Britain and France the awaited opportunity to "smash Nasser".[78] At length, the State Department agreed to ensure payment of tolls by ships under American registry, but it declined to apply this rule to American-owned vessels under foreign registry.[79] In fact, American ships never stopped paying tolls to the Egyptian Canal Authority.[80]

Another example of the American leadership's lack of zeal was its refusal to block both new and private Egyptian assets in the United States. Moreover, while the State Department advised against the employment of American canal pilots by the Egyptian Canal Authority, no legal restrictions were imposed, and some ten pilots were so employed.[81]

The divergence between the American approach and that of its allies, who were determined to force SCUA on Egypt if necessary, became crystal clear in Dulles's press statement of 2 October:

The United States cannot be expected to identify 100 percent either with colonial powers or the powers uniquely concerned with the problem of getting independence, as rapidly and fully as possible. There were, I admit, differences of approach by the three nations to the Suez dispute, which perhaps arise from fundamental concepts. For while we stand together. . .any areas encroaching in some form or manner on the problem of so-called colonialism, find the United States playing a somewhat independent role.[82]

Commenting on SCUA, he declared: "There is talk about teeth being pulled out of the plan, but I know of no teeth in it."[83] Dulles thus specifically linked the canal issue to the larger problem of colonialism; revealed his sensitivity to Third World opinion; and weakened the threat of force in relation to SCUA that America's allies had tried to render credible.[84]

The American position, coupled with Egypt's a priori rejection of SCUA, showed the allies that there was even less chance of implementing Dulles's users' association now than when the Menzies Mission had been undertaken. Eden, who had used the time Dulles sought to gain for more ominous purposes of his own, was fed up: "American torpedoing of their own plan. . .left no alternative but to use force or acquiesce in Nasser's triumph."[85]

After the conference, Britain and France decided — against American opposition — to go through the motions of appealing to the United Nations. Their proposal that an international board should operate the canal received the expected Soviet veto on 13 October.[86]

Whether, at this point, the American Administration was unaware of the gravity of the situation or chose to ignore it cannot be ascertained. Efforts to encourage peaceful exchanges between the governments of Egypt, Britain, and France were now pursued through the good offices of United Nations Secretary-General Hammarskjold.[87] Despite knowledge of advanced military preparations by Britain, France, and Israel, Dulles sounded a note of optimism as late as 27 October in the belief that no action would be taken before the elections in November.[88]

Describing the American role in the Suez crisis as an instance of "waging peace", Dulles reviewed the six "peace efforts" so far undertaken: (1) his initial trip to London in early August; (2) the First Session of the London Conference; (3) the Menzies Mission; (4) the Second Session of the London Conference; (5) recourse to the Security Council; (6) the private and informal conversations between Britain, France, and Egypt. He foresaw that "effort number seven" would be the continuation of these private and informal exchanges.

Instead, information from the allies suddenly ceased to arrive in mid-October. "It's darned funny," observed Dulles to Under-Secretary Murphy, "We haven't heard anything from the British or French for two weeks. I wonder what they are up to. . . ."[89] When the answer came, Dulles found that he had in fact lost control of the situation, just as the Egyptians predicted in early August 1956.[90]

A more thorough examination of the Egyptian position during this period of intense diplomatic activity is now in order. For the Egyptian leadership, the chief objective was to maintain its acquisition of the Canal Company against the opposition of Britain and France. Because Nasser realized that he needed the United States to mollify its allies, Egypt found it expedient to temper the hostility manifested immediately after Dulles withdrew the American offer of aid for the Aswan Dam. Although Egypt knew it could count on the Soviet Union and the Afro-Asian Bloc to support its nationalization of the Canal Company,[91] the potential ability of the United States to restrain Britain and France from resorting to force was signaled by the American leadership and could hardly be ignored.

The American government had early indicated that one key to its attitude concerning the use of force would be Egyptian assurance of an uninterrupted flow of traffic through the canal. Accordingly, Egypt endeavored to prove its ability to operate the canal efficiently. In a 31 July announcement Nasser asserted that nationalization in no way affected Egypt's international obligations regarding freedom of navigation through the canal as guaranteed by the 1888 Constantinople Convention. In addition, the Egyptian government announced on 6 August that a large part of the revenue from the canal would be reinvested for its improvement and upkeep.[92]

Actions that might be deemed provocative were carefully avoided. For example, the foreign community was protected by the Egyptian government against local manifestations of hostility. Foreign canal pilots, though encouraged by generous offers to continue their work, were allowed to leave at will. Even ships that refused to pay tolls to the Egyptian Canal Authority were allowed to pass through the Canal.[93]

However, the American position as a whole was far from clear to Egypt. While the United States dominated the various negotiations with elaborate proposals and plans that were uniformly unacceptable to Egypt, the American leadership declared its unwillingness to back strong-arm measures to ensure implementation. In these circumstances, the half-hearted economic measures taken by America against Egypt[94] could further have indicated nominal rather than genuine commitment to the policy of its allies.

Part of the ambiguity may have derived from reactions by the United States to Egypt's own remonstrances. The time sequence between certain stern Egyptian protests against the American stance during this period and the corresponding demonstrations of American moderation toward Egypt are such as to suggest a causal relation. For example, on the eve of the departure of the Menzies Mission, Nasser's personal protest to the American Ambassador to Cairo appears at least partly responsible for Eisenhower's pacifying statement of 31 August. A similar relation seems to exist between a 13 September warning to Dulles by the Egyptian Ambassador in Washington that forcible implementation of the SCUA scheme was tantamount to a declaration of war and Dulles's official denial, later that same day, that the United States intended to allow SCUA "to shoot its way through the canal".[95]

The explanation is not likely to be found in any real American desire to appease Egypt. Rather, Egypt's warnings showed the United States how potentially grave the situation was becoming, and the American responses appear to have been primarily aimed at keeping the allies from finding some pretext for military intervention. Egypt was thus increasingly reassured by the high-level statements that the United States would not readily join its allies in armed action.

After 15 September Egypt knew that its demonstrated capacity to maintain the regular flow of traffic through the canal without British and French pilots had removed the one criterion for enforcement action that the United States might have accepted. Moreover, signs that the differences between the United States and its allies kept growing sharper were assuredly welcome to the Egyptian leadership.

Even without the reassuring signals it received from the American leadership, Egypt knew it could rely on the Soviet Union as well as the emerging Afro-Asian Bloc to defend its cause. The grounds for holding that Egypt would in any case have resisted Anglo-French pressure therefore seem strong.

In view of the advanced stage of military preparations that Britain and France had reached by October, it was in the interest of both the United States and Egypt to keep the negotiations going. Anthony Nutting reports that Dulles advised the Egyptian Foreign Minister to continue the talks at all costs. According to Heikal, the United States warned Egyptian leaders about Eden's health and unpredictability. Dulles reportedly stated that he felt Eden would use force if no satisfactory solution were found and advised Nasser to compromise.[96]

On 5 October Egyptian Foreign Minister Fawzi proposed that direct negotiations between Egypt, Britain, and France be held under United Nations auspices.[97] In a conciliatory gesture, Egypt also accepted the possibility that an international advisory board could enable canal users to participate in the discussion of matters of common concern.[98]

A further show of Egyptian moderation occurred in the course of talks between Fawzi, Pineau, and Lloyd in early October. On this occasion, Egypt accepted six basic principles for the operation of the Suez Canal:

1. Free and open transit through the canal without discrimination;
2. Egyptian sovereignty to be respected;
3. The insulation of the operation of the canal from the politics of any country;
4. Tolls and charges to be decided by agreement between Egypt and the users;
5. A fair proportion of the revenue to be allocated to the development of the canal;
6. Disputes to be settled by arbitration.[99]

However, Egypt would undoubtedly have continued to exclude Israel, which it did not recognize, since prior to nationalization Israel had never succeeded in gaining access to the canal for its vessels.

Britain and France submitted a draft resolution to the Security Council that included a rider insisting that Egypt had "not yet formulated sufficiently precise proposals to meet the requirements set above [the six principles]." They demanded, among other things, that Egypt promptly submit proposals no less effective than those delivered by Menzies, which Nasser had already rejected. Moreover, Britain and France insisted that Egypt, pending a definitive agreement, should cooperate with SCUA; this included the payment of tolls.[100]

Insistence by Britain and France that an international board should operate the canal deadlocked discussions at the United Nations. On 8 October the Soviet Union vetoed that part of the Anglo-French draft resolution to the Security Council that called for such action.[101] Dulles himself reportedly commented to Eisenhower that the rider attached to the resolution by the allies rejected those minor modifications needed to make the resolution palatable to Egypt. Nevertheless, further negotiations under the good offices of Secretary-General Hammarskjold were scheduled for 29 October.[102]

On 19 October Nasser offered to negotiate personally with Eden and Mollet. By then, however, the Anglo-French determination to strike Nasser down had rendered further Egyptian efforts futile.

Israel invaded the Sinai on the evening of 29 October 1956. The next day France and Britain, without consulting their American ally, issued a joint ultimatum to Egypt and Israel to cease fighting and to withdraw to positions ten miles from the Suez Canal within twelve hours.[103] On 31 October, citing the need to enforce the ultimatum in order to protect the canal, Britain and France launched an attack against Egypt. In collusion with Israel they had found the excuse they needed to deal with Nasser.[104]

Although intelligence and diplomatic sources had forewarned the American leadership of the pending aggression, news of the actual event was reportedly received with "profound shock".[105] Information on Israeli mobilization had been telegraphed from the American military attaché in Israel;[106] but a high-placed Paris source reported that the pending attack was to have been launched sometime after the American elections.[107]

The three friends of the United States had thus decided to carry out their aggression against Egypt without consulting the United States. Moreover, they had acted only one week before the American elections and may well have calculated that fears concerning the pro-Israeli vote would soften the reaction.[108]

Allen Dulles, Chief of the American Central Intelligence Agency and brother of Secretary Dulles, described the deep disappointment of the American leadership:

> We were surprised that the British and French — and I know my brother was terribly surprised and he was terribly hurt — that this conference [Sèvres] had taken place and those plans had been made at the secret meeting in Paris, which he knew had taken place — without knowing exactly what they had decided at that meeting.[109]

Eisenhower was even more candid. Despite constant surveillance by American intelligence agencies, he admitted that "we couldn't figure out exactly what was happening because. . .finally all communications just ceased between us. . . ."[110] In plain words, having lost contact with its allies after 14 October, the United States stood helpless and — despite the various warnings issued to Israel and the allies — could not begin to regain the initiative until these allies had shown their real intentions.

If Britain, France, and Israel had counted on the presidential elections scheduled for 6 November to hinder the United States from taking a strong position, this assumption proved very shortsighted. On the contrary, the American leadership, with a determination rarely witnessed in its approach to Middle East issues, clearly defined its opposition to the action of its friends[111] and moved quickly to disassociate American policy from what seemed a demonstration of nineteenth centry colonialist methods.

President Eisenhower, in a 31 October nationwide broadcast, emphasized not only American noninvolvement in this recourse to arms but also its disapprobation:

> The United States was not consulted in any way about any phase of these actions. Nor were we informed of them in advance. . . .As it is the manifest right of any of these nations to take such decisions and actions, it is likewise our right, if our judgement so dictates, to dissent. We believe these actions to have been taken in error. For we do not accept the use of force as a wise and proper instrument for the settlement of international disputes.[112]

In private, Eisenhower reportedly declared that he "wanted to establish the fact that we were not a colonial power." Hence, "in this struggle, they [Britain and France] are not our allies."[113]

From the moment this issue was first introduced into the United Nations General Assembly, the United States showed sensitivity to the opinion of the Afro-Asian community and, according to the evidence, worked closely with this community throughout the Suez War. After Secretary Dulles was hospitalized on 3 November, Henry Cabot Lodge, Ambassador to the United Nations, took a more active role in decision-making. It was well-known that the Afro-Asian Bloc had more influence on him than on Dulles because of the former's association with the United Nations.

The overriding aim was to terminate hostilities and bring about the withdrawal of the attacking forces in the shortest possible time. Formulating its position on the basis of its 1950 Tripartite commitment, the United States took the lead in the United Nations Security Council and submitted its first proposal on 30 October. Israel was called upon to "immediately withdraw its armed forces behind the established armistice lines," and all member states were urged "to refrain from giving any military, economic, or financial assistance to Israel so long as it had not complied with this resolution."[114]

The United States, which had previously protested against the Anglo-French ultimatum, now openly sided with Egypt. But Britain and France vetoed the American resolution as well as a more moderate one proposed by the Soviet Union,[115] and the Security Council was paralyzed as a result.

Not to be put off, the United States next joined the Soviet Union in supporting a Yugoslav resolution to bring the issue before the General Assembly where decisions were not subject to the veto power vested in Britain and France. In the General Assembly the United States again seized the initiative. On 1 November Secretary Dulles personally introduced the draft resolution that formed the basis for further United Nations action.

In his introductory remarks, he admitted that the disagreement between the United States and "its trusted allies" and friends caused him to take the rostrum with a "heavy heart". Nevertheless, he declared that "because the disagreement involves principles which far transcend the immediate issue, we feel impelled to make our point of view known to you and, through you, to the world." Dulles then briefly reviewed the history of the canal question and chided Egypt for "repeated expressions of hostility. . .toward other governments. . . ." However, he concluded "that these provocations — serious as they were — cannot justify the resort to armed force which has occurred."[116]

He then put forward the American draft resolution which requested "an immediate ceasefire" and a prompt withdrawal of all forces behind the Armistice lines. The same resolution recommended that "all members refrain from introducing military goods in the area of hostilities" and urged that, once the ceasefire took effect, steps should be taken to reopen the canal and restore freedom of navigation.[117] The Secretary-General was requested to observe the compliance of the belligerents and to report to the Security Council and the General Assembly. These two bodies were subsequently to take such further action as was deemed appropriate in accordance with the Charter.

The American resolution was adopted on 2 November by an overwhelming majority of 64 to 6.[118] However, an American attempt on 3 November to incorporate into a general settlement two further resolutions that called for long-term solutions for the Suez and Palestine questions was defeated.[119]

To facilitate an Anglo-French withdrawal with a minimum loss of face, the United States supported a Canadian resolution calling upon the Secretary-General to produce a plan for the creation of the United Nations Emergency Forces (UNEF). These forces were to supervise and secure the termination of hostilities.[120] This proposal was adopted on 4 November 1956, and the UNEF was born on 5 November.[121]

While the role of the United States within the United Nations thus greatly contributed to the creation of an organized framework for ending the Suez War, the role that America played on other levels was even more decisive. One example was the unwillingness of the United States to serve as an alternative source of British petroleum requirements once Britain was cut off from its Middle East supply. This possibility, which had been a paramount concern of Britain throughout the crisis, became a reality when the blockage of the Suez Canal and the blowing up of important oil pipelines to the Mediterranean by Syria reduced British reserves to the minimum.[122]

Britain duly applied to the United States in the knowledge that a Middle East Emergency Committee of thirteen major American oil companies had been formed to pool oil production and shipping facilities in view of a possible petroleum shortage. The American leadership replied by categorically refusing to alleviate the allies' shortage of oil unless they accepted a ceasefire and demonstrated a real intention of withdrawing their troops.[123]

A rapidly developing financial crisis in Britain offered the United States a further opportunity to exert pressure. By the first week in November a run on Sterling had placed Britain in a difficult situation and its need for a loan from the International Monetary Fund (IMF) was pressing. Again Britain found itself at the mercy of the United States, whose agreement to such a loan was a necessary precondition. The United States intimated that its agreement was contingent on a ceasefire and a British decision to withdraw its troops from Egypt.[124]

Still another development was to increase Britain's dependence on the United States. On 5 November the Soviet Union proposed joint Soviet-American action against the aggressors, and stern Soviet notes to Britain, France, and Israel implied the threat of nuclear intervention against these powers.[125] As the risk of superpower confrontation was by now greatly reduced — since both Israel and Egypt had agreed to a ceasefire — the Soviet threats were probably conceived for their propaganda value.[126] Nevertheless, they posed the major question of whether the United States would extend a nuclear umbrella to its allies within the framework of its NATO commitments.

The answer of the United States was evasive. Assurances that it would come to the aid of its allies should Britain and France be attacked still left open the question of whether this aid would be forthcoming if the attack occurred on foreign territory. Anglo-French uneasiness about this issue no doubt increased their willingness to accept a ceasefire.[127]

Although the importance of other factors should not be discounted — including the force of world public opinion, Commonwealth opposition, internal dissent, and threats by the Soviet Union — it seems clear that the pressure exerted by the United States was the crucial factor in persuading Britain and subsequently France to accept the ceasefire that took effect on 7 November.[128] Following the Anglo-French agreement to cease fire, the American leadership maintained its stern stand toward these countries and Israel in order to constrain them all to withdraw their troops from Egyptian territory. A request by Eden and Mollet to visit the United States in this period was denied.[129]

The American government continued to refuse to assist Britain with its financial and petroleum problems. Lloyd and Pineau were also denied direct contact with the American administration.[130] During November the American government refused to authorize operations of the Middle East Emergency Committee because "the international situation was extremely delicate." Aside from the pressure value of this decision on Britain, practical considerations were involved—namely, the fear of jeopardizing American Middle East oil interests.[131]

On 10 November the Soviet Union announced that unless Britain, France, and Israel agreed to comply with the United Nations resolution, it would permit "volunteers" to join Egyptian forces.[132] Evidence exists that the Soviet Union was bluffing. The formation of UNEF troops to replace those of France and Britain had reached an advanced stage, and Nasser had reportedly informed American officials that the Soviet offer would not be accepted.[133] However, a Soviet build-up was reportedly underway in Syria.[134] On balance the Soviet announcement could not be ignored and made the need for a prompt withdrawal more urgent than ever. At the same time it gave the United States still another means of applying pressure on its allies.

By 20 November 700 troops under UNEF command had already been dispatched to Egypt and some 3,000 more were on the way. But Britain, France, and Israel still declined to accept a total withdrawal. Faced with their continued intransigence, the United States again sided with the Afro-Asian and Communist Blocs in the United Nations General Assembly by supporting a 24 November Indian resolution that once more called upon the invaders to withdraw their forces.[135]

An imminent energy crisis, a dire need for American financial aid, and adverse pressures from many quarters finally compelled Britain to yield. On 3 December 1956 that country and France agreed to a total withdrawal; generous American assistance was promptly forthcoming.[136]

Israel's deep penetration into the Sinai Peninsula followed by the Anglo-French attack gave the Egyptian regime the feeling that it was fighting for its very survival. The attitudes adopted by the two superpowers were therefore of paramount importance. Although Soviet friendship toward Egypt had been firmly established, the Soviet Union's involvement in Eastern European troubles, the great distance separating it from Egypt, and the relative strength of the American Sixth Fleet in the Eastern Mediterranean at that time cast doubts on the credibility of the Soviet threat to intervene militarily. Moreover, the risk of a great power confrontation if such intervention did occur was far too high, as Nasser himself reportedly recognized.

In a discussion on this subject with then American Ambassador to Cairo Raymond Hare, Nasser revealed that he was wary of allowing the Soviet Union to increase its influence in Egypt. He assured Hare that the United States need not worry about the possibility that Egypt would ask for Soviet military intervention, since Egypt had struggled many years to rid itself of foreign domination and did not intend to repeat the experience.[137]

Furthermore, the possibility that the United States itself could assist in arresting the aggression became tangible once the American government resolutely censured the attack on Egypt. The Egyptian leadership accordingly took steps to secure that country's support, and the American Ambassador was asked to convey to President Eisenhower Egypt's request for American "help". When asked to define what this meant, Nasser specified that it was military help that was needed.[138]

The formal American response to Egypt's plea indicated a willingness to aid Egypt only within the framework of the United Nations.[139] As has been seen, however, American efforts to halt the war and force the invaders to withdraw went well beyond the limits of that promise. Nasser later credited both the Soviet Union and the United States for their support, but he admitted that the role of the latter had been decisive for Egypt.[140]

The United States thus regained Egypt's goodwill, and Egypt expressed hopes that relations would continue to improve. A new chapter in American-Egyptian relations seemed to have opened. Yet, while this period undoubtedly constitutes a high point in the relationship,[141] its long-term importance should not be exaggerated.

The position adopted by the United States during the crisis appears to be largely the result of its displeasure with its allies and Israel and of the need to recoup the loss of Western prestige and influence their combined action had produced. Dulles gave still another reason in an off-the-record press briefing on 6 December 1956:

> If we had not stood up for this principle [the UN Charter], it would have involved the collapse of the United Nations and would have given justification to the charge of the Soviet Union and of some neutralists like Nehru that our collective security arrangements are in fact a cover for aggression. . . .[142]

The evidence strongly suggests that the American position reflected no basic change in the attitude of the American leadership toward the Egyptian regime. On the contrary, the United States government continued to freeze certain Egyptian assets despite numerous appeals for their release and suspended all American aid programs to Egypt including CARE. The United States also refused to supply Egypt with fuel, wheat, and medicine during the crisis or to release blocked funds for their purchase.[143] Many of these items were instead immediately airlifted by the Soviet Union.[144]

Fundamental differences, especially the Egyptian brand of neutralism that was such a thorn in the Americans' side, continued to hinder the development of better relations between the two countries. It was expediency that required both to maintain cordial relations and to shelve controversial issues for the time being. Egypt especially needed American support in order to dislodge Israeli troops from Egyptian soil. As will be seen, the United States hoped that Egypt would take a moderate stance toward the American leadership's next approach to Middle East politics — the Eisenhower Doctrine.

Persuading the Israelis to withdraw proved a difficult task. Once they had gained their principal objectives of eliminating fedayeen bases from the Sinai and securing control over Sharm El Sheikh, the Israeli leaders accepted only a partial withdrawal from the Sinai and adamantly refused to relinquish control over Gaza and Sharm El Sheikh.[145]

In the meantime Egypt had made the reopening of the Suez Canal contingent on Israel's total withdrawal from Egyptian territory. The United States' allies needed the canal reopened quickly, and the American leadership hoped to coax Egypt into taking a favorable or at least benevolent view of major United States policy decisions on the future of the Middle East.[146]

For these reasons, the United States exerted strenuous pressures on Israel, both in and out of the United Nations. Economic aid was suspended and economic sanctions were threatened if Israel's withdrawal was not forthcoming. At the same time, Dulles assured Israel that the United States would support the principle of free navigation in the Gulf of Aqaba and that UNEF troops would be stationed in Gaza and Sharm El Sheikh.[147]

On 20 February Eisenhower, in a public address, admitted that he had written Ben Gurion on 3 February urging Israel to complete its withdrawal. Eisenhower asserted that "I believe that. . .the United Nations has no choice but to exert pressure upon Israel to comply with the withdrawal resolutions."[148] In fact, the United States was consistent in its support of United Nations resolutions calling upon Israel to withdraw its troops.[149]

In the end Israel yielded to these pressures and inducements, the last Israeli troops were withdrawn by 7 March 1957, and American economic aid to Israel was resumed in April.[150]

Following the Israeli withdrawal, Egypt agreed to complete the clearance of the canal, and this vital international waterway was declared open to all but the largest ships on 10 April.[151]

Further attempts by Britain, France, and the United States to obtain Egyptian agreement to a Canal Users Association received only scant attention.[152] The Egyptian government asserted its sovereignty over the operations of the newly opened canal. To allay canal users' fears, this government issued an official statement on 13 April setting forth Egypt's intention to respect the principle of freedom of navigation in the canal.[153]

Thus Nasser's Egypt had succeeded in making its will prevail.

The consequences of the Suez crisis on both the regional and global planes were vast. Egypt, the victim of a domineering style of politics characteristic of the nineteenth century, had managed with the aid of the United States, the Soviet Union, and world public opinion to transform its military defeat into a re-sounding political victory. Nasser's position both at home and in the region was enhanced rather than diminished as Britain and France had intended. The potential strength of the Arab world—derived from its ability to withhold oil and to close the Suez Canal to Europe—had demonstrably become a factor to be reckoned with.

In contrast, the position and prestige of Britain and France were irreparably compromised as a result of their Suez adventure with Israel. Britain lost its treaty rights in Egypt and found that even its relations with the Baghdad Pact countries had been severely strained.[154] The very purpose of the Baghdad Pact, i.e., to contain the Soviet enemy, could now be put in question by any Arab leaders. It was not the Soviet Union that had attacked Egypt; on the contrary, the Soviets had once against demonstrated solidarity with the Arab world by coming to Egypt's aid. The Soviet Union, which had shared the spotlight with the United States during this period, thus verified that its only rival of any importance in the Middle East was the United States.

By its own role during the war, the United States managed to salvage a modicum of the Western prestige and influence that had otherwise been so badly damaged. From this point onward the American leadership's need to counterbalance the surge in Soviet influence would dictate a new willingness to make commitments.

American-Egyptian relations during this period improved to the point of cordiality. But the American leadership's disinclination to reappraise the basis of its habitual attitude toward Egypt and the Arab nationalist cause in general continued to plague this relationship and ultimately rendered the new warmth merely a transitory phenomenon. Still, America's leaders had demonstrated considerable courage in opposing Israel only one week before a presidential election. This was a positive development in Arab eyes, and one that seems to have paid unlooked for dividends at home: Eisenhower won the election with a large majority and even carried the state of New York where the "Jewish vote" is traditionally strong.[155]

The Suez crisis also confirmed that major changes had been taking place in the international power structure. The fact that Britain and France were no longer dominant powers was plain to all. They had dared to act without American consent, and their dependence on the United States had become painfully apparent. Moreover, the breach in Western solidarity that had occurred during the Suez War shook the very foundations of the Western alliance. Only after the December 1956 NATO Foreign Ministers' Conference and the March 1957 Bermuda Conference was some semblance of unity restored.

The Suez crisis also became an instructive point of reference for cold war policymakers and strategists. The fear that this conflict might escalate into total war exerted a moderating influence on the policies of the two superpowers. It can even be argued that the cautious restraint shown by these powers at this time was a way station on the long and tortuous road that finally led to a gradual easing of international tension. If nothing else, the lesson had been learned that when regional conflicts reached the boiling point, neither superpower desired or could afford a confrontation.

Finally, the Suez crisis clearly demonstrated that limited wars could still occur despite the pervasive influence of the superpowers. "Brinkmanship", rather than a means of preventing such wars, was now reduced to a technique by which one superpower restricted the other's possibilities of action when limited wars did erupt. At the same time the Egyptian example demonstrated the extent to which a small country could effectively manipulate and profit from superpower rivalries for its own ends, a lesson that was to be learned and applied by many others in the years to come.

Notes

1. *Le Journal d'Egypte*, 19 December 1955.

2. *New York Times*, 2 April 1956.

3. Mansoor, ed., *The Arab World* (3), 21 July 1956.

4. *Le Journal d'Egypte*, 25 July 1956; Mansoor, ed., *The Arab World* (3), 24 July 1956.

5. Egypt's leaders later contended that it was they who had declined to persue the Soviet offer so as not to increase Egyptian indebtedness to the Soviet Union. See Ali Sabri's comments in this vein to Kennett Love, *Suez: The Twice-Fought War*, p. 323. Also see Nasser's denial of having approached the Soviet Union concerning aid at that time. *New York Times*, 8 October 1956.

6. Nasser's statement of 26 July 1956, Foreign Broadcast Information Service; *Daily Report*, 27 July 1956, Foreign Radio Broadcasts.

7. See statement by Nasser, *Egyptian Gazette*, 18 November 1954.

8. Trevelyan, *The Middle East in Revolution*, pp. 82-84. See also Terence Robertson, *Crisis* (New York: Atheneum, 1965), pp. 59-60.

9. These studies were reportedly carried out by Zachariya Mohieddin. Trevelyan, *The Middle East in Revolution*, p. 84. In support of the hypothesis that nationalization had been considered before the events of July 1956, see Egyptian Home Service, Cairo, 12 August 1956; *Egyptian Gazette*, 18 November 1954. See also Robertson, *Crisis*, pp. 60-62.

10. Egyptian Home Service, Cairo, 12 August 1956. Both Eden and Macmillan, British Chancellor of the Exchequer, believed "Dulles's clumsy handling of the final stages played into Nasser's hands." Macmillan, *Riding the Storm*, p. 100. Dulles, in his own defense, echoed Nasser in insisting that the latter had been "studying" the possibility of nationalizing the Company for over two years. Dulles Press Conference, U.S. Department of State, Press Release 450, 28 August 1956.

11. Thomas, *Suez*, p. 31.

12. Eden, *Full Circle*, 3: 427-28, 465-66.

13. Nutting, *No End of a Lesson*, p. 47.

14. Eden's 5 August 1956 letter to Eisenhower quoted in Love, *Suez: The Twice-Fought War*, p. 394. Eden described the task as follows: "to reduce the stature of the megalomaniacal dictator at an early stage" (*Full Circle*, 3: 431).

15. *Le Monde*, 26 June 1960, Ambassador Dillon's report to Eisenhower (Eisenhower, *Waging Peace*, p. 36).

16. Telegram from Eden to Eisenhower, quoted in Eden, *Full Circle*, 3: 428. Robert D. Murphy, Under-Secretary of State for Political Affairs, had been sent by Eisenhower to survey the London situation and to prevent impulsive action. Eisenhower, *Waging Peace*, pp. 32 and 644. After extensive discussion with high-ranking British and French officials, Murphy "was left in no doubt that the British Government believed that Suez was a test which would be met only by the use of force." Robert Murphy, *Diplomat among Warriors* (London: Collins, 1964), pp. 462-64.

17. *Orient*, no. 1, 1957, p. 68. See also Dillon's message to Eisenhower (Eisenhower, *Waging Peace*, p. 36).

18. Robertson, *Crisis*, pp. 75-77.

19. See, for example, Eden, *Full Circle*, 3: 430; André Beaufre, *The Suez Expedition, 1956* (New York: Praeger, 1969).

20. Murphy, *Diplomat among Warriors*, p. 465.

21. See the report by Andrew Foster, American Attaché in London, to Eisenhower on 27 July: "The question confronting (the British) Cabinet tonight was of course (the) extent to which (the) U.S. would go in supporting and participating in (a) firm position vis-à-vis Nasser in terms of economic sanctions and, beyond that if necessary, military action." Eisenhower papers, Gettysburg, quoted in Love, *Suez: The Twice-Fought War*, p. 355. See also Eden's 27 July 1956 telegram to Eisenhower urging a firm stand to prevent "our influence and yours throughout the Middle East. . .(from being) finally destroyed." Eden, *Full Circle*, 3:427.

22. Unpublished disclosure by high-ranking American diplomat. The same source holds that the American leadership planned to take a new initiative to prevent its allies from resorting to force after the elections.

23. See Dulles's 29 July 1956 statement, U.S. Department of State, Press Release 415.

24. Only 4 percent of total U.S. domestic oil consumption came from the Middle East in 1956 (J. H. Lichtblau, "Is the Tank Running Low," *The Reporter*, 21 March 1957, p. 17).

25. Eisenhower, *Dulles Oral History Collection*; Secretary Dulles's 28 August 1956 press statement, U.S. Department of State, Press Release 450.

26. These were made explicit in a joint statement by Nasser and Soviet Ambassador Kiselev. *Le Journal d'Egypte,* 20 August 1956.

27. Eisenhower to Eden, telegram dated 8 September 1956 (Eisenhower, *Waging Peace*, pp. 669-71.).

28. See Eisenhower comment: "We sat down and we were determined to pursue a course that would not lead to war. We were certain a negotiation could settle this problem." Quoted in R. P. Stebbins, *The United States in World Affairs, 1956* (New York: Harper and Brothers, 1957), p. 260.

29. Unpublished declaration by middle-ranking State Department source.

30. According to Under-Secretary Robert D. Murphy in *Dulles Oral History Collection*.

31. U.S. Department of State, *Bulletin*, 6 August 1956, p. 221 and 13 August 1956, pp. 262-63.

32. Eisenhower, *Dulles Oral History Collection*. Since the right of a state to nationalize is well accepted in international law if adequate compensation is made to the shareholders, the Egyptian nationalization decree of 26 July 1956 may arguably have met the standards of international legal requirements. However, compensation for the shareholders remained to be negotiated. See *Documents on International Affairs, 1956*, p. 113. Concerning the question of Egypt's termination of the Company's concession, if one accepts the premise that the Company was an Egyptian limited entity, this issue would fall within the purview of Egypt's domestic jurisdiction. For interesting analyses of the legal issues involved, see T. F. Huang, "Some International and Legal Aspects of the Suez Canal Question," *American Journal of International Law*, 51 (1957): 277; J. A. Obieta, *The International Status of the Suez Canal* (The Hague, 1960).

33. Eden, *Full Circle*, 3: 427-28.

34. U.S. Department of State, Press Release 415, 29 July 1976; Eisenhower, *Waging Peace*, p. 39.

35. Ibid.

36. Dulles address, 3 August 1956, U.S. Department of State, *Bulletin*, 13 August 1956, p. 260.

37. *New York Times*, 1 August 1956. This measure had been taken by Britain on 28 July and France on 29 July. See Mansoor, ed., *The Arab World* (3), 28 and 29 July 1956.

38. Adams, *Firsthand Report*, p. 251.

39. Murphy, *Dulles Oral History Collection*.

40. Eden, *Full Circle*, 3: 430; André Beaufre, *The Suez Expedition, 1956*; Thomas, *Suez*, p. 48; Robertson, *Crisis*, p. 75.

41. Eisenhower, 31 July 1956 telegram to Eden (*Waging Peace*, pp. 664-65).

42. Dulles according to Eden, *Full Circle*, 3: 437. Eisenhower, *Dulles Oral History Collection*.

43. Eisenhower, telegram to Eden, 31 July 1956 (*Waging Peace*, pp. 664-65); U.S. Department of State, 3 August 1956, Press Release 425. The principle that members of the United Nations were committed to seeking peaceful solutions was also mentioned.

44. Eden, *Full Circle*, 3: 437.

45. Ibid., pp. 437 and 434.

46. Quoted in Love, *Suez: The Twice-Fought War*, p. 387. However, it also gave Britain and France time to complete military preparations.

47. *Le Journal d'Egypte*, 6 August 1956.

48. See Dulles's statement of 3 August 1956, U.S. Department of State, *Bulletin*, 13 August 1956, pp. 261, 263.

49. U.S. Department of State, *The Suez Canal Problem, July 26 - September 22, 1956: Documents* (Washington, D.C.: Government Printing Office, 1956), pp. 51-52.

50. Ibid.

51. U.S. Department of State, *The Suez Canal Problem*, p. 44. For final text with amendments by Ethiopia, Iran, Pakistan, and Turkey incorporated, see U.S. Department of State, *Bulletin*, 3 September 1956, pp. 373-74. Also see The Indian Minority Plan, *Documents on International Affairs, 1956*, p. 174.

52. U.S. Department of State, *The Suez Canal Problem*, pp. 51-52.

53. *Documents on International Affairs, 1956*, p. 174; Eisenhower, *Waging Peace*, p. 46.

54. Quoted in Love, *Suez: The Twice-Fought War*, p. 405.

55. Mansoor, ed., *The Arab World* (3), 7 August 1956.

56. U.S. Department of State, *Bulletin*, 5 September 1956, p. 371-73.

57. Macmillan, *Riding the Storm*, p. 108.

58. *Washington Post and Times Herald*, 31 August 1956. Note that the American commitment to a peaceful solution was again stressed by Eisenhower on 4 September. Mansoor, ed., *The Arab World* (3), 5 September 1956.

59. Press Conference, 28 August 1956, U.S. Department of State, Press Release 450.

60. Heikal, *The Cairo Documents*, p. 102.

61. Nasser's reply to Menzies, 9 September 1956, *Documents on International Affairs, 1956*, p. 194.

62. Henderson, *Dulles Oral History Collection*; Henderson to the author.

63. Sir Robert Menzies, *Afternoon Light* (London: Cassel, 1966), p. 450.

64. Heikal, *The Cairo Documents*, p. 103.

65. Statement of 10 September 1956, U.S. Department of State, *Bulletin*, 24 September 1956, p. 464.

66. *Documents on International Affairs, 1956*, p. 201; note that the deadline had been put off from 15 August to this date. Ibid., p. 158.

67. *Documents on International Affairs, 1956*, pp. 202-4.

68. Macmillan, *Riding the Storm*, p. 113; Robertson, *Crisis*, pp. 98-100.

69. Loy Henderson quotes Anthony Eden (*Dulles Oral History Collection*).

70. Dulles was informed of the intention on 28 August (Eden, *Full Circle*, 3: 456-61; Eisenhower, *Waging Peace*, p. 52. Eden on Dulles's position, *Full Circle*, 3: 460.

71. Macmillan, *Riding the Storm*, p. 119; Eisenhower, *Waging Peace*, pp. 672-75.

72. Eden, *Full Circle*, 3:476-79; Macmillan, *Riding the Storm*, p. 121.

73. Eden, *Full Circle*, 3:479-81.

74. U.S. Department of State, Press Conference Release 486, 13 September 1956.

75. E. J. Hughes, *Ordeal of Power* (New York: Atheneum, 1963), p. 178. Dulles, apparently attempting to stretch the matter out, told Macmillan that it should take six months to organize such a system (Macmillan, *Riding the Storm* p. 126).

76. Murphy, *Diplomats among Warriors*, p. 470.

77. *Egyptian Gazette*, 16 September 1956. See Egyptian case on the question presented by the Representative of Egypt to the President of the Security Council, 17 September 1956, *Documents on International Affairs, 1956*, pp. 230-32.

78. See Eden's remarks on this issue (*Full Circle*, 3: 489-90).

79. *New York Times*, 27 September 1956. American ships were frequently registered under Panamanian and Liberian registry.

80. See comments by Dulles, U.S. Department of State, Press Release 273, 23 April 1957.

81. Eden, *Full Circle*, 3:455; Macmillan, *Riding the Storm*, p. 111.

82. Dulles News Conference, 2 October 1956, U.S. Department of State, *Bulletin*, 15 October 1956, pp. 574-80.

83. Ibid.

84. Eden, *Full Circle*, 3: 499. See also 13 September News Conference, U.S. Department of State, *Bulletin*, 24 September 1956, pp. 476-83. Moreover, in later statements, Dulles emphasized that the aim was to seek an agreement whereby Egypt would allow SCUA to "supervise" the operation of the canal. For Dulles, SCUA was to "help" the Egyptian authorities, "not to be an obstacle"; "nor is it our purpose to coerce Egypt". Extemporaneous remarks by Dulles at the Second Plenary Session of the Suez Canal Conference, 19 September 1956, in U.S. Department of State, *Bulletin*, 1 October 1956, pp. 503-6; U.S. Department of State, Press Release 497, 20 September 1956.

85. Eden, *Full Circle*, 3: 484.

86. United Nations Documents, S/3671, 13 October 1956.

87. United States Mission to the United Nations, Press Release 2472, 13 October 1956.

88. For examples of Dulles's optimism, see his statement of 16 October 1956, U.S. Department of State, *Bulletin*, 29 October 1956, pp. 655-62 and that of 27 October 1956, ibid., 5 November 1956, pp. 698-99. Even after the elections, Dulles felt America could find means to deter Britain and France from pursuing a policy contrary to its wishes. At least one unpublished statement by a high-ranking State Department official suggests that a plan to prevent the allies from using force after the elections was already in existence.

89. Murphy, *Dulles Oral History Collection*. One reliable source dates the information blackout from 14 October. See also Love, *Suez: The Twice-Fought War*, p. 471; Eisenhower, *Waging Peace*, p. 56.

90. *Le Journal d'Egypte*, 6 August 1956.

91. For examples, see Mansoor, ed., *The Arab World* (3) 29 July 1956 and *Pravda*, 9 August 1956 as regards the Soviet Union. For others, see Mansoor, ed., *The Arab World* (3), 28 July 1, 5, 8, 10, 12, 14, 15 August 1956. The Egyptian press announced that 32 nations had recognized Egypt's right to nationalize the Canal Company. *Le Journal d'Egypt*, 3 August 1956.

92. *Le Journal d'Egypte*, 1 and 7 August 1956.

93. Trevelyan, *The Middle East in Revolution*, pp. 107, 99-100.

94. Eden, *Full Circle*, 3:455; Macmillan, *Riding the Storm*, p. 111.

95. *Le Journal d'Egypte*, 31 August and 14 September 1956.

96. Nutting, *Nasser*, p. 156; Heikal, *The Cairo Documents*, pp. 98-99.

97. Mansoor, ed., *The Arab World* (3), 5 October 1956.

98. Stephens, *Nasser: A Political Biography*, p. 220.

99. United Nations Documents, S/3675, 13 October 1956.

100. Love, *Suez: The Twice-Fought War*, p. 446.

101. U.N. Security Council, *Official Records*, 11th year 736; 8 October 1956, p. 17.

102. Love, *Suez: The Twice-Fought War*, pp. 446-47.

103. Dayan, *Diary of the Sinai Campaign 1956*, pp. 12-21, gives the background of the Israeli decision. Anglo-French ultimatum to Egypt and Israel, 30 October 1956, *Documents on International Affairs, 1956*, p. 261.

104. The charge of collusion has now been amply confirmed by those directly involved in the events. See Anthony Nutting, *No End of a Lesson*; André Beaufre, *The Suez Expedition 1956*.

105. W. W. Aldrich, "The Suez Crisis: A Footnote to History," *Foreign Affairs*, April 1967, p. 547; Adams, *Firsthand Report*, p. 256.

106. Murphy, *Dulles Oral History Collection*.

107. Unpublished disclosure by high-ranking American diplomat.

108. According to Loy Henderson, *Dulles Oral History Collection*.

109. Quoted by Sherman Adams, *Firsthand Report*, p. 256. Adams also remarks Eisenhower's disappointment in Eden for his not having confided in the United States about the attack.

110. Eisenhower, *Dulles Oral History Collection*.

111. See Hagerty's statements of 29 October on the Israeli attack and 30 October on the Anglo-French ultimatum. U.S. Department of State, *Bulletin*, 12 November 1956, p. 749.

112. U.S. Department of State, *Bulletin*, 12 November 1956.

113. Unpublished disclosure by an informed, official source; see also Robertson, *Crisis*, p. 196.

114. United Nations Documents, S/3710. Dayan reports that Eisenhower telegraphed Ben Gurion, suggesting that if Israel withdrew its forces from the Sinai he would immediately declare his deep appreciation (*Diary of the Sinai Campaign, 1956*, p. 95).

115. United Nations Documents, S/3713/Rev. 1.

116. U.S. Department of State, *Bulletin*, 12 November 1956, pp. 751-57.

117. United Nations Documents, A/3256. The Canal had been blocked by scuttled ships. Love, *Suez: The Twice-Fought War*, pp. 527-28.

118. Mansoor, *The Arab World* (3), 2 November 1956.

119. United Nations Documents, A/3272 and A/3273.

120. United Nations Documents, A/3276, 3 November 1956. Note that Britain and France claimed they had intervened for the purpose of separating the belligerents and safeguarding the canal.

121. United Nations Documents, A/Res/391, A/Res/394.

122. British reserves were estimated to last six weeks. Eden, *Full Circle*, 3: 429.

123. Macmillan, *Riding the Storm*, p. 165; U.S. Department of State, *Bulletin*, 3 September 1956, p. 374; Adams, *Firsthand Report*, pp. 252, 262; Mansoor, ed., *The Arab World* (3), 31 October 1956.

124. Macmillan, *Riding the Storm*, p. 164.

125. See 5 November 1956 United Nations Documents, S/3736, and letter from Soviet Premier Bulganin to Eisenhower, *Documents on International Affairs, 1956*, pp. 292-94. The United States quickly labelled this possibility as "unthinkable" in its response of 5 November 1956 before the Security Council. U.S. Department of State, *Bulletin*, 19 November 1956, p. 791. Also see White House Statement of 5 November 1956, ibid., pp. 795-96. *Documents on International Affairs, 1956*, pp. 288-92.

126. The UNEF had also been established by the time the Soviet Union decided to make its willingness to extend all-out aid to Egypt a matter of record. Khrushchev commented that the American refusal to collaborate in a joint action with Russia had been anticipated. Nikita Khrushchev, *Khrushchev Remembers*, ed., Edward Crankshaw (London: André Deutsch Ltd., 1971), p. 435. See ibid., p. 436, for the Soviet threats. Robert Murphy, among others, believed that no action by the President was dictated by fear of Soviet participation. *Dulles Oral History Collection*.

127. Love, *Suez, The Twice-Fought War*, pp. 612-13.

128. Mansoor, ed., *The Arab World* (3), 6 and 7 November 1956. The importance of the American role may be deduced from Macmillan's comments (*Riding the Storm*, pp. 163-66). Once the British decision had been made, France had little choice but to accept it since French forces and supplies were well integrated with those of Britain.

129. Adams, *Firsthand Report*, p. 260.

130. Ibid., pp. 264-69; Robertson, *Crisis*, p. 303; Nutting, *Nasser*, p. 180.

131. U.S. House Committee on Interstate and Foreign Commerce, *Petroleum Survey*, Preliminary Report, 85th Cong., 1st sess. (Washington, D.C.: Government Printing Office, 1957), pp. 14-22; Adams, *Firsthand Report*, pp. 264-69.

132. *Tass*, 11 November 1956.

133. Adams, *Firsthand Report*, p. 261.

134. Michel Bar-Zohar, *Suez: Ultra Secret* (Paris: Fayard, 1964), p. 208; J. R. Tournaux, *Secrets d'Etat* (Paris: Plon, 1960), pp. 162-63.

135. Robertson, *Crisis*, p. 299; United Nations Documents, A/Res/410, 24 November 1956.

136. *New York Times*, 4 December 1956. Once the coming acceptance became known on 30 November, the United States immediately dispatched needed petroleum to Britain. Adams, *Firsthand Report*, p. 270. Israeli withdrawal was to present a much more difficult problem.

137. Raymond Hare to the author. See also Eisenhower Papers, Gettysburg, quoted by Love, *Suez: The Twice-Fought War*, p. 644; Nasser's statement of 19 November 1954 (*Le Journal d'Egypte*, 20 November 1956).

138. Raymond Hare to the author. Nasser in his 1966 interview with Kennett Love held that "help"

had not been defined at the time (*Suez: The Twice-Fought War*, p. 557).

139. Raymond Hare to the author.

140. Ibid. See also Nasser's 9 November speech, *Le Journal d'Egypte*, 10 November 1956; Love *Suez: The Twice-Fought War*, p. 558.

141. *New York Times*, 28 November 1956 and 11 December 1956; Nutting, *Nasser*, p. 182, including comments of Fawzi and Nasser.

142. Dulles, Off-the-Record Background Press Conference, 6 December 1956, *Dulles Private Papers*.

143. *New York Times*, 1 and 15 January, 17 March, and 1 and 3 May 1957; Nutting, *Nasser*, p. 184.

144. Ibid.

145. Mansoor, ed., *The Arab World* (3), 8 and 24 November and 2 December 1956.

146. Eisenhower to Kennett Love, *Suez: The Twice-Fought War*, p. 633; Eisenhower, *Waging Peace*, p. 185.

147. See 3 February cable to Ben Gurion, ibid., p. 184; *New York Times*, 6 February 1957.

148. U.S. Department of State, *Bulletin*, 11 March 1957, pp. 387-91.

149. See Ambassador Lodge's statements, ibid., 18 February 1957, pp. 269-71. For text of the American *aide mémoire* on assurances to Israel, issued on 11 February 1956, see ibid., 11 March 1957, p. 392; see also letter from Eisenhower to Ben Gurion (with assurances), Bar-Zohar, *Suez: Ultra Secret*, p. 218; Love, *Suez: The Twice-Fought War*; Mansoor, ed., *The Arab World* (3), 20 April 1957.

150. *New York Times*, 28 and 29 February 1957, 7 and 8 March 1957; Mansoor, ed., *The Arab World* (3), 20 April 1957.

151. *New York Times*, 10 April 1957.

152. Ibid., 10 April and 19 and 28 February 1957. See statements by Dulles on 2 April 1957 (U.S. Department of State, Press Release 184) and 23 April 1957 (ibid., Press Release 237). The problem had been left in the hands of United Nations Secretary General Hammarskjold.

153. *Le Journal d'Egypte*, 14 April 1957.

154. Mansoor, ed., *The Arab World* (3), 1 January 1957.

155. Eisenhower, *Waging Peace*, p. 186.

8

The Eisenhower Doctrine

The United States was the only Western great power to emerge from the Suez crisis with some semblance of prestige and influence in the Middle East. Since it was unwilling to allow the Soviet Union to step into the position previously occupied by Britain, the American leadership began unilaterally to assert itself in the region. "The existing vacuum in the Middle East must be filled by the United States before it is filled by Russia," is the way President Eisenhower subsequently characterized the situation.[1]

Signs that America would take a firm stand were already apparent in November 1956. Warnings to the Soviet Union over its offer to dispatch "volunteers" to Egypt's aid were followed by an announcement of America's intention to view any hostile move against the Middle East members of the Baghdad Pact "with the utmost gravity".[2]

Then, on 5 January, before a joint session of Congress, President Eisenhower made it clear that the United States would assume the major Western responsibility for the security of the Middle East. Introducing a bill subsequently referred to as the Eisenhower Doctrine, he emphasized the American commitment "without reservation" to "the full sovereignty and independence of each and every nation" in the region:

> Weakness in the present situation and the increased danger from International Communism convince me that basic United States policy should now find expression in joint action by the Congress and the Executive. Furthermore, our joint resolve should be so couched as to make it apparent that if need be our words will be backed by action.[3]

He formulated three main proposals:

1. The President should be authorized by the Legislature to employ as he deems necessary the armed forces of the United States to secure and protect the integrity and independence of any nation or group of nations in the general area of the Middle East that requests such aid against overt armed aggression from a nation controlled by communism.
2. The President should be authorized to undertake programs of military aid.

    3. The United States should participate in the economic development of will-
ing Middle East states.

Toward the realization of the last two proposals, the President requested that
$200 million be made available by the Legislature on which the Executive could
draw without prior consent and without being subject to the restrictions imposed
by existing statutes.[4]

    The presidential bill was passed by the House of Representatives on 30
January 1957. After lengthy discussion by the Senate it became law on 9 March,[5]
thereby satisfying the administration's desire to loosen the hold of the
Legislature over the Executive branch in the particularly delicate matters of
economic and military aid to the Arab world. Preallocated appropriations freed
of existing restrictions helped to avoid congressional debate; prior legislative
authorization to the President to employ the armed forces as he deemed
necessary gave the Executive greater flexibility.

    Wary of the approach that had led to the Korean conflict, the American
leadership this time chose to leave the precise geographical limits to which the
new Doctrine applied undefined. This was believed to reinforce the deterrent
character of the Doctrine since an aggressor could otherwise be encouraged "to
seize any area outside the boundary."[6]

    Moreover, the American leadership indicated that it wished to disassociate
itself from the policies of Britain and France, and it now showed some consideration for local nationalist sentiments. In view of entrenched Arab nationalist
aversion to pacts with the great powers, no request or requirement was made
that a potential beneficiary of the Doctrine adhere to such a pact.[7] Instead President Eisenhower emphasized the importance of the political independence of the
region and elaborated on this theme in a letter to Nehru:

> We have no thought that any country in the group would want, or
> indeed could afford, great armaments. When we speak of assisting in a
> military way, we mean only to help each nation achieve the degree of
> strength that can give it reasonable assurance of protection against any
> internal rebellion or subversion and make certain that any
> external aggression would meet resistance....It is my belief that this an-
> nouncement will tend to diminish, if not eliminate, any chance of this
> kind of aggression.[8]

The Doctrine gave the Executive the power it wanted to strengthen the
military capacity of those countries that had been willing to join the Baghdad
Pact. This point was stressed by Dulles in his 24 March Background Press Conference:

> The Joint Resolution [the Eisenhower Doctrine] on the Middle East
> provided that the U.S. might cooperate militarily, not only with individ-
> ual countries but with groups of countries. That phrase 'groups of

countries' appears twice in the Joint Resolution. That was put in there deliberately, with the Baghdad Pact group in mind....This will enable us to cooperate more fully, more effectively, and more advantageously in the military planning for that area, particularly among the Northern Tier.[9]

Having thus proclaimed its Doctrine, the American leadership's next task was to find the means of applying it. This, however, opened a new phase in the contest between the Egyptian-led neutralist axis and the pro-Western regional supporters of American policy.

Not long after President Eisenhower announced his Doctrine, the four regional members of the Baghdad Pact expressed satisfaction with the pronouncement. Hence the American leaders centered their attention on the area to the south, i.e., the Arab world.

They received a mixed reaction. Egypt's initial posture was conditioned by its urgent need for American support in bringing about the departure of Israeli troops. Overtly reserved toward the new American plan, Egypt relied on its Arab allies to voice its real attitude. The factors that probably determined this attitude are easily identified.

First, the continued American insistence on viewing local developments in terms of cold war power politics could hardly be appreciated, given the Soviet Union's warm championship of Egypt during the Suez crisis. Although Nasser continued to maintain a firm anti-communist stance in internal matters,[10] friendship with the Soviet Union during this period remained a basic tenet of Egyptian policy.

Second, the American perception of the Middle East in terms of a vacuum of power was totally objectionable precisely because the United States refused to recognize the Egyptian-led Arab nationalists as a valid regional force capable of filling that vacuum. This unwillingness to come to terms with Arab nationalism had three main reasons. According to Robert D. Murphy, Nasser was responsible for allowing the Soviets to expand their influence in the region, and the general consensus in Washington was that the Soviet Union was using Nasser for this very purpose.[11] Besides, the anti-Israeli orientation of the Arab nationalists rendered it difficult for American policymakers to deal with them, while these same policymakers had yet to accept the principle that local nationalist resistance could be a highly effective bulwark against Soviet encroachment.

American intransigence was particularly resented by Egypt, whose regional position had been greatly strengthened by the tremendous surge in popularity following Nasser's political victory in the Suez crisis. Through the pro-Egyptian regimes in Syria and Jordan, as well as by crypto-diplomatic methods, Egypt attempted to ensure that its will prevailed in the Arab world and appeared to be making its own bid to fill the former British position. Hence insistence by the United States that it alone could prevent Soviet expansion in the region was viewed with suspicion, and the Eisenhower Doctrine could be portrayed as a disguised American essay to take over Britain's role in the name of preventing Soviet encroachment.

The Egyptian leadership accordingly proceeded to influence Arab public opinion without at first appearing to reject the Doctrine outright. The object was to force the United States to modify its approach, especially as regarded Arab nationalism. A partial success was recorded in a joint Egyptian-Syrian-Saudi Arabian communiqué, issued on 19 January 1957, in which the "vacuum" theory was rejected and Arab nationalism was again declared to be the sole basis for Arab policy.[12] Since this occurred even before the withdrawal of Israeli troops, the American leadership should have entertained no illusions that its role during and after the Suez crisis would have induced Egypt to toe the American line.

The new dynamism in Egyptian policy, however, led certain Arab circles to fear Egyptian domination, a development that, for a while, favored the promotion of the American Doctrine. Those Arab leaders who seemed more receptive to the Doctrine did not seriously fear a communist take-over; rather, they were concerned to strengthen their own resistance to the spread of Egyptian influence.

Saudi Arabia provides an early case in point. King Saud was alarmed by the new Egyptian activism and its impact on the Arab masses. The potential disruption that Egyptian liberalism could cause to his feudalistic political system was obvious. Hence he began to venture out of the Egyptian orbit and, as will be seen, was soon joined by the more conservative Arab elements whose common aim was to curb Nasser's influence.

The American leadership promptly moved to exploit these rifts. President Eisenhower invited King Saud to the United States and sought to promote him as a counterpoise to Nasser.[13] The king was received in February as the recognized leader of the Arab people; his willingness to assume a more pro-Western stance and generally to endorse the Eisenhower plan became apparent during his stay. He left the United States with an American agreement to supply him with arms in exchange for the renewal of a five-year lease on the Dhahran Air Base. King Saud visited the Sultan of Morocco, Tunisian Premier Bourguiba, and King Iris of Libya on the way home.[14] Back in his own country, the king seemed to assume a new leadership role in the Middle East,[15] and signs of a breach between the king and Nasser became evident at the Cairo Summit Conference that began on 25 February 1957.[16]

America's next step was to send Ambassador James P. Richards on a mission to fifteen nations in and around the Middle East excluding Egypt, Syria, and Jordan.[17] The stated purpose of this mission was "to devise effective methods of cooperating with interested nations for the improvement of their security and for their economic progress . . . to determine what countries wished to cooperate in this effort, and to make commitments for assistance within the limitations of funds."[18]

Richards was given a positive reception in the countries he visited. The declared purpose of extending American economic and military aid to willing nations could hardly be dismissed. Another factor was the fears that renewed Egyptian political dynamism engendered among many of the regimes in the area. Moreover, the activities of the Arab nationalist Baath Party in coalition with Syrian communist elements appeared on the verge of overflowing the Syrian border into Lebanon and Jordan, which inclined conservative forces to draw closer to the United States.

In the months following the announcement of the American plan the United States seemed to hold the advantage in the impending struggle with Egypt over the propagation of its Doctrine. This is shown by the positive statements issued by many of the regional governments, the warm reception extended to the Richards Mission, and the agreements on the extension of American aid that were reached between the United States and eight of the nations visited, including Lebanon, Libya, Saudi Arabia, and Iraq.[19]

The official reason for the exclusion of Egypt, Syria, and Jordan from the countries to be visited was the existence of an adverse political climate.[20] Syria was outspoken against the Doctrine from the first. Although there were indications that a request by Ambassador Richards to visit Egypt would have been accepted,[21] no request was forthcoming.

Egypt interpreted this snub, especially in the light of America's courtship of Saudi Arabia, as proof of American determination to isolate it. In fact, the Egyptian and Syrian governments, which enjoyed Soviet and — for the moment — Jordanian support, were nearly alone in resisting America's attempt to enhance its influence in the region in these early months.

Two major opportunities to test the effectiveness of the Eisenhower Doctrine arose in the course of 1957. These crises, chiefly manifestations of the regional contest between pro- and anti-Nasserist elements, occurred in Jordan and Syria. The United States was drawn into these local struggles by anti-Nasserist elements whose claims that a serious communist threat existed appear to have been designed to gain American support.

The Jordanian crisis of April 1957 grew out of the changed political situation that had developed in that country since the end of October 1956. In response to growing fears of an invasion by Israel and to the pressure exerted on Egypt by Britain and France, the pro-Nasserist National Socialist Party registered an overwhelming victory in the Jordanian national elections held in October. The formerly outlawed Communist Party also emerged to capture 3 of the 40 seats in the Jordanian House of Representatives.[22] Jordan thus entered the Egyptian orbit under the leadership of Prime Minister Nabulsi.

The new Jordanian government embraced the tenets of neutralism and began to expand its relations with the Soviet Union.[23] In January an agreement was reached between Jordan on the one hand and Egypt, Syria, and Saudi Arabia on the other, by which the three countries would replace the annual British subsidy to Jordan. The Anglo-Jordanian treaty of alliance was terminated in March.[24]

However, King Hussein was encouraged to reassert himself as master of Jordan by the growing dissension between King Saud and Nasser and by the fact that Lebanon had overtly endorsed the Eisenhower Doctrine. On 10 April 1957 he used the Nabulsi government's move to solidify relations with the Soviet Union as a pretext for demanding the resignation of both Prime Minister Nabulsi and Chief-of-Staff Nuwar. Tension mounted quickly as King Hussein, backed by his loyal Bedouin troops, attempted to enforce this decision against strong pro-Nasserist resistance.

Externally, Egypt unleashed a war of words against the king, while a Syrian armored regiment reportedly entered the northern part of Jordan to reinforce a 3,000-troop Syrian brigade already there.[25] Internally, the king's action touched off anti-American demonstrations and clashes between troops loyal to him and the pro-Nasserist faction in the army.

King Hussein was undeterred. He replaced pro-Nasserist elements in the army with loyal Bedouins and set up a conservative government under Hussein Fakhri El Khalid, who was later replaced by Ibrahim Hashem. Martial law was declared on 25 April.

In order to carry out these measures, the king relied in part on Iraqi and Saudi backing. The traditional feud between the Saudi and Hashemite families was put aside, and King Saud placed his troops at King Hussein's disposal. Iraq re-enforced its troops along Jordan's borders.[26] Then, charging that international communism was the cause of Jordan's troubles, Hussein invoked the Eisenhower Doctrine.

The United States hastened to his aid. An announcement by White House spokesman James Hagerty on 24 April endorsed the claim that "the threat to the independence and integrity of Jordan" came from "international communism." The American Sixth Fleet was dispatched to the Eastern Mediterranean as a "precautionary move against the threat to Jordan."[27] The American government granted $10 million in aid to bolster the king, followed by an additional $10 million extended in June. The king thus succeeded in re-establishing his control over the country, and the American Sixth Fleet withdrew from the area on 3 May 1957.

In retrospect, it seems clear that King Hussein's real enemy was not international communism, as he alleged, so much as the nationalist elements who looked to Nasser for leadership and guidance. True, the Soviet Union had definitely gained in popularity and the local Communist Party appears to have become more influential. But there is no proof that this group ever posed a serious threat, unlike the pro-Nasserist Arab nationalists that had drawn Jordan closer to Egypt than ever before and had thereby succeeded in restricting the king's power to an intolerable degree.

If the crisis in Jordan was of the king's own creation, it would seem that he had little popular support for the governmental changes effected in the course of re-establishing his power. The Palestinians, who constituted two-thirds of Jordan's population, were particularly against these changes.

King Hussein's claims that Jordan's troubles were communist inspired appear primarily intended to elicit American backing under the tenets of the Eisenhower Doctrine. If he carefully avoided direct mention of the Doctrine, it was most likely to avoid further antagonizing the Arab nationalists. American support, coupled with the aid of the conservative Saudi and Iraqi regimes, then enabled the king to weaken the power of pro-Nasserist elements in Jordan.

This first application of the Eisenhower Doctrine hardly squares with the declared aim of preventing Soviet or communist encroachment on the independence of nations in the Middle East. Those who nonetheless regard it as a success for the United States stress that America's support for King Hussein was rewarded by Jordan's resumption of a more pro-Western posture.[28] This meant that Jordan now moved closer to Iraq, Saudi Arabia, and Lebanon, whose common interest in preventing the expansion of Egyptian influence had brought them together. Egypt and Syria, because of their disagreement with Saudi Arabia and the new Jordanian stance, found themselves isolated.

On closer analysis, however, America appears to have scored only a qualified success. In the name of pro-Westernism, certain regimes had played on America's obsession with cold war politics in order to secure the support of the United States for unpopular policies, which in turn served only to heighten the Arab nationalists' anti-Westernism. The American leadership's inability or unwillingness to distinguish between nationalist manifestations and those of communist inspiration was actually driving the nationalists and communists closer together against a common enemy. Threatened by indiscriminate American hostility, the Arab nationalists were forced to seek support from the Soviet Union.

If the Eisenhower Doctrine nonetheless provided a workable framework for dealing with the Jordanian crisis, the opposite was true in the case of Syria. Indeed, the existence of the American Doctrine was an important contributing factor in the development of the Syrian political crisis that climaxed during the summer of 1957.

In the early years after gaining its independence from France, Syria was plagued by the internal political struggles of army officers competing for power. After the overthrow of the Shishakli regime in 1954 this instability continued as external powers fanned the strife between the political parties in order to influence Syrian policy. The National Socialist Party had strong leanings toward Iraq and the West. The Baath Party, which spoke for the Arab nationalists, identified with the neutralist policies of Nasser's Egypt. The Communist Party was pro-Soviet.

Such external intervention, most often of a crypto-diplomatic nature, greatly contributed to the internal chaos that had fast become a constant feature of Syria's political life. As Nasser's popularity among the masses rose, the influence of the Baath Party was greatly enhanced to the detriment of pro-Western elements. The April 1955 disclosure of a Western-inspired plot to bring the pro-Baghdad National Socialist Party to power caused this party to be disbanded. When still another plot to establish a pro-Iraqi regime in Syria was uncovered at the end of November 1956, the faction favoring the West was dealt an overwhelming blow. The evidence strongly suggests that this time the United States was implicated along with Britain and Iraq.

While Britain was hostile to Nasser and the spread of Egyptian influence, the United States had become alarmed by reports of growing Soviet influence in Syria. Eisenhower later expressed this concern by comparing the situation in Syria with that in Egypt:

> Syria was far more vulnerable to Communist penetration than Egypt. In Egypt where one strong man prevailed, Colonel Nasser was able to deal with Communists and accept their aid with some degree of safety simply because he demanded that all Soviet operations be conducted through himself. In Syria, where a weak man was in charge of the government, the Soviet penetration by-passed the Government and dealt directly with various agencies, the army, the foreign ministry, and the political parties.

For the American leadership, according to Eisenhower, the important question was this: "If the government comprised only radical Arab nationalists and pro-Nasserites, that was one thing; if they were to go completely communist, that could call for action."[29]

The United States had apparently agreed to the establishment of an Anglo-American committee in Beirut for the purpose of exchanging intelligence on the Syrian situation. Reports of rapidly growing Soviet influence were magnified and used by neighboring pro-Western govenments to spur the American leadership into action against the regime in power. For this purpose, Iraq played the role of intermediary between the plotting pro-Western Syrian faction and the United States and Britain.[30]

With the disclosure of the plot, the Syrian regime took punitive action against pro-Western elements and virtually eliminated their influence. However, Iraq, Lebanon, and Turkey, later to be joined by Jordan, overtly continued their campaign to undermine the Syrian regime. Their clamor about Soviet and communist penetration of Syria caught and held the attention of the United States and may in part have been responsible for the issuance of the Eisenhower Doctrine.

Whatever the validity of these allegations about the spread of communist influence, it is clear that Iraq, Lebanon, and eventually Jordan were very troubled by the threat that pro-Nasserist forces in Syria posed to their own regimes. The unpopular policies of these regimes rendered Jordan and Iraq particularly vulnerable to the war of words waged against them from Cairo and Damascus. Constantly fearful of a Nasser-inspired Syrian plot to overthrow them, these governments sought American support to bolster their internal position.[31] Iraq, moreover, with its major oil pipeline to the Mediterranean passing through Syria, felt that its vital interests were more secure if a pro-Iraqi regime ruled Syria.

In Lebanon it was feared that the growing strength of the Arab nationalists could upset the precarious balance between the Moslem and Christian communities. Hence the possibility that the crises in Syria could extend into Lebanon was in part responsible for the Lebanese government's shift from a fairly neutral stance toward the Baghdad Pact to outright acceptance of the Eisenhower Doctrine. Frequent official Lebanese references to the communist menace were probably intended to secure American backing for the Lebanese leadership's own delicate position vis-à-vis the pro-Nasserist Arab nationalists. This inference is supported by the banning of all Egyptian publications prior to elections, the sealing of the border with Syria,[32] and other measures taken to limit Egyptian and Syrian influence in Lebanon.

American policy was definitely influenced by the hue and cry raised by Syria's neighbors against an alleged communist threat. When the American leadership again failed to distinguish between nationalists and communists, it brought about a temporary alliance between these two forces. This led to an even greater crisis that came to a head during the summer of 1957.[33]

One factor that set off the new crisis was the mounting evidence that Syria was moving closer to the Soviet Union. During the visit from 24 July to 14 August by the Syrian Defense Minister, Khaled El Azm, to the Soviet Union and Czechoslovakia, an important economic and technical agreement was concluded. On 15 August the well-known leftist, Afif Bizri, replaced the more conservative Syrian Chief of Staff Nizam Eddin, and this appointment was followed by a purge of conservative elements in the army. Thirteen Syrian army officers fled to Beirut, and ten officers were arrested for allegedly conspiring with the United States.[34]

In mid-August three American Embassy officials were expelled for their reported role in a new plot against the Syrian regime.[35] This was followed by strong verbal attacks against the United States by Syrian officials, who insisted that the American government was conspiring to force Syria to accept the Eisenhower Doctrine.[36]

How to cope with the new crisis was a difficult problem for the American leadership, which had not been invited to intervene in Syria (as it had in Jordan) and which had not managed to condition the Syrian political situation from within. Under-Secretary of State Loy Henderson was dispatched on 22 August on what was called a fact-finding tour. In Istambul Henderson met with Turkish President Menderes and the kings of Iraq and Jordan. Journeying to Beirut, he further discussed the Syrian situation with leading Lebanese officials. After another brief meeting with high-ranking Jordanian, Iraqi, and Turkish officials, again in Istambul, he returned to the United States.

In a report on his mission dated 4 September, Henderson declared that the Syrian situation was extremely serious.[37] The United States, having already alerted the Strategic Air Command, dispatched the Sixth Fleet to the Eastern Mediterranean and moved auxiliary aircraft to Turkey. Airlifts of arms to Jordan, Lebanon, Iraq, and Turkey were ordered.[38]

Secretary Dulles, in a 7 September statement, called attention to the "subversive activities directed toward the overthrow of the newly constituted governments of Syria's Arab neighbors" and reaffirmed America's commitments under the Eisenhower Doctrine. On the same day President Eisenhower pledged to use all necessary means to protect pro-Western Arab governments from any attempt to overthrow them by the "pro-Soviet" Syrian government.[39] This statement was expressly worded so as to bring the Syrian threat to its neighbors within the purview of the Doctrine.

It soon became clear that the United States counted on non-Arab Turkey to take the lead in exerting pressure against Syria.[40] Unlike the Arab regimes, the Turkish government was not susceptible to the influence exerted by Arab nationalists. Loy Henderson claims that Turkey possessed information that the Soviet Union had promised to aid Syria in taking back areas ceded to Turkey following the First World War.[41] If so, Turkey found a direct reason to intervene.

However, America's reliance on Turkey caused certain staunch opponents of the Syrian regime to backtrack. Iraq suddenly became less preoccupied with the type of political regime in Syria than with the risk that its oil pipeline to the Mediterranean might be cut in an act of reprisal. King Hussein suddenly departed for Spain, and even King Saud began to attenuate his earlier pro-Western stance in order not to jeopardize his potential leadership of the Arab world.[42]

Only Lebanon and Turkey now maintained their original hostility toward Syria, and Lebanon modified its position by October.[43] Turkey, instead, with apparent American backing, began massing its troops on the Syrian border, and the Turkish armed forces were increased from 32,000 to 50,000 troops.[44]

Eisenhower later denied that the United States had ever intended to encourage a Turkish attack against Syria, and he insisted that Turkey pursued an independent policy.[45] But these assertions, in light of the American dispatch of aircraft and arms to Turkey and America's later support for the Turkish position in the United Nations, are open to question.

The Syrian regime was obliged to rely more heavily than ever on the Soviet Union as the only power capable of effectively countering the pressure exerted against it by America and its regional allies. A visit by Khrushchev and Bulganin was announced; economic aid was extended; Soviet warships were dispatched to Syria; and jets and other arms were reportedly to be supplied.[46] Accusing the United States of planning armed intervention against Syria through its regional representative, Turkey, the Soviet Union warned that it would not remain indifferent to any American move against the Syrian regime.[47]

By October, in the United Nations as well as in other forums, the Syrian issue was treated as part of the cold war struggle. The Soviet Union, on one side, lent its full support to Syria; the United States, on the other, backed Turkey.

The American-Turkish approach toward Syria had thus strengthened communist influence there, regardless of whether the threat of a communist takeover in Syria ever really existed. The new surge of Soviet popularity in Syria rendered the already chaotic situation especially serious in view of the known pro-Soviet leanings of certain of the Syrian army's leading officers.

The result was that a realignment within the Arab world began to take shape. Many of the nations that had initially supported the Eisenhower Doctrine now reversed their positions and backed the Arab nationalist forces in Syria. Apparently, it was felt that these forces alone could enable Syria to resist mounting Soviet influence. Radio Cairo railed against the coercion of Syria; the West, this time including the United States, was once again labeled as the aggressor.

Saudi Arabia called upon the United States to modify its stand toward Syria and pledged support to both Syria and Egypt in the event of aggression. The Saudi Arabian leadership thus set out to bring the Syrian issue back within a purely regional framework, and it offered its aid in mediating Turco-Syrian and inter-Arab differences. By mid-October, Iraq, Lebanon, and Jordan had joined with Saudi Arabia and Egypt in support of Syria.[48]

The Syrian crisis thus brought the feuding Arab community momentarily closer to unity than any other Arab development with the exception of the 1948 and 1956 wars with Israel. Many of the Arab nations had proclaimed international communism to be the true regional threat when their principal enemy was in fact Nasser-led Arab nationalism. Now, these same nations—to varying degrees—backed the Arab nationalists against what was deemed an American threat to Syria precisely at a time when the communist threat in Syria had become a reality.

The Eisenhower Doctrine, rather than preventing this threat, had proved a contributing factor to its emergence. Support for the Arab nationalist forces paradoxically became the principal means of preventing further deterioration in Syria and of providing the Syrian regime with an alternative to the Soviet Union.

The Egyptian role in these developments deserves special attention. Syria, under the leadership of the Baath party, had been Egypt's constant and loyal friend and ally since 1955. That either a pro-Western coup d'état could occur or that Syria could fall under Soviet control were possibilities viewed with equal consternation by the Egyptian leadership. Accordingly, it struggled on two fronts to sustain the pro-Nasserist Arab nationalist regime: overtly against American-backed Turkey and covertly against the Soviet Union.

Paralleling Saudi Arabian action on Syria's behalf, Egypt and the Syrian government leaders remained in constant contact through high-level exchanges and through the presence in Syria of Egyptian representative Mahmoud Riad. In response to heightened Western pressure and the growing Soviet influence in Syria, steps were taken as early as September to bring about the unification of Syria with Egypt.[49] Egypt also championed the Syrian case before the United Nations, together with the Soviet Union.[50] The dispatch of Egyptian troops to Syria in October to reinforce Syria's defense capacity overshadowed Saudi Arabia's earlier efforts on Syria's behalf.[51]

Confronted by extreme external pressures and internal chaos bordering on anarchy, the Syrian regime looked increasingly to Nasser for salvation. Union with Egypt appeared to be the Baathists' only satisfactory solution, especially since the conservative elements that could have balanced the growing communist influence had been greatly weakened.[52]

Egypt's reluctance to enter the proposed union has been recognized by several authorities. According to disclosures by former Ambassador Raymond Hare, Nasser informed him personally that Egypt was unprepared for the union, but that it would acquiesce in order to keep Syria out of the hands of the communists.[53]

The United Arab Republic was proclaimed on 1 February 1958. By this act Nasser, as the leader of Arab nationalism, stepped in to fill the power vacuum that the West had both feared and helped to create. Characteristically, one of his first decrees banned political parties in Syria and thus dealt a heavy blow to the Syrian Communist Party.[54]

When an explanation is sought for the failure of the Eisenhower Doctrine to meet the specific challenges of the Jordanian and Syrian crises described above, it is the refusal of the American leadership to come to terms with Arab nationalism that stands out over time. Paradoxically, this refusal was so pernicious in its effects precisely because the cold war thinking that spawned it was capable of converting regional problems and contests into instances of actual global confrontation.

America insisted on perceiving every threat to the region as external, a blinkered view expressed by Dulles during the 1957 congressional hearings on the Eisenhower Doctrine.[55] Ignoring Nasser's earlier counsel that the Western "hammering" for pacts set loose internal forces from which only the extremists benefited, the American leadership sought to impose its own preconceived definition of cooperation upon the regional states and linked the security of the United States with the need to bolster these states militarily.

Far from stabilizing the region, this military aid only intensified regional rivalries as certain client states proceeded to use American weaponry for their own ends. Iraq and Turkey, for example, used Western arms to coerce Syria, which in turn rendered Syria increasingly dependent on the Soviet Union for similar military support. By the summer of 1957, chaos reigned in Syria, the two superpowers both resorted to "brinkmanship" to keep each other at bay, and Syria found itself sucked into the cold war struggle. The net result was the enhancement of Soviet influence.

In this perspective the application of the Eisenhower Doctrine was bound to strain American-Egyptian relations. Initially, the American leadership seemed to expect that Nasser would show his gratitude for the American role in the Suez crisis and for the pressure then exerted on Israel by tolerating the new American approach. Once Israeli troops had departed from Egypt, the discrepancies between the desired attitude and Egyptian policy quickly surfaced.

This rift was deepened by American courtship of King Saud and the application of the Doctrine in the Jordanian crisis. Although the true extent of Egyptian involvement in Jordan and later in Syria is difficult to appraise because of its crypto-diplomatic nature, one fact stands out: Nasser was certain to oppose the application of any doctrine aimed against pro-Nasserist Arab nationalist elements. The constant American failure to discriminate between these nationalists and the communists that were their avowed target alienated the Arab nationalists and inevitably damaged American-Egyptian relations.

The Egyptian leadership soon came to view the Doctrine as one more attempt to isolate Egypt and to curb its influence by strengthening its rivals. America's intentions were stigmatized as follows:

A revival of the Arab League with a strong Saudi and Hashemite tendency was envisaged and hopes were entertained that a new Arab political entity might be created in which the activist nationalist ardours of Cairo could be balanced by a strongly pro-Western Baghdad and Riad.[56]

Egypt also resented the American policy embodied in the Doctrine as yet another attempt by a great power to install itself in the region and to counteract the Egyptian neutralist stance by drawing the region into the cold war.

By mid-1957 the very force that had been weakened by the application of the Doctrine regained sufficient strength to save the critical Syrian situation. The Arab nationalists under Nasser's lead rallied even the most conservative regimes to the Syrian cause while Egypt stepped in to bolster the Baathists and to fill the political vacuum. Nasser thus proved that local forces were better able to cope with local situations than any of the great powers, including the United States, whose Doctrine had in fact aggravated the severity of the Syrian crisis. If there had been a serious threat of a Soviet or communist take-over in Syria, it was Egypt, not the United States, that prevented it.

This inability to recognize the capacity of regional forces to deal with their own political problems followed from the patronizing attitude consistently adopted by the American leadership toward the emerging Third World nations in this period. It also went hand-in-glove with the failure of the American Doctrine to offer solutions for deep-rooted regional problems such as the fate of the

Palestine refugees, the Arab-Israeli feud, and the need to reduce poverty through economic development.

These problems, apparently of secondary importance to the American leadership, were again to be dealt with by ad hoc approaches, a failing that was criticized by Senator Michael J. Mansfield in the following terms:

> Our use of military force in the Middle East may be a positive act, but a positive military act is not to be confused with a positive foreign policy. On the contrary, it is the antithesis of such a policy. The use of military force signifies the absence of policy or the breakdown of policy. In this case it is the former. We have not had a Middle Eastern policy or, at best, we have had only the generalities of such a policy.[57]

By the end of 1957 it should have been evident to the American leaders that their approach to the Middle East was likely to fail if it conflicted with Arab nationalist interests promoted by Nasser. By lending its support to unpopular regimes America could perhaps momentarily have subdued nationalist resistance, but such regimes were not able to resist indefinitely the internal pressures from this force. In fact, American policy unified and strengthened Arab nationalist resistance while ignoring its tremendous popular appeal.

A slow learner, the United States was not to re-evaluate its approach toward Egypt until after the 1958 crises in Lebanon and Iraq. Only then did the American leadership come gradually to recognize that, along with their opposition to Western interference in regional affairs, the Arab nationalists were equally determined not to succumb to the Soviet influence that had otherwise proved a useful counterweight in the struggle for full independence.

Notes

1. Eisenhower, *Waging Peace*, p. 178.
2. U.S. Department of State, *Bulletin*, 10 December 1956, p. 918. This statement was chiefly motivated by reports of a Soviet build-up in Syria.
3. U.S. Department of State, *Bulletin*, 21 January 1957, pp. 83-86.
4. Ibid., p. 86.
5. *Public Law 85-7*, 85th Cong. 1st sess., House Joint Resolution 117, 9 March 1957.
6. Eisenhower, *Waging Peace*, pp. 180-81. The American definition of its defense periphery had excluded Korea.
7. U.S. Department of State, *Bulletin*, 27 May 1957, p. 841.
8. Eisenhower, *Waging Peace*, p. 181.
9. Unpublished Background Press Conference, 24 March 1957, *Dulles Private Papers*.
10. The Communist Party remained outlawed, and on 30 August 1957, 18 Egyptians were arrested and charged with being members. Mansoor, ed., *The Arab World* (3), 30 August and 19 October, 1957.
11. Murphy, *Dulles Oral History Collection*.
12. *Egyptian Gazette*, 20 January 1957.

13. Adams says that Eisenhower told Republican Congressional leaders that his principal aim was to strengthen Saud for this purpose (*Firsthand Report*, p. 278).

14. Mansoor, ed., *The Arab World* (3), 10, 21, and 22 February 1957.

15. *New York Times*, 31 January and 9 February 1957.

16. See Eisenhower, *Waging Peace*, p. 190.

17. The countries visited were Lebanon, Libya, Turkey, Pakistan, Afghanistan, Iran, Iraq, Saudi Arabia, Yemen, Ethiopia, Sudan, Greece, Israel, Tunisia, and Morocco.

18. Eisenhower, *Waging Peace*, pp. 193-94.

19. *Documents on American Foreign Relations*, 1957, pp. 214-15.

20. Eisenhower, *Waging Peace*, p. 194.

21. Note Egyptian spokesman Ali Sabri's announcement in April that he would welcome a visit by Ambassador Richards and that the Foreign Ministry was making diplomatic preparations for the visit. *New York Herald Tribune*, 25 April 1957.

22. Mansoor, ed., *The Arab World* (3), 22 and 25 October 1956.

23. The government extended its thanks for Soviet support to the Arabs during the Suez Crisis, and for the first time since Communism was banned, a statement by the Jordanian Communist Party was published in the Jordanian press. Ibid., 7 and 18 November 1956. There were reports of Jordan's decision to establish diplomatic relations with the USSR and the People's Republic of China. Ibid., 19 November 1956 and 3 April 1957. Premier Nabulsi gave indications of Jordan's willingness to accept Soviet aid if offered. Ibid., 4 April, 1957.

24. Ibid., 19, 22, and 26 January, 13 February, and 13 March 1957.

25. Ibid., 10, 13 and 14 April 1957.

26. Ibid., 16 and 17 April 1957.

27. U.S. Department of State, *Bulletin*, 13 May 1957, p. 768; *New York Times*, 26 April and 1 July 1957.

28. King Hussein, following the dismissal of the Nabulsi government, rejected establishment of diplomatic relations with the Soviet Union. Mansoor, ed., *The Arab World* (3), 27 April 1957.

29. Eisenhower, *Waging Peace*, p. 197-98.

30. Seale, *The Struggle for Syria*, p. 273.

31. Loy Henderson to the author.

32. Mansoor, ed., *The Arab World* (3), 8 May 1957 and 6 June 1957. See also Camille Chamoun, *Dulles Oral History Collection*.

33. Scale, *The Struggle for Syria*, p. 278.

34. Mansoor, ed., *The Arab World* (3), 5, 15, and 21 August 1957.

35. *New York Times*, 14 August 1957. See Seale, *The Struggle for Syria*, p. 293. The United States responded by expelling the Syrian Ambassador and protesting against the Syrian accusations.

36. *New York Times*, 19 and 20 August 1957.

37. *New York Times*, 5 September 1957. Note that Henderson had also conveyed to Eisenhower that "a surprising amount of rivalry among the Arabs" existed. Eisenhower, *Waging Peace*, p. 202. According to Eisenhower, "Syria's neighbors...had come to the conclusion that the present regime...had to go." Ibid., p. 197.

38. Ibid., p. 199; *New York Times*, 5, 6, and 7 September 1957.

39. Ibid., 8 September 1957.

40. Eisenhower, *Waging Peace*, pp. 198-200.

41. Loy Henderson to the author.

42. Mansoor, ed., *The Arab World* (3), 26 August and 17, 19, and 20 Septemer 1957.

43. Ibid., 8 October 1957.

44. Eisenhower, *Waging Peace*, p. 203.

45. Ibid., p. 201.

46. Mansoor, ed., *The Arab World* (3), 28 August; 2, 4, 7, 18 and 19 September; 27 and 28 October 1957.

47. Ibid., 24 August; 9, 10 and 11 September 1957.

48. Mansoor, ed., *The Arab World* (3) , 26 and 28 September and 2, 8, 17 and 20 October 1957.

49. On 3 September, an agreement between Egypt and Syria was signed establishing a joint committee to facilitate the economic unification of the two countries (Ibid., 3 September 1957). Efforts were also made to unify the two armies (Ibid., 11 and 12 September 1957).

50. *Egyptian Gazette* 10 and 29 September 1957. See the 3 October declaration of Egyptian Foreign Minister Mahmoud Fawzi. Ibid., 4 October 1957.

51. Ibid., 14 October 1957. The Saudi offer to mediate between Syria and Turkey was withdrawn at Syria's request. Mansoor, ed., *The Arab World* (3), 24 and 26 October 1957.

52. Kerr, *The Arab Cold War*, p. 10.

53. See also Seale, *The Struggle for Syria*, p. 312; Kerr, *The Arab Cold War*, p. 11.

54. *Egyptian Gazette*, 2 February 1958.

55. *Hearings, 1957*, p. 41. Also see H. H. Humphrey's criticism of the lack of attention to the threat of subversion. *Congressional Record*, Senate, 85th Cong. 1st sess., 103, pt. 1, 7 January 1957: p. 295.

56. "The Americans in the UAR," 7:7.

57. "Beyond the Middle East Crisis" *Congressional Record* (Senate, 85th Cong., 2nd sess.) 104, pt. 13 (8 August 1958): 16,644. See also Dean Acheson's statement, 10 January 1957 before the House Committee on Foreign Affairs: "The Administration's New Mid-East Doctrine," *Congressional Digest*, 36, no. 3 (March 1957): 77.

Bibliography

OFFICIAL PUBLICATIONS

United States

Papers Relating to the Foreign Relations of the United States, vol. 2, 1922. Washington, D.C.: Government Printing Office, 1938.

Public Papers of the President of the United States, Dwight D. Eisenhower, 1953, et seq. Washington, D.C.: Government Printing Office, 1960-1961.

U.S. Congress. House of Representatives, Committee on Foreign Affairs. *Hearings of H. J. Res. 117, A Joint Resolution to Authorize the President to Undertake Economic and Military Cooperation with Nations in the General Area of the Middle East in Order to Assist in the Strengthening and Defense of Their Independence.* 85th Cong., 1st sess., 7-22 January 1957. Washington, D.C.: Government Printing Office, 1957.

U.S. Congress. House of Representatives, Committee on Foreign Affairs. *The Arab Refugees and Other Problems in the Near East, Report of the Special Study Mission to the Near East, February 8, 1954.* 83rd Cong., 2d sess. Washington, D.C.: Government Printing Office, 1954.

U.S. Congress. House of Representatives, Committee on Foreign Affairs. *Foreign Policy and Mutual Security. . .December 24, 1956.* Washington, D.C.: Government Printing Office, 1956.

U.S. Congress. House of Representatives, Committee on Foreign Affairs. *Mutual Security Act of 1956: Bill to Amend Further the Mutual Security of 1954 as Amended, and for Other Purposes.* 84th Cong., 2d sess., on H.R. 10082. Washington, D.C.: Government Printing Office, 1956.

U.S. Congress. House of Representatives, Committee on Foreign Affairs. *Mutual Security Act of 1957: On the Executive Branch Proposed Draft Bill to Amend the Mutual Security Act of 1954.* 85th Cong., 1st sess., Washington, D.C.: Government Printing Office, 1958.

U.S. Congress. House of Representatives, Committee on Foreign Affairs. *Report of the Special Study Mission to the Middle East, Southeast Asia and the Western Pacific. Report No. 2147*, 84th Cong., 2d sess., Washington, D.C.: Government Printing Office, 10 May 1956.

U.S. Congress. House of Representatives, Committee on Interstate and Foreign Commerce. *Petroleum Survey.* Preliminary Report. 85th Cong., 1st sess., Washington, D.C.: Government Printing Office, 1957.

U.S. Congress. House of Representatives, *Hearing on the Mutual Security Act of 1954.* 83rd Cong., 2d sess., Washington, D.C.: Government Printing Office, 1953.

U.S. Congress. House of Representatives, Subcommittee of the Committee on Appropriations. *Mutual Security Appropriations for 1957.* 84th Cong., 2d sess., Washington, D.C.: Government Printing Office, 1958.

U.S. Congress. Senate, Committee on Appropriations. *Financing of the Aswan High Dam in Egypt.* 84th Cong., 2d sess., 26 January 1956. Washington, D.C.: Government Printing Office, 1956.

U.S. Congress. Senate, Committee on Appropriations. *Mutual Security Appropriations for 1957: An Act Making Appropriations for Foreign Operations for the Fiscal Year Ending July 30, 1957, and for Other Purposes.* 84th Cong., 2d sess., on H.R. 12130. Washington, D.C.: Government Printing Office, 1957.

U.S. Congress. Senate, Committee on Foreign Relations. *Hearing on the Situation in the Middle East.* 84th Cong., 2d sess., 24 February 1956. Washington, D.C.: Government Printing Office, 1956.

U.S. Congress. Senate, Committee on Foreign Relations. *Review of Foreign Policy, 1958.* 85th Cong., 2d sess., on Foreign Policy, 3 February-10 March 1958. Washington, D.C.: Government Printing Office, 1958.

U.S. Congress. Senate, Committee on Foreign Relations. *A Select Chronology and Background Documents Relating to the Middle East,* 1st rev. ed., 91st Cong., 1st sess., May 1969. Washington, D.C.: Government Printing Office, 1969.

U.S. Congress. Senate, Committee on Foreign Relations and the Committee on Armed Services. *The President's Proposals on the Middle East.* Hearings on S.J. Res. 19 and H.J. Res. 117, pts. 1-2, 14 January-4 February 1957. 85th Cong., 1st sess., Washington, D.C.: Government Printing Office, 1957.

U.S. Congress. Senate, Subcommittee on Reorganization and International Organization of the Committee of Government Operations. *Report of a Study of United States Foreign Aid in Ten Middle Eastern and African Countries.* 88th Cong., 1st sess., Washington, D.C.: Government Printing Office, 1963.

U.S. *Congressional Record,* 1918 and 1953 et seq.

U.S. Department of State. *Bulletin,* 1950 et seq.

U.S. Department of the Army. *Middle East: Tricontinental Hub—A Strategic Survey.* Washington, D.C.: Government Printing Office, 1965.

U.S. Department of State. *American Foreign Policy, 1950-1955: Basic Documents.* Washington, D.C.: Government Printing Office, 1957.

U.S. Department of State. Historical Division, Bureau of Public Affairs. *American Foreign Policy, Current Documents, 1956,* et seq. Washington, D.C.: Government Printing Office, 1959.

U.S. Department of State. *Nazi-Soviet Relations: 1939-1941.* U.S. Department of State Publication 3023.

U.S. Department of State. *The Suez Canal Problem, July 26-September 22, 1956: Documents.* Washington, D.C.: Government Printing Office, 1956.

U.S. Department of State. *United States Policy in the Middle East: September 1956-June 1957.* Washington, D.C.: Government Printing Office, 1957.

U.S. Treaties and Other International Agreements. Washington, D.C.: Government Printing Office, 1952-1963.

Egypt

Egypt. *Arab Political Encyclopedia: Documents and Notes.* Cairo: Documentation Research Center Information Department, n.d.

Egypt. Ministry of Foreign Affairs. *Records of Conversations, Notes and Papers Exchanged Between the Royal Egyptian Government and the United Kingdom Government* (March 1950-November 1951). Cairo, 1951.

Egypt. *President Abdel-Nasser's Speeches and Press Interviews*. Cairo: Information Department, 1959.

United Arab Republic. Central Agency for Public Mobilization and Statistics. *Statistical Abstract of the United Arab Republic, 1951/1952. . .1967/1968*. Cairo, June 1969.

United Arab Republic. Ministry of National Guidance. *President Gamal Abdel Nasser on Consolidation of the Cause of World Peace*. Cairo: State Information Service, n.d.

United Arab Republic. Ministry of National Guidance. *The U.A.R. and the Policy of Non-Alignment*. Cairo: The Arab Publishers, n.d.

United Arab Republic. Ministry of Power. *The High Dam*. High Dam Public Relations Department. Aswan, n.d.

United Arab Republic. *Egypt's High Dam*. Cairo: State Information Service, n.d.

Great Britain

Great Britain. Foreign Office. *Papers Regarding the Negotiations for a Revision of the Anglo-Egyptian Treaty of 1936*. Cmd. 7179. London: Stationer's Office, 1947.

Great Britain. *Parliamentary Papers*. vol. 125. London, 1908.

Great Britain. *Treaties Series*. Nos 50 and 9544, London, Stationer's Office, 1955.

United Nations

United Nations General Assembly. *Official Records, 1951*, et seq.

United Nations Security Council. *Official Records, 1951*, et seq.

World Bank

International Bank of Reconstruction and Development. *Loans, United Arab Republic (Egypt)*. September 1951-December 1959. Unpublished Board Reports.

UNOFFICIAL PUBLICATIONS

Documentary Collections

Anglo-Egyptian Conversations on the Defence of the Suez Canal and on the Sudan. December 1950-November 1951. Egypt, no. 2, 1951, Cmd. 8419. London: Oxford University Press, 1952.

Arab Political Documents, 1952-1958. Edited by W. Khalidi and Y. Ibish. Beirut: American University Press, 1964.

The Arab States and the Arab League: *A Documentary Record*. vols. 1 and 2. Edited by M. Khalil. Beirut: Khayats, 1962.

Diplomacy in the Near and Middle East. Edited by J. C. Hurewitz. vols. 1 and 2. New York: D. Van Nostrand Company, 1956.

A Documentary History of American Life. Edited by Donald David. The Johns Hopkins University. New York: McGraw-Hill Book Company, 1966.

Documents on American Foreign Relations, 1952, et seq. New York: Council on Foreign Relations, Harper and Brothers, 1953 et seq.

Documents on International Affairs, 1951, et seq. London: Oxford University Press, Royal Institute of International Affairs, 1952 (New York: Oxford University Press, 1954).

The Israel-Arab Reader. Edited by Walter Laqueur. New York: Bantam Books, 1969.

Great Britain and Egypt, 1914-1936, Royal Institute of International Affairs. London: Chatham House, 1936.

The Middle East, 1948, et seq. London: Europa Publications, Ltd., 1948, et seq.

Memoirs and Other Major Sources

Abdel Nasser, Gamal. "The Egyptian Revolution." *Foreign Affairs* 33, no. 2 (January 1955): 199-211.

— — —. *Egypt's Liberation: The Philosophy of the Revolution.* Cairo, n.d.

— — —. *Where I Stand and Why.* Washington, D.C.: Embassy of the U.A.R., Press Department, 1959.

Acheson, D. G. *Present at the Creation.* New York: New American Library, 1970.

Adams, Sherman. *Firsthand Report: The Story of the Eisenhower Administration.* New York: Harper & Brothers, 1961.

Aldrich, W. W. "The Suez Crisis: A Footnote to History." *Foreign Affairs* (April 1967), p. 541.

Beaufre, André. *The Suez Expedition, 1956.* New York: Praeger, 1969.

Ben Gurion, David. *Israel: Years of Challenge.* London: Anthony Blond, 1964.

Chamoun, Camille. *Crise au Moyen-Orient.* Paris: Gallimard, 1963.

Dayan, Moshe. *Diary of the Sinai Campaign 1956.* London: Sphere Books, Ltd., 1967.

— — —. "Israel's Border and Security Problem." *Foreign Affairs* (January 1955), p. 259.

Dulles, John Foster. *The John Foster Dulles Oral History Collection.* Seeley G. Mudd Manuscript Library. Princeton University, Princeton, N.J.

— — —.*The Papers of John Foster Dulles, 1888-1959.* Seeley G. Mudd Manuscript Library. Princeton University, Princeton, N.J.

Eddy, William. *F.D.R. Meets Ibn Saud.* New York: American Friends of the Middle East, Inc., 1954.

Eden, Sir Anthony. *Full Circle.* vol. 3, London: Cassell, 1960.

Eisenhower, Dwight D. *Mandate for Change: 1953-1956.* London: Heinemann, 1963.

— — —. *Waging Peace.* Garden City, N.Y.: Doubleday, 1965.

Forrestal, James. *The Forrestal Diaries.* Edited by Walter Millis. New York: Viking Press, 1951.

Gallman, W. J. *Iraq under General Nuri.* Baltimore, Md.: The Johns Hopkins Press, 1964.

Hughes, E. J. *Ordeal of Power.* New York: Atheneum, 1963.

Hull, Cordell. *The Memoirs of Cordell Hull.* vol. 2, New York: Macmillan Company, 1948.

Hussein I, King of Jordan. *Uneasy Lies the Head.* New York: Bernard Geis Associates, 1963.

Hutchison, E. H. *Violent Truce*. New York: Devin-Adair, 1956.

Kennan, George. *Memoirs (1925-1950)*. New York: Bantam Books, 1969.

Khrushchev, Nikita. *Khrushchev Remembers*. Edited by Edward Crankshaw. London: André Deutsch Ltd., 1971.

Macmillan, Harold. *Riding the Storm, 1956-1959*. London: Macmillan and Company, 1971.

Meir, Golda. *My Life*. London: Futura Publications Ltd., 1976.

Menzies, Sir Robert. *Afternoon Light*. London: Cassell, 1966.

Murphy, Robert. *Diplomat among Warriors*. London: Cassell, 1964.

Naguib, Mohammed. *Egypt's Destiny*. Garden City, N.Y.: Doubleday, 1955.

Nutting, Anthony. *Nasser*. London: Constable, 1972.

— — —. *No End of a Lesson*. New York: Clarkson N. Potter, 1967.

El Sadat, Anwar. *Revolt on the Nile*. New York: J. Day Company, 1957.

Trevelyan, Humphrey. *The Middle East in Revolution*. London: Macmillan and Company, 1970.

Truman, H. S. *Memoirs: Years of Trial and Hope, 1946-1955*. vol. 2. Garden City, N.Y.: Doubleday, 1955.

Books and Dissertations

Abidi, A. H. H. *A Political Study, 1948-1957*. New York: Asia Publishing House, Taplinger, 1968.

Adams, Michael. *Suez and After: Year of Crisis*. Boston: Beacon Press, 1958.

Agwani, M. S. *The United States and the Arab World, 1945-1952*. Aligarh: Institute of Islamic Studies, Muslim University, 1955.

Allen, Robert Loring. *Middle Eastern Economic Relations with the Soviet Union, East Europe, and Mainland China*. Charlottesville: University of Virginia Press, 1958.

Alliance Policy in the Cold War. Edited by Arnold Wolfers. Baltimore, Md.: The Johns Hopkins Press, 1959.

American Diplomacy in a New Era. Edited by S. D. Kertesz. Notre Dame, Ind.: Notre Dame University Press, 1961.

Antonius, George. *The Arab Awakening*. London: Hamish Hamilton, 1945.

Apetheker, Herbert. *American Foreign Policy and the Cold War*. New York: New Century Publishers, 1962.

Assima, George. *La crise de Suez, 1956*. Lausanne: L'Age d'Homme, 1970.

Badeau, J. S. *The American Approach to the Arab World*. New York: Harper and Row, 1968.

The Baghdad Pact: Origins and Political Setting. London: Royal Institute of International Affairs, 1956.

Baldwin, D. A. *Economic Development and American Foreign Policy, 1943-1962*. London, The University of Chicago Press, 1967.

Bar-Zohar, Michel. *Suez: Ultra Secret*. Paris: Fayard, 1964.

El Barawy, Rashed. *The Military Coup in Egypt*. Cairo: The Renaissance Bookshop, 1952.

Baulin, Jacques. *The Arab Role in Africa*. Baltimore, Md.: Penguin Books, 1962.

Beal, J. R. *John Foster Dulles*. New York: Harper and Brothers, 1957.

Beaton, Leonard. *The Struggle for Peace*. London: George Allen and Unwin, 1966.

Berger, M. *Military Elite and Social Change: Egypt Since Napoleon*. Princeton, N.J.: Princeton University Press, 1960.

Berliner, J. S. *Soviet Economic Aid*. New York: Praeger, 1958.

Beyssade, Pierre. *La Ligue Arabe*. Paris: Edition Planète, 1968.

Binder, Leonard. *The Ideological Revolution in the Middle East*. New York: John Wiley and Sons, 1964.

Birdwood, Lord. *Nuri As-Said: A Study in Arab Leadership*. London: Cassell, 1959.

Blaxland, Gregory. *Egypt and Sinai: Eternal Battleground*. New York: Funk and Wagnalls, n.d.

Boutras-Ghali, B. *Egyptian Foreign Policy and the Arab League*. Cairo: Cairo University Press, 1956.

British Interests in the Mediterranean and Middle East. Royal Institute of International Affairs. London: Oxford University Press, 1958.

Bullock, Sir Reader. *The Middle East: A Political and Economic Survey*. London: Oxford University Press, 1958.

Bustani, Emile. *Doubts and Dynamite*. London: Allan Wingate, 1958.

— — —. *March Arabesque*. London: Trinity Press, 1961.

Calvocoressi, Peter. *Suez Ten Years After*. London: Broadcasts from the B.B.C., Third Program, B.B.C., 1967.

Campbell, J. C. *Defense of the Middle East*. New York: Praeger, 1960.

Childers, E. B. *The Road to Suez: A Study of Western-Arab Relations*. London: MacGibbon and Kee, 1960.

Childs, Marquis. *Eisenhower: Captive Hero*. New York: Harcourt, Brace and Company, 1958.

Connell, John. *The Most Important Country*. London: Cassell, 1957.

Conte, Arthur. *Bandoung, tournant de l'histoire*. Paris: Robert Laffont, 1965.

The Contemporary Middle East: Transition and Innovation. Edited by B. Rivlin and J. S. Szyliowicz. New York: Random House, 1965.

Cooke, M. L. *Nasser's Aswan Dam: Panacea or Politics?* Washington, D.C.: Public Affairs Institute, 1956.

Copeland, Miles. *The Game of Nations*. London: Weidenfeld and Nicolson, 1969.

Crabb, Cecil V. *American Foreign Policy in the Nuclear Age: Principles, Problems and Prospects*. Evanston, Ill.: Row, Peterson and Co., 1960.

Crabitès, Pierre. *Americans in the Egyptian Army*. London: George Routledge & Sons, Ltd., 1938.

Cremeans, Charles. *The Arabs and the World: Nasser's Arab Nationalist Policy*. New York: Praeger, 1963.

Crisis in the Middle East. Edited by Edward Latham. New York: H. W. Wilson, 1952.

Crum, B. C. *Behind the Silken Curtain*. New York: Simon and Schuster, 1947.

Davison, R. H. *The Near and Middle East: An Introduction to History and Bibliography*. Washington, D.C.: n.p., 1959.

Dekmejian, R. H. *Egypt Under Nasser: A Study in Political Dynamics*. Albany State University of New York Press, 1971.

DeNovo, J. A. *American Interests and Policies in the Middle East*. Minneapolis: University of Minnesota Press, 1963.

Draper, Theodore. *Israel and World Politics*. London: Secker and Warburg, 1968.

Drummond, R., and Coblentz, G. *Duel at the Brink: John Foster Dulles' Command of American Power*. Garden City, N.Y.: Doubleday, 1960.

Dulles, Allen. *The Craft of Intelligence*. New York: Harper and Row, 1963.

The Dynamics of Neutralism in the Arab World. Edited by Fayez Sayegh. San Francisco: Chandler Publishing Co., 1964.

Ellis, H. B. *Heritage of the Desert*. New York: The Ronald Press Co., 1956.

———. *Israel and the Middle East*. New York: The Ronald Press Co., 1957.

———. *Challenge in the Middle East*. New York: The Ronald Press Co., 1960.

Egypt and the United Nations. Edited by the Egyptian Society of International Law. New York: Manhattan Publishing Co., 1957.

Egypt Since the Revolution. Edited by P. J. Vatikiotis. London: George Allen and Unwin, Ltd., 1968.

El Erian, Tahany. *References Dealing with the Arab World: A Selected and Annotated List*. New York: Organization of Arab Students in the U.S.A. and Canada, 1966.

Evolution in the Middle East. Edited by S. N. Fisher. Washington, D.C.: Middle East Institute, 1953.

Farnie, D. A. *East and West of Suez*. Oxford: Clarendon Press, 1969.

Finer, Herman. *Dulles Over Suez*. London: Heinemann, 1964.

Fisher, C. A. and Krinsky, Fred. *Middle East in Crisis: A Historical and Documentary Review*. Syracuse, N. Y.: Syracuse University Press, 1959.

Fisher, Louis. *The Soviets in World Affairs*. New York: Vintage Books, 1960.

Fisher, S. N. *The Middle East: A History*. New York: Alfred A. Knopf, 1959.

Gelber, Lionel. *America in Britain's Place: The Leadership of the West and Anglo-American Unity*. New York: Frederick A. Praeger, 1961.

Gerson, L. L. *The American Secretaries of State and Their Diplomacy*. vol. 17, *John Foster Dulles*. New York: Cooper Square Publishers, Inc., 1967.

Glubb, Sir John Bagot. *A Soldier with the Arabs*. New York: Harper and Brothers, 1957.

———. *Britain and the Arabs: A Study of 50 Years, 1908-1958*. London: Hodder and Stoughton, 1959.

Goold-Adams, Richard. *The Time of Power: A Reappraisal of J. F. Dulles*. London: Weidenfeld and Nicolson, 1962.

Goss, H. P. *The Middle East: Dilemma and Challenge*. Santa Barbara, Calif.: Technical Military Planning Operation, General Electric Corporation, 1958.

Groves, J. C. "The Arab Attitude to Communism with Special Reference to Nasser's Egypt." Unpublished Mémoire de Diplôme No. 88, Geneva, Institute Universitaire de Hautes Études Internationales, 1962.

Hadawi, Sami. *Bitter Harvest*. New York: The New World Press, 1967.

Halperin, Samuel. *The Political World of American Zionism*. Detroit, Mich.: Wayne State University Press, 1961.

Halpern, Manfred. *The Politics of Social Change in the Middle East and North Africa*. Princeton, N. J.: Princeton University Press, 1965.

Hammond, and Alexander, S. S. *Political Dynamics In the Middle East*. New York: American Elsevier, 1971.

Harari, M. *Government and Politics of the Middle East*. Englewood Cliffs, N. J.: Prentice-Hall, Inc., 1962.

Hare, Raymond A. *American Interests in the Middle East*. Washington, D.C.: Middle East Institute, 1969.

Harris, C. P. *Nationalism and Revolution in Egypt*. The Hague: Mouton and Co., 1965.

Heikal, Mohamed H. *Nahnu Wa Amrika* (We and America). Cairo: Al Ahram Press, 1965.

―――. *The Cairo Documents*. Garden City, N.Y.: Doubleday and Company, Ltd., 1973.

Heller, Dean, and Heller, David. *John Foster Dulles: Soldier For Peace*. New York: Holt, Rinehart, and Winston, 1960.

Hesseltine, W. B., and Wolf, H. C. *The Blue and Grey on the Nile*. Chicago: University of Chicago Press, 1961.

Hilton, Richard. *The Thirteenth Power*. London: Christopher Johnson, 1958.

Historical Documents of World War I. Edited by L. Snyder. Princeton, N. J.: Van Nostrand Co., 1958.

Hitti, Philip K. *History of the Arabs*. New York: Macmillan Company, 1956.

Holt, P. M. *Egypt and the Fertile Crescent*. London: Longmans, 1966.

Hopkins, Harry. *Egypt: The Crucible*. London: Secker and Warburg, 1969.

Hoskins, H. L. *The Middle East, Problem Area in World Politics*. New York: Macmillan Company, 1957.

Hottinger, Arnold. *The Arabs*. London: Thames and Hudson, 1963.

Humbaraci, Arslan. *Middle East Indictment*. London: Robert Hale Ltd., 1958.

Hurewitz, J. C. *Middle East Dilemmas: The Background of United States Policy*. New York: Harper and Brothers, 1953.

―――. *Middle East Politics: The Military Dimension*. New York: Frederick A. Praeger, 1969.

―――. *The Struggle for Palestine*. New York: W. W. Norton and Co., 1950.

Hurst, H. E. *The Nile*. London: Constable and Co., 1952.

Ionides, Michael. *Divide and Lose: The Arab Revolt of 1955-1958*. London: Geoffrey Bles, 1960.

Johnson, Paul. *Suez War*. London: MacGibbon and Key, 1957.

Jones, Joseph. *The Fifteen Weeks*. New York: Harcourt, Brace and Co., 1955.

Karanjia, R. K. *Arab Dawn*. Bombay: Blitz, 1958.

Kerr, Malcolm. *The Arab Cold War*. New York: Oxford University Press, 1967.

Kimche, Jon. *The Second Arab Awakening*. New York: Holt, Rinehart and Winston, 1970.

Kirk, George. *The Middle East in the War 1939-1946*. London: R.I.I.A., Oxford University Press, 1952.

―――. *The Middle East 1945-1950*. London: R.I.I.A., Oxford University Press, 1954.

―――. *Contemporary Arab Politics*. New York: Frederick A. Praeger, 1961.

―――. *A Short History of the Middle East*. London: Praeger, 1964.

Kirkpatrick, Byron. *Year of Crisis*. New York: n.p., 1956.

Lacouture, Jean and Lacouture, Simone. *Egypt in Transition*. London: Methuen and Co., 1962.

Langer, W. L. *The Diplomacy of Imperialism*. New York: Alfred A. Knopf, 1965.

———. *European Alliances and Alignments*. New York: Alfred A. Knopf, 1962.

Laqueur, Walter. *Communism and Nationalism in the Middle East*. London: Routledge and K. Paul, 1956.

———. *The Soviet Union and the Middle East*. New York: Praeger, 1959.

———. *The Struggle for the Middle East.* London: Routledge and Kegan Paul, 1969.

Lawrence, E. *Egypt and the West: Salient Facts Behind the Suez Crisis*. New York: American Institute of International Information, 1956.

Layid, M. Y. *Egypt's Struggle for Independence*. Beirut: Khayats, 1965.

Lenczowski, George. *The Middle East in World Affairs*. Ithaca, N. Y.: Cornell University Press, 1952.

———. *United States Interests in the Middle East: Special Analysis*. Washington, D.C.: American Enterprise Institute for Public Policy Research, 1968.

Lengyel, Emil. *Egypt's Role in World Affairs*. Washington, D.C.: Public Affairs Press, 1957.

Leopold, R. W. *The Growth of American Foreign Policy: A History*. New York: Alfred A. Knopf, 1964.

Lewis, Bernard. *The Middle East and the West*. Bloomington: Indiana University Press, 1964.

Lilienthal, A. M. *The Other Side of the Coin: An American Perspective of the Arab-Israeli Conflict*. New York: Devin-Adair Co., 1965.

———. *There Goes the Middle East*. New York: Devin-Adair Co., 1957.

———. *What Price Israel*. Chicago: Henry Regnery Co., 1953.

Little, Tom. *Egypt*. London: Ernest Benn Ltd., 1958.

———. *High Dam at Aswan*. New York: John Day, 1965.

———. *Modern Egypt*. New York: Praeger, 1967.

Love, Kennett. *Suez: The Twice-Fought War*. New York: McGraw-Hill, Inc., 1969.

Lubell, Harold. *Middle East Oil Crises and Western Europe's Energy Supplies*. Baltimore, Md.: Johns Hopkin's Press, 1963.

Mansfield, Peter. *Nasser's Egypt*. Baltimore, Md.: Penguin Books, 1965.

Marlowe, John. *Arab Nationalism and British Imperialism*. New York: Praeger, 1961.

Mehdi, M. T. *An Arab Looks at America*. San Francisco: New World Press, 1962.

The Middle East, A Political and Economic Survey. R.I.I.A. London: Oxford University Press, 1958.

The Middle East in the Cold War. Edited by G. S. McClellan. New York: H. W. Wilson Co., 1956.

The Middle East in Transition. Edited by W. Z. Laqueur. London: Routledge and Kegen Paul, 1958.

The Military in the Middle East: Problems in Society and Government. Edited by S. N. Fisher. Columbus, Ohio: n.p., 1963.

Monroe, Elizabeth. *Britain's Moment in the Middle East: 1914-1956*. London: Chatto and Windus, 1963.

Morris, James. *Islam Inflamed*. New York: Pantheon, 1957.

Moussa, Farag. *Les négociations Anglo-Egyptiennes de 1950-1951 sur Suez et le Soudan*. Geneva: Librairie E. Drog, 1955.

Mowat, R. C. *Middle East Perspective*. London: Blandford Press, 1958.

Oakes, J. B. *The Edge of Freedom*. New York: Harper and Brothers, 1961.

Obieta, J. A. *The International Status of the Suez Canal*. The Hague: n.p., 1960.

Osgood, R. E. *Limited War: The Challenge to American Strategy*. Chicago: University of Chicago Press, 1957.

Peretz, Don. *Israel and the Palestine Arabs*. Washington, D.C.: The Middle East Institute, 1958.

Polk, W. R. *The United States and the Arab World*. Cambridge, Mass.: Harvard University Press, 1965.

Ra'Anan, Uri. *The USSR Arms the Third World: Case Studies in Soviet Foreign Policy*. Cambridge, Mass.: MIT Press, 1969.

Regional Development for Regional Peace: A New Policy and Program to Counter the Soviet Menace in the Middle East. Washington, D.C.: Public Affairs Institute, 1957.

Renouvin, Pierre. *Histoire des Relations Internationales*. vol. 5. Paris: Librairie Hachette, 1954.

Robertson, Terence. *Crisis: The Inside Story of the Suez Conspiracy*. New York: Atheneum, 1965.

Rodinson, Maxime. *Israel and the Arabs*. Aylesbury: Penguin Books, 1968.

Rondot, Pierre. *The Changing Patterns of the Middle East*. New York: Frederick A. Praeger, 1961.

Rustow, D. A. *The Politics of the Developing Areas*. Princeton, N.J.: Princeton University Press, 1960.

Saab, Gabriel. *The Egyptian Agrarian Reform: 1952-1962*. London: Oxford University Press, 1967.

Safran, Nadav. *Egypt in Search of Political Community: An Analysis of the Intellectual and Political Evolution of Egypt, 1804-1952*. Cambridge, Mass.: Harvard University Press, 1961.

― ― ―. *From War to War*. New York: Pegasus, 1969.

― ― ―. *The United States and Israel*. Cambridge, Mass.: Harvard University Press, 1963.

Said, Raouf. "The Baghdad Pact in World Politics", Thesis, Graduate Institute of International Studies, Geneva, 1971.

Sands, William. *Tensions in the Middle East*. Washington, D.C.: Middle East Institute, 1956.

Seale, Patrick. *The Struggle for Syria*. London: Oxford University Press, 1965.

Sedar, Irving and Greenberg, Harold. *Behind the Egyptian Sphinx*. Philadelphia: Chilton Books, 1960.

Sharabi, Hisham B. *Governments and Politics of the Middle East*. Princeton, N.J.: Princeton University Press, 1962.

― ― ―. *Nationalism and Revolution in the Arab World*. New York: D. Van Nostrand Co., Inc., 1966.

Shwadran, Benjamin. *Jordan, A State of Tension*. New York: Council of Middle East Affairs Press, 1959.

― ― ―. *The Middle East Oil and the Great Powers*. New York: Frederick A. Praeger, 1955.

Sources of Conflict in the Middle East. London: Institute for Strategic Studies, 1966.

Soustelle, Jacques. *The Long March of Israel*. New York: American Heritage Press, 1969.

Soviet-American Rivalry in the Middle East. Edited by J. C. Hurewitz. New York: Frederick A. Praeger, 1969.

Spanier, J. W. *American Foreign Policy Since World War II*. New York: Frederick A. Praeger, 1960.

Spector, Ivar. *The Soviet Union and the Muslim World, 1917-1958*. Seattle: University of Washington Press, 1959.

Spencer, William. *Political Evolution in the Middle East*. New York: J. P. Lippincott Co., 1962.

Spielman, Carl. *The United States in the Middle East*. New York: Pageant Press, 1959.

Steindorff, G. and Seele, H. C. *When Egypt Ruled the East*. Chicago: University of Chicago Press, 1963.

Stephens, Robert. *Nasser: A Political Biography*. London: Allen Lane The Penguin Press, 1971.

Stewart, Desmond. *Young Egypt*. London: Allen Wingate, Ltd., 1958.

St. John, Robert. *The Boss: The Story of Gamal Abdel Nasser*. New York: McGraw-Hill Book Co., Inc., 1960.

Suez: Ten Years After. Edited by Anthony Moncrieff. New York: Random House, 1967.

A Survey of American Interests in the Middle East. Washington, D.C.: Middle East Institute, 1953.

Survey of International Affairs, 1952, et seq. London: Royal Institute of International Affairs, Oxford University Press.

Tansky, Leo. *US and USSR Aid to Developing Countries: A Comparative Study of India, Turkey and the UAR*. New York: Foreign Affairs, Praeger, 1967.

Tensions in the Middle East. Edited by P. W. Thayer. Baltimore, Md.: The Johns Hopkins Press, 1958.

Thomas, Hugh. *Suez*. New York: Harper and Row, 1966.

Tournaux, J. R. *Secrets d'Etat*. Paris: Plon, 1960.

The United States and the Middle East. Edited by Georgiana Stevens. Englewood Cliffs, N.J.: Prentice-Hall, 1964.

United States Interests in the Middle East. Edited by G. Lenczowski. Washington, D.C.: American Enterprise Institute for Public Policy Research, 1968.

The United States in World Affairs, 1952, et seq. New York: Harper Bros., Council on Foreign Affairs.

Utley, Fredo. *Will the Middle East Go West*. Chicago: Henry Regnery Co., 1957.

Vatikiotis, P. J. *The Egyptian Army in Politics: Pattern For New Nations?* Bloomington: Indiana University Press, 1961.

— — —. *The Modern History of Egypt*. London: Weidenfeld and Nicolson, 1969.

Warner, Oliver. *Battle of the Nile*. New York: Macmillan Company, 1960.

Waterfield, Gordon. *Egypt*. London: Thames and Hudson, Ltd., 1967.

Wheelock, Keith. *Nasser's New Egypt*. New York: Praeger, 1960.

Wint, G., and Calvocoressi, P. *Middle East Crisis*. Middlesex: Penguin Books, 1957.

Wright, A. T. *The Suez Canal, Its Past, Present and Future*. London: Oxford University Press, 1939.

Wright, L. C. "United States Policy Toward Egypt, 1830-1914." Ph.D. dissertation, Columbia University.

Wynn, Wilton. *Nasser of Egypt: The Search for Dignity.* Cambridge, Mass.: Arlington Books, Inc., 1959.

Yale, William. *The Near East: A Modern History.* Ann Arbor: University of Michigan Press, 1958.

Yost, Charles. *The Insecurity of Nations.* New York: Praeger, 1968.

Articles

Aboof-Adams, M. "Egypt and the Middle East." *Australian Outlook* (September 1951), pp. 140-48.

Abueltan, Barid. "East-West Middle East Policies." *Middle Eastern Affairs,* 7 (August-September 1956), p. 269.

Acheson, Dean. "Middle East Policy." *Vital Speeches of the Day,* February 1, 1957, p. 234.

— — —. "The Administration's New Mid-East Doctrine." *Congressional Digest. XXXVI,* no. 3, March, 1957, p. 77.

— — —. "Foreign Policy and Presidential Moralism." *Reporter,* 16, no. 9 (May 2, 1957), p. 10.

Agostini, Regis. "Egypt et Inde: deux conceptions du neutralisme." *Orient* (April 1958), p. 73.

Alan, Roy. "Western Pactomania in the Middle East." *Reporter,* June 15, 1955, p. 24.

"The Americans in the U.A.R." *Egyptian Economic and Political Review,* 7 (January 1961).

Atyeo, H. C. "Arab Politics and Pacts." *Current History* (June 1956), p. 339.

— — —. "The United States in the Middle East." *Current History* (March 1957), p. 160.

Babaa, Khalid I. "Arab Positive Neutrality." *Middle East Forum* (Winter 1965), p. 9.

— — —. "Recent Arab-American Relations." *Arab Journal* (Spring 1965), p. 8.

Badeau, J. S. "The Emergence of Modern Egypt." *Headline Series,* no. 98 (March-April 1953).

— — —. "Role in Search of a Hero." *Middle East Journal* (Autumn 1955), p. 373.

— — —. "The Middle East: Conflict in Priorities." *Foreign Affairs* (January 1958), p. 232.

— — —. "The Soviet Approach to the Arab World." *Orbis* (April 1959), p. 75.

— — —. "U.S.A. and U.A.R.: Crisis in Confidence." *Foreign Affairs* (January 1965), p. 281.

— — —. "The Arab World: Paths to Modernization." *Journal of International Affairs* (January 1965), p. 1.

— — —. "Development and Diplomacy in the Middle East." *Bulletin of the Atomic Scientists* (May 1966), p. 17.

— — —. "Internal Contest in the Middle East." *American-Soviet Rivalry in the Middle East.* Edited by J. C. Hurewitz. Praeger: New York, 1969, p. 170.

Bagley, F. R. C. "Nasserism." *Journal of International Affairs* (1958), p. 150.

Baldwin, H. W. "Strategy of the Middle East." *Foreign Affairs* (July 1957), p. 655.

Beer, J. "The Strategic Situation in the Middle East." *Nations,* 15, no. 8 (1959), p. 75.

Beling, W. A. "The Record of American Achievement in the Middle East." *Institute of World Affairs: Proceedings,* no. 38, 1962.

Ben-Tzur, Abraham. "Egyptian-United States Economic Relations." *New Outlook* (January 1964), p. 16.

Berger, Elmer. "Realities in United States National Interests in the Middle East." *Arab Journal* (Winter 1965), p. 26.

— — —. "The United States and the Middle East." *Vital Speeches of the Day,* January 1, 1966, p. 184.

Berreby, J. J. "L'Egypte et la Syrie après le R.A.U." *Politique Etrangère,* nos. 5 & 6 (1961), p. 425.

Bertier, F. "L'Egypte et le Pacte de Baghdad." *Politique Etrangère* (October 1957), p. 535.

— — —. "Reflexions sur la politique exterieure et interieure de l'Egypte." *Orient,* 3 (July 1959), p. 31.

Biddle, A. J. D., Jr. "Current Russian Designs in Europe and the Middle East." *Annals* (July 1957), p. 69.

Bloomfield, L. P. and Leiss, A. L. "Arms Transfers and Arms Control." *American-Soviet Rivalry in the Middle East.* Edited by J. C. Hurewitz. New York: Praeger, 1969, p. 37.

Boutras-Ghali, B. "The Arab League: 1945-1955." *International Conciliation* (May 1954).

— — —. "Middle Eastern Security Pacts." *Revue Egyptienne de Droit International,* 13 (1957), p. 31.

— — —. "Arab Blocs and Western Policy." *Internationales Recht und Diplomatie.* vol. 1, 1960, p. 63.

Bowles, Chester. "Long Term Issues in the Middle East." *Proceedings of the Academy of Political Science* (May 1957), p. 292.

Bustani, Emile. "The Arab World and Britain." *International Affairs* (October 1959), p. 427.

Campbell, J. C. "America and the Middle East." *India Quarterly* (15 April-June 1959), p. 142.

— — —. "From 'Doctrine' to Policy in the Middle East." *Foreign Affairs* (April 1957), p. 441.

— — —. "American Search for Partners." *Soviet-American Rivalry in the Middle East.* Edited by J. C. Hurewitz. New York: Praeger, 1969. p. 198.

Capil, M. "Middle East-1961: A Political Review." *Middle Eastern Affairs* (January 1962), p. 34.

— — —. "Political Survey, 1962: The Arab Middle East." *Middle Eastern Affairs* (February 1963), p. 34.

Castleberry, H. P. "The Arab's View of Postwar American Foreign Policy: Retrospect and Prospect." *Western Political Quarterly* (March 1959), p. 9.

Cater, Douglass. "Dulles and Congress: Playing at Partnership." *The Reporter,* February 7, 1957.

Chaudhri, M. A. "New Egypt and the West." *Pakistan Horizon* (September 1956), p. 130.

Chejne, A. G. "Egypt's Attitudes Toward Pan-Arabism." *Middle East Journal* (Summer 1957), p. 253.

Clubb, O. E. "Suez and the Indian Ocean." *U.S. Naval Institute Proceedings* (August 1957), p. 829.

Colombe, Marcel. "Interpretations orientales de la Doctrine Eisenhower." *Orient*, no. 3 (July 1957), p. 131.

――― . "Egypt Yesterday and Today." *Middle East Journal* (April 1959), p. 134.

――― . "La nouvelle politique arabe de la République Arabe Unie." *Orient*, no. 11, (1959).

――― . "Où va l'Egypte?" *Orient*, no. 5 (1961), p. 57.

――― . "Vers une union Egypte-Irakienne?" *Orient*, no. 3 (1964), p. 75.

Crabb, C. V., Jr. "The United States and the Neutralists: A Decade in Perspective." *Annals* (November 1965), p. 92.

Dajani, Burhan. "American and Soviet Aid: A Comparison." *Middle East Forum* (June 1961).

Davids, Jules. "The United States and the Middle East: 1955-1960." *Middle Eastern Affairs* (May 1961), p. 130.

Davidson, R. H. "Where is the Middle East?" *Foreign Affairs* (July 1960).

Dean, V. M. "Aswan and Suez." *Foreign Policy Bulletin*, 26 (September 15, 1956), p. 6.

Deney, Nicole. "Les Etats-Unis et le financement du barrage d'Assouan." *Revue Française de Science Politique*, 12 (June 1962), p. 360.

Dimeshkie, N. "The Impact of the Cold War on the Arab World." *Middle East Forum* (December 1963), p. 15.

Doherty, Kathryn B. "Jordan Waters Conflict." *International Conciliation* (May 1965).

Dougherty, J. E. "The Aswan Decision in Perspective." *Political Science Quarterly* (March 1959), p. 21.

"Egypt Since the Coup d'Etat of 1952." *The World Today* (April 1954), p. 140.

"The Egyptian Imbroglio." *Round Table* (March 1952), p. 113.

"The Eisenhower Doctrine: Beginnings of a Middle East Policy." *Round Table* (March 1957), p. 141.

Eller, E. M. "U.S. Destiny in the Middle East." *U.S. Naval Institute Proceedings*, 82 (November 1956), p. 1160.

Ellis, Harry. "The United States and the Arab World." *Middle East Forum* (March 1960).

Entelis, J. P. "Nationalism, Nasserism, and the Arab World: Contemporary Arab Nationalism Under Nasser and Its Effects on Egypt's Approach Toward Inter-Arab Affairs." *Arab Journal*, 4, no. 1 (1966-1967), p. 35.

Fatemi, N. S. "The United States in the Changing Middle East." *Annals* (July 1954), p. 598.

Feis, Herbert. "Suez Scenario: A Lamentable Tale." *Foreign Affairs* (July 1960), p. 598.

Ferrell, R. H. "United States Policy in the Middle East." *American Diplomacy in a New Era*. Edited by S. D. Kertesz. Notre Dame, Ind.: Notre Dame University Press, 1961, p. 270.

Fitzsimmons, M. A. "The Suez Crisis and the Containment Policy." *Review of Politics* (October 1957), p. 419.

Fleming, D. F. "Is Containment Moral?" *Annals* (November 1965), p. 18.

Focsaneau, Lazar. "La Doctrine Eisenhower pour le proche orient." *Annuaire Français de Droit International*, 4 (1958), p. 33.

Foudah, E. D. "Principles of Arab Policy in 12 Years." *Egyptian Political Science Review*, no. 40 (July 1964), p. 71.

Ghobashy, O. Z. "Arab-American Cooperation." *The Egyptian Economic and Political Review* (January 1960).

Glubb, Sir J. B. "Britain and the Middle East." Parts 3 and 4. *Royal Central Asian Journal* (July-October 1957), p. 216.

— — —. "The Middle East." *Asian Review* (July 1959), p. 163.

Hall, H. P. "American Interests in the Middle East." *Headline Series*, no. 72 (November-December 1948).

Halpern, Manfred. "Dulles in the Suez Crisis: Responses to Law, Agression and Revolution." *World View* (October 1964), p. 12.

Hanna, P. J. "America in the Middle East." *Middle Eastern Affairs* (May 1959), p. 178.

Hinterhoff, E. "The Middle East in the Perspective of a Decade." *Revue militaire générale* (March 1967), p. 379.

Horrocks, Brian. "Middle East Defense, A British View." *Middle Eastern Affairs* (February 1955), p. 33.

— — —. "The Guardianship of the Suez Canal." *Middle East Journal* (April 1950), p. 143.

Hoskins, H. L. "Some Aspects of the Security Problem in the Middle East." *American Political Science Review* (March 1953), p. 188.

— — —. "The Quest for Security in the Middle East." *Annals* (July 1954), p. 138.

— — —. "The Suez Canal." *Current History* (November 1957), p. 257.

— — —. "The United States Posture in the Middle East." *Current History* (April 1962), p. 193.

— — —. "The United States in the Middle East: Policy in Transition." *Current History* (May 1965), p. 257.

— — —. "Aid and Diplomacy in the Middle East." *Current History* (July 1966), p. 14.

Hottinger, Arnold. "The United States and Egypt." *Swiss Review of World Affairs* (October 1962), p. 13.

Hourani, Albert. "The Anglo-Egyptian Agreement: Some Cause of Implication." *Middle East Journal* (Summer 1955), p. 239.

— — —. "The Middle East and the Crisis of 1956." *St. Antony's Papers*, no. 4. London: Chatto and Windus, 1958

Howard, H. N. "The American Tradition and U.S. Policy in the Middle East." *Middle East Forum* (April 1964), p. 17.

— — —. "The United States and Israel: Conflicts of Interest and Policy." *Issues* (Summer 1964), p. 14.

— — —. "Postmortems on the Suez Conflict of 1956." *Orbis* (November 1967), p. 14.

— — —. "United States Interest in the Middle East." *Military Review* (January 1970), p. 64.

— — —. "Problems in American Relations With the Near East: A Review Essay." *Balkan Studies*, p. 12, no. 2 (1971), 485-89.

— — —. "The Regional Pacts and the Eisenhower Doctrine." *Annals* (May 1972), p. 85.

Huang, T. F. "Some International and Legal Aspects of the Suez Canal Question." *American Journal of International Law*, 51 (1957), p. 277.

Hudson, G. F. "America, Britain and the Middle East." *Commentary* (June 1956), pp. 516-21.

Hurewitz, J. C. "Our Mistakes in the Middle East." *Atlantic Monthly* (December 1956), p. 46.

— — —. "The U. N. and Disimperialism in the Middle East." *International Organization* (Summer 1965), p. 749.

Al-Husry, Khaldun. "The Iraqi Revolution of July 14, 1958." *Middle East Forum* (Autumn 1964), p. 25.

Issawi, Charles. "United States Policy and the Arabs." *Current History* (March 1958), p. 136.

— — —. "Negotiation from Strength? A Reappraisal of Western-Arab Relations." *International Affairs* (January 1959).

— — —. "The United Arab Republic." *Current History* (February 1959), p. 165.

— — —. "Middle East Dilemmas: An Outline of Problems." *Journal of International Affairs* (1959), p. 102.

Johnson, D. "The Struggle for the Middle East — America Takes Over." *New Statesman*, July 6, 1957, p. 19.

Joston, Joachim. "Nasser's Daring Dream: The Aswan Dam." *World Today* (February 1960), p. 55.

Kemp, Geoffrey. "Strategy and Arms Levels, 1945-1967." *American-Soviet Rivalry in the Middle East*. Edited by J. C. Hurewitz. New York: Praeger, 1969, p. 21

Kerr, M. H. "Coming to Terms with Nasser: Attempts and Failures." *International Affairs* (January 1967), p. 65.

— — —. "Egyptian Foreign Policy and the Revolution." *Egypt Since the Revolution*. Edited by P. J. Vatikiotis. London: George Allen and Unwin, 1968, p. 114.

— — —. "Persistence of Regional Quarrels." *American-Soviet Rivalry in the Middle East*. Edited by J. C. Hurewitz. New York: Praeger, 1969, p. 228.

Khadduri, Majid. "The Role of the Military in Middle Eastern Politics." *American Political Science Review* (June 1953), p. 22.

Khar, M. A. "Strategic Problems of the Middle East." *Islamic Review* (July-August 1958), p. 9.

El Khatib, M. F. "American Economic Aid to the Middle East." *L'Egypte Contemporaire*, no. 319 (1965), p. 99.

Laqueur, Walter. "Soviet Prospects in the Middle East." *Problems of Communism* (July-August 1957).

Laurent, François. "L'U.R.S.S. et le moyen orient." *Orient*, no. 2 (April 1957), p. 53, and no. 3 (July 1957), p. 15.

Leiden, Carl. "Egypt: The Drift to the Left." *Middle Eastern Affairs*. pt. 1 (December 1962), p. 290; pt. 2 (January 1963), p. 2.

Lenczowski, George. "The Objects and Methods of Nasserism." *Journal of International Affairs* (January 1965), p. 63.

Lengyel, Emil. "Middle East Power Vacuum." *Annals* (July 1953), p. 47.

Lewis, Bernard. "The Middle East Reaction to Soviet Pressures." *Middle East Journal* (Spring 1956), p. 125.

Lichtblau, J. H. "Oil: How Long Can Nasser Strangle the Flow." *The Reporter,* 16, no. 3, p. 29.

– – –. "Is the Tank Running Low?" *The Reporter* (March 1957).

Linebarger, P. M. A. "Air Power in the Modern Middle East." *Annals* (May 1955), p. 109.

Little, Tom. "Britain, Egypt, and the Canal Zone Since July 1952." *The World Today.* Royal Institute of International Affairs (May 1954), p. 186.

– – –. "Nasser and the Cold War Strategy." *Middle East Forum* (April 1959).

London, Issac. "Evolution of the U.S.S.R. Policy in the Middle East 1950-1956." *Middle Eastern Affairs* (May 1956), p. 169.

Loya, A. "Radio Propaganda of the United Arab Republic: An Analysis." *Middle Eastern Affairs* (April 1962), p. 62.

Lyautey, P. "Duel russo-americain au moyen orient." *Revue des Deux Mondes* (June 1957), p. 395.

Malley, Simon. "And the Answer Was Suez." *Reporter* (September 6, 1956), p. 30.

Martin, H. G. "The Soviet Union and the Middle East." *Middle Eastern Affairs* (February 1956), pp. 49-56.

Martin, L. W. "The Changing Military Balance." *American-Soviet Rivalry in the Middle East*. Edited by J. C. Hurewitz. New York: Praeger, p. 61.

Masannat, G. "Arab Neutrality and American Foreign Policy in the Middle East." *General Political Quarterly*, 1, no. 3 (1967), p. 19.

El Messiri, A. W. "Toward Better Arab-American Understanding." *Arab Journal* (1966-67), p. 63.

"The Middle East." *Atlantic Monthly* (July 1959), p. 4.

"Middle East." *Time* (March 29, 1963), p. 22.

"The Middle East and the Balance of Power." *Current History* (November 1957), p. 257.

Mohieddin, Khaled. "Foreign Policy Since 1952: An Egyptian View." *Egypt Since the Revolution*. Edited by P. J. Vatikiotis. London: George Allen and Unwin Ltd., 1968, p. 135.

Mones, Hussein. "Our Foreign Policy: An Egyptian View." *Current History* (December 1956), p. 357.

Monroe, Elizabeth. "John Foster Dulles and the Middle East: Appraisal of the Late Secretary of State's Accomplishments." *Western World* (August 1959), p. 41.

"New Egypt Displays Its Power." *Life* (April 16, 1956), p. 29.

Nimer, Benjamin. "Dulles, Suez, and Democratic Diplomacy." *Western Political Quarterly* (September 1959), p. 784.

Nimrod, Y. "The Jordan's Angry Waters." Part 1, *New Outlook* (July-August 1965), p. 19.

– – –. "Conflict Over the Jordan." Part 2, *New Outlook* (September 1965), p. 5.

Nolte, R. H. "Year of Decision in the Middle East." *Yale Review* (Winter 1956), p. 228.

– – –. "American Policy in the Middle East." *Journal of International Affairs*, 23 (1958), p. 113.

― ― ―. "Arab Nationalism and the Cold War." *Yale Review* (Autumn 1959), p. 1.

Nolte, R. H. and Polk, W. R. "Towards a Policy For the Middle East." *Foreign Affairs* (July 1958), p. 645.

"Our Stake in the Middle East." *Current History* (November 1957), p. 272.

Pal, K. C. "An Estimate of the Eisenhower Doctrine for the Middle East." *Modern Review* (January 1960), p. 21.

Peretz. Don. "United States Aid in the Middle East." *Current History* (August 1957), p. 55.

― ― ―. "If There Were No Nasser." *New Republic* (August 4, 1958), p. 12.

― ― ―. "Democracy and the Revolution in Egypt." *Middle East Journal* (Winter 1959), p. 26.

― ― ―. "Nonalignment in the Arab World." *Annals* (November 1965), p. 36.

Perlmann, M. "Baghdad-Gaza-Bandung." *Middle Eastern Affairs* (May 1955), p. 141.

― ― ―. "The Middle East in the Summer of 1955." *Middle Eastern Affairs* (August 1955), p. 258.

― ― ―. "Facts Versus Pacts." *Middle Eastern Affairs* (December 1955), p. 373.

― ― ―. "Egypt Versus the Baghdad Pact." *Middle Eastern Affairs* (March 1956).

― ― ―. "The Voice of Cairo." *Middle Eastern Affairs* (August-September 1956), p. 294.

― ― ―. "Between the Devil and the Deep Red Sea." *Middle Eastern Affairs* (December 1956), p. 425.

― ― ―. "New Doctrine, Old Realities." *Middle Eastern Affairs* (March 1957), p. 97.

― ― ―. "Aswan and After." *Middle Eastern Affairs* (February 1960), p. 63.

"Point Four and the U.A.R." *Egyptian Economic and Political Review* (January 1961), p. 14.

Polk, William R. "A Decade of Discovery: America in the Middle East, 1947-1958." *St. Antony's Papers.* London: Chatto and Windus, 1961.

Raleigh, J. S. "Middle East Politics: The Past Ten Years." *Middle Eastern Affairs* (January 1959), p. 3.

― ― ―. "The Middle East in 1959: A Political Survey." *Middle Eastern Affairs* (January 1960).

― ― ―. "The Middle East in 1960: A Political Survey." *Middle Eastern Affairs* (February 1961), p. 24.

― ― ―. "The West and the Defense of the Middle East," *Middle Eastern Affairs* (June-July 1955), p. 178.

Ramagani, R. K. "Toward a United States Policy in the Middle East." *Quarterly Review* (January 1960), p. 1.

Range, Willard. "An Interpretation of Nasserism." *Western Political Quarterly* (December 1959), p. 1005.

"Relations with America." *Egyptian Economic and Political Review* (January 1961), p. 5.

"Report on Assistance." *Egyptian Economic and Political Review* (January 1961), p. 26.

Rondot, P. "Les Etats-Unis devant l'orient d'aujourd'hui." *Orient*, no. 2 (April 1957, p. 19; no. 3 (July 1957), p. 31; no. 4 (October 1957), p. 63.

— — —. "Crises orientales: été 1958, été 1961." *L'Afrique et l'Asie* (4th quarter, 1961), p. 41.

— — —. "La Nouvelle crise du proche-orient." *L'Afrique et L'Asie* (2nd quarter, 1963), p. 2.

— — —. "Dix Ans après: Quelques remarques sur l'affaire de Suez." *L'Afrique et l'Asie*, 76 (1966), p. 31.

Roosevelt, Kermit. "The Partition of Palestine: A Lesson in Pressure Politics." *Middle East Journal* (January 1948).

Roucek, J. "Politics versus Policies and the Problem of American Zionism." *Issues* 20, no. 2 (1966), p. 42.

Rountree, W. M. "The Middle East Policy of the United States." *Social Science* (October 1957), p. 220.

Rustow, D. A. "Defense of the Near East." *Foreign Affairs* (January 1956), p. 271.

Sablier, Edouard. "La Tension en proche-orient et la politique des grandes puissances." *Politique Etrangère* (February 1956), p. 21.

Saleme, E. "The Arabs Between East and West." *Free World Review* (Fall-Winter 1957), p. 19.

— — —. "The Search for Arab-American Understanding." *World Affairs* (Spring 1959), p. 17.

Sayegh, Fayez A. "Arab Nationalism and Soviet-American Relations." *Annals* (July 1959), p. 103.

— — —. "Anatomy of Neutralism in The Arab World." *The Dynamics of Neutralism in the Arab World;* Edited by Fayez A. Sayegh. San Francisco: Chandler, 1964.

Shwadran, Benjamin. "The Middle East: Pressures Within and Without." *Current History* (March 1960), p. 257.

Spain, J. W. "Middle East Defense: A New Approach." *Middle East Journal* (Summer 1954), p. 251.

Sterling, Claire. "How the United States Saved Nasser." *The Reporter,* 15, no. 12 (December 13, 1956), p. 9.

— — —. "The Never Ended War in the Middle East." *The Reporter*, 29 (July 18, 1963), p. 24.

Stevens, Georgiana. "Arab Nationalism and Bandung." *Middle East Journal* (Spring 1957), p. 139.

Strausz-Hupé, Robert. "The Middle East." *U.S. Naval Institute Proceedings* (January 1959).

Suleiman, M. "An Evaluation of Middle East News Coverage in Seven American News Magazines, July-December 1956." *Arab Journal*, 4, nos. 2-4 (1967).

Thompson, C. L. "American Policy in the Middle East." *Current History* (October 1958), p. 234.

Thompson, E. M. "Egyptian Crisis and Middle Eastern Defense." *Editorial Research Report* (January 29, 1952), p. 83.

Tutsch, Hans E. "Middle East Problems." *Swiss Review of World Affairs* (June 1956), p. 12.

Vatikiotis, P. J. "Dilemmas of Political Leadership in the Arab Middle East: The Case of the U.A.R." *International Affairs* (April 1961), p. 189.

— — —. "Foreign Policy of Egypt." *Foreign Policy in World Politics.* Edited by R. C. Macridis, Englewood Cliffs, N.J.: Prentice-Hall, 1962, p. 335.

Venicataramari, M. S. "Oil and U.S. Foreign Policy During the Suez Crisis." *International Studies* (October 1960).

Vernant, J. "L'Heure de Baghdad ou l'heure du Caire?" *Revue de défense nationale* (March 1958), p. 505.

Weinberger, S. J. "The Suez Canal Issue 1956." *Middle Eastern Affairs* (February 1957), p. 46.

Wheeler, G. E. "Russia and the Middle East." *International Affairs,* 35 (July 1959), p. 295.

Wright, Esmond. "Foreign Policy Since Dulles." *Political Quarterly* (April-June 1963).

Wright, Quinsy. "Intervention, 1956." *American Journal of International Law* (April 1957), p. 257.

— — —. "American Historical and Present Concerns in the Middle East." *Issues* (Autumn 1965), p. 44.

Yin'am, S. "The Middle East in 1953: Annual Political Survey." *Middle Eastern Affairs* (January 1954), p. 1.

Zartman, I. W. "The Mediterranean: Bridge or Barrier?" *U.S. Naval Institute Proceedings* (February 1967), p. 63.

— — —. "Military Elements in Regional Unrest." *American-Soviet Rivalry in the Middle East.* Edited by J. C. Hurewitz, New York: Praeger, 1969, p. 75.

NEWSPAPERS, JOURNALS, AND SURVEYS

Al Ahram

Akhbar Al Yaum

L'Afrique et l'Asie

Arab Journal (New York)

The Arab World (Beirut)

Arab World. Vol. 3 (1953-59). Edited by M. Mansoor. Washington, D. C.: NCR Microcard Editions, 1973.

La Bourse Egyptienne

Cahiers de l'Orient Contemporain (Paris)

Christian Science Monitor

Current Digest of the Soviet Press

Economic Review-National Bank of Egypt

Economist

L'Egypte Contemporaine (Cairo)

Egyptian Economic and Political Review

Egyptian Gazette

Egyptian Political Science Review (Cairo)

Foreign Policy Bulletins

Al Gomhouria

Jewish Observer and Middle East Review

Journal d'Egypte

Keesing's Contemporary Archives, Vols. 9 et seq. London: Keesing's Publications Ltd.

Middle East Forum (Beirut)

Middle East Journal (Washington, D. C.)

Middle East Mirror (Lebanon)

Middle Eastern Affairs (New York)

Al Misri

New Outlook-Middle East Monthly

New York Herald Tribune

New York Times

L'Orient (Lebanese daily)

Orient (Paris)

Oriente Moderno (Rome)

Al Tahrir

The Times (London)

Washington Post and Herald Tribune

Index